This book is due for return on or before the last date shown below.

Marketing Research

A Practical Approach

Bonita Kolb

Los Angeles • London • New Delhi • Singapore

First published 2008

SAGE Publications Ltd
1 Oliver's Yard
55 City Road
London EC1Y 1SP

SAGE Publications Inc.
2455 Teller Road
Thousand Oaks, California 91320

SAGE Publications India Pvt Ltd
B 1/I 1 Mohan Cooperative Industrial Area
Mathura Road
New Delhi 110 044

SAGE Publications Asia-Pacific Pte Ltd
33 Pekin Street #02-01
Far East Square
Singapore 048763

Library of Congress Control Number: 2007934524

British Library Cataloguing in Publication data

A catalogue record for this book is available from the
British Library

ISBN 978-1-4129-4796-1
ISBN 978-1-4129-4797-8 (pbk)

Typeset by C&M Digitals (P) Ltd, Chennai, India
Printed in Great Britain by TJ International, Padstow, Cornwall
Printed on paper from sustainable resources

Contents

**PART I INTRODUCTION TO USES AND METHODS OF
MARKETING RESEARCH**   **1**

1 INTRODUCTION TO MARKETING RESEARCH   3

  1.1 Research and Marketing Strategy   4

    1.1.1 Stages of marketing development   5

  1.2 Defining Marketing Research   7

  1.3. The Development of Marketing Research as a Profession   8

    1.3.1 Marketing research today   9

  1.4 Marketing Research and the Development of the Marketing Plan   10

    1.4.1 The relationship between data, information and knowledge   12

  1.5 Ethics in Marketing Research   13

    1.5.1 Ethical research issues   13
    1.5.2 Guidelines for conducting ethical research   14

2 RESEARCH AS A PROCESS   19

  2.1 The Uses of Marketing Research   20

    2.1.1 Marketing research and the organization   21
    2.1.2 Research issues   21

  2.2 The Research Process   23

    2.2.1 Determine the research question   23
    2.2.2 Sources of information   23
    2.2.3 Choose the research approach   24
    2.2.4 Planning the research method   24
    2.2.5 Conducting research and reporting findings
           and recommendations   25

	2.3	Research Approaches	25
		2.3.1 Descriptive research	25
		2.3.2 Exploratory research	26
		2.3.3 Causal research	27
	2.4	Research Methods	28
		2.4.1 Quantitative vs. qualitative research	29
		2.4.2 Research methodologies	29
3		DETERMINING THE RESEARCH QUESTION	35
	3.1	Critical Thinking	36
		3.1.1 Critical thinking and faulty assumptions	37
	3.2	The Critical Thinking Process	38
		3.2.1 Challenging assumptions	38
		3.2.2 Using internal data to challenge assumptions	39
		3.2.3 Generating new ideas	40
		3.2.4 Making a correct assumption	40
	3.3	Obtaining Internal Secondary Data to Help in Critical Thinking	42
		3.3.1 Obtaining existing internal data from people	43
		3.3.2 Conducting internal interviews	44
		3.3.3 Deciding not to conduct additional research	44
	3.4	Determining the Research Question	45
		3.4.1 Decision-making process	45
		3.4.2 Purpose of the research question	46
		3.4.3 Research questions and research approaches	46
		3.4.4 Writing the question	47
4		THE RESEARCH PROPOSAL	52
	4.1	The Research Proposal	53
		4.1.1 Reasons for writing a research proposal	53
	4.2	Components of a Research Proposal	54
		4.2.1 Components of a research proposal – the problem	54
		4.2.2 Components of a research proposal – the methodology	57
		4.2.3 Components of a research proposal – analysis and findings	59
		4.2.4 Appendices	59

4.3	The Research Industry	61
4.3.1	Structure of internal marketing research departments	62
4.3.2	External providers of marketing research	63
4.3.3	Guidelines for choosing a research company	65
4.3.4	The global research industry	65
4.3.5	Marketing research associations	65

5	CULTURAL CONSIDERATIONS FOR MARKETING RESEARCH	69
5.1	International Marketing Research Challenges	69
5.1.1	Cross-cultural research at home	70
5.1.2	Unique research questions	71
5.1.3	Availability and comparability of secondary data	71
5.1.4	Level of cultural difference	72
5.2	Language Issues	73
5.2.1	Translation needs	73
5.2.2	Translation during the research process	74
5.2.3	Back translation	75
5.3	Hofstede's Dimensions of Culture	75
5.3.1	Power distance	77
5.3.2	Uncertainty avoidance	78
5.3.3	Individualism versus collectivism	79
5.3.4	Masculinity versus femininity	80
5.4	Marketing Ethics and Cultural Values	80
5.4.1	Stereotyping	81
5.4.2	Prejudice	82

6	CONDUCTING SECONDARY RESEARCH	86
6.1	External Secondary and Primary Research Data	86
6.1.1	Institutions that collect secondary data	87
6.1.2	Benefits of conducting secondary research	88
6.1.3	Requirements of secondary data	88
6.2	Secondary Research Issues	89
6.2.1	Secondary research on the external environment	89
6.2.2	Secondary research on the industry	90
6.2.3	Secondary research on the consumer	91
6.2.4	Organizing secondary data	92

Contents

	6.3	Sources of Quantitative and Qualitative Secondary Data	92
		6.3.1 Quantitative secondary data	92
		6.3.2 Types of qualitative secondary data	94
		6.3.3 Competitor secondary data	96
	6.4	Steps in the Secondary Research Process	96
		6.4.1 Finding data online	97
		6.4.2 Planning the search	98
		6.4.3 Online search strategy	99
		6.4.4 Retrieving online information	99
		6.4.5 Combining the uses of secondary and primary data	100

PART II QUALITATIVE MARKETING RESEARCH   **105**

7		CHOOSING PARTICIPANTS FOR QUALITATIVE RESEARCH	107
	7.1	Choosing Participants for Qualitative Research	108
		7.1.1 Focus group research participant selection issues	108
		7.1.2 Interview research participant selection issues	109
		7.1.3 Observation research participant selection issues	109
		7.1.4 Professional recruiters	109
	7.2	Constructing a Sample for Qualitative Research	110
		7.2.1 Convenience sampling	110
		7.2.2 Snowballing	111
		7.2.3 Purposive sampling	112
	7.3	The Purposive Sampling Process	113
		7.3.1 Identifying characteristics	113
		7.3.2 Identifying organizations or groups	113
		7.3.3 An invitation to participate	115
	7.4	Using Segmentation Characteristics to Develop a Profile	115
		7.4.1 Choosing participants based on demographics	116
		7.4.2 Psychographic characteristics	117
		7.4.3 Geographic characteristics	120
		7.4.4 Usage characteristics	120
8		PLANNING AND CONDUCTING FOCUS GROUPS	124
	8.1	Rationale for Using Focus Group Methodology	124
		8.1.1 Advantages of using focus groups	125
		8.1.2 Disadvantages of conducting focus groups	126
		8.1.3 Combining focus group and survey research	127

8.2	Steps in Developing the Focus Group Methodology	128
	8.2.1 Focus Group Preparation	128
	8.2.2 Conducting a focus group	131
	8.2.3 Focus group analysis	132
8.3	Desirable Moderator Characteristics and Skills	133
	8.3.1 Desirable personal characteristics	133
	8.3.2 Required skills	134
8.4	Handling Group Conflict	135
	8.4.1 Stages of Group Development	135
	8.4.2 Focus groups using nominal grouping	135
8.5	Other Venues for Focus Groups	137
	8.5.1 Videoconferencing focus groups	137
	8.5.2 Online focus groups	137

9	IN-DEPTH, INTERCEPT AND EXPERT INTERVIEWS	141
9.1	The Rationale for Conducting Interview Research	141
	9.1.1 Interview stages	142
	9.1.2 Advantages of using interviews	142
	9.1.3 Disadvantages of using interviews	144
9.2	Types of Interviews	145
	9.2.1 In-depth interviews	145
	9.2.2 Expert interviews	146
	9.2.3 Intercept interviews	147
9.3	Writing Questions	148
	9.3.1 Descriptive questions	148
	9.3.2 Causal questions	148
	9.3.3 Consequence questions	149
	9.3.4 Non-directional questions	149
9.4	Screening Participants	149
	9.4.1 In-depth interviews	150
	9.4.2 Intercept interviews	150
	9.4.3 Expert interviews	151
9.5	Constructing Questions	152
	9.5.1 General rules on writing questions	152
	9.5.2 Testing questions	153
	9.5.3 Location of interviews	154

10 PROJECTIVE, OBSERVATIONAL, ETHNOGRAPHY AND GROUNDED THEORY TECHNIQUES   **158**

10.1   Projective Techniques   159

    10.1.1   Advantages of using projective techniques   159
    10.1.2   Disadvantages of using projective techniques   159
    10.1.3   Types of projective techniques   159
    10.1.4   The process of conducting projective research   163

10.2   Observational Research   163

    10.2.1   Advantages of observational research   164
    10.2.2   Disadvantages of observational research   164
    10.2.3   Types of observations   164
    10.2.4   Designing the observational research process   166

10.3   Ethnography Research   168

    10.3.1   Advantages and disadvantages of conducting
             ethnographic research   169
    10.3.2   The process of conducting ethnographic research   169
    10.3.3   Participant involvement in ethnographic research   169

10.4   Grounded Theory   171

    10.4.1   Advantages and disadvantages of conducting
             grounded theory   171
    10.4.2   The process of conducting grounded theory   171

PART III   QUANTITATIVE MARKETING RESEARCH   **175**

11   DETERMINING PROBABILITY SAMPLES   177

11.1   Sampling Issues   177

    11.1.1   Using a census   178
    11.1.2   Using a sample   178
    11.1.3   Sampling errors   179
    11.1.4   Nonsampling errors   179

11.2   Determining the Target Population and the Sample Frame   180

    11.2.1   Sampling frame   181
    11.2.2   Probability versus nonprobability sampling   182

11.3   Probability Sampling   183

    11.3.1   Simple random sampling   184
    11.3.2   Systematic sampling   184

Marketing Research

	11.3.3	Stratified sampling	185
	11.3.4	Cluster sampling	186
11.4		Determining a Sample Size	187
	11.4.1	Calculating the size of a sample	188
	11.4.2	Normal distribution and variation	189
	11.4.3	Calculating the sample size when estimating a population proportion	190

12		QUESTIONNAIRE DESIGN	194
	12.1	Survey Research Methodology	195
	12.1.1	Uses of survey research	195
	12.1.2	Questionnaire development needs	196
12.2		The Questionnaire Design Process	196
	12.2.1	Question topic areas	197
	12.2.2	Writing the draft and management review	197
	12.2.3	Coding the question answers	198
	12.2.4	Pretesting the survey form	198
12.3		Writing the Question and Answers	199
	12.3.1	General guidelines for question writing	200
	12.3.2	Writing the answers	202
12.4		Questionnaire Layout	205
	12.4.1	Question sequence	206
12.5		Electronic Survey Forms	206
	12.5.1	Using technology to design new types of responses	208

13		CONDUCTING SURVEYS	212
	13.1	Methods of Conducting Researcher-Administered Surveys	213
	13.1.1	Researcher-administered surveys	213
	13.1.2	Self-administered surveys	214
13.2		Researcher-Administered Survey Methods	214
	13.2.1	Personally-administered surveys	215
	13.2.2	Location of personal surveying	215
	13.2.3	Computer-aided personal surveys	216
	13.2.4	Researcher-administered telephone surveys	216

13.3	Methods of Conducting Self-Administered Surveys	217
	13.3.1 Mail surveys	218
	13.3.2 Web-based self-completion	218
13.4	Motivating Participation	219
	13.4.1 Providing information to potential participants	220
	13.4.2 The use of incentives	221
13.5	The Survey Process	222
	13.5.1 Training survey takers	222
	13.5.2 Conducting a survey	223

PART IV   ANALYZING AND REPORTING FINDINGS   **227**

14   ANALYZING VERBAL AND OTHER QUALITATIVE DATA   229

14.1	Analysis of Quantitative versus Qualitative Data	230
	14.1.1 The art of qualitative research	231
14.2	The Analysis Process	231
	14.2.1 Data organization	232
	14.2.2 The art of transcribing recordings	234
14.3	Coding Qualitative Data	235
	14.3.1 Using coding to develop recommendations	238
	14.3.2 Software tools for coding	238
14.4	Analysis of Qualitative Data Content	239
	14.4.1 Consumer segments	240
	14.4.2 Consumer behavior processes	240
	14.4.3 Comparing and contrasting consumer traits	241
	14.4.4 Development of hypotheses	241
	14.4.5 Analysis of ethnographic and observational research data	241

15   ANALYZING NUMERICAL DATA   246

15.1	Measuring Differences	247
	15.1.1 Scales of measurement	247
15.2	The Process of Quantitative Data Analysis	248
	15.2.1 Pre-analysis of survey data	250

Marketing Research

15.3   Data Analysis using Descriptive Statistics   251

     15.3.1   Frequency   252
     15.3.2   Central tendency   254
     15.3.3   Dispersion measures   255

15.4   Data Analysis using Inferential Statistics   257

     15.4.1   Statistical testing process   257
     15.4.2   Hypothesis   257
     15.4.3   Level of confidence   259
     15.4.4   Chi-square tests   259

16   REPORT WRITING AND PRESENTATION   262

16.1   The Importance of a Written Report   263

     16.1.1   Reasons for preparing a report   263
     16.1.2   Types of research report   264

16.2   Components of a Written Report   266

     16.2.1   Introduction   266
     16.2.2   Research methodology   267
     16.2.3   Findings and recommendations   268
     16.2.4   Appendices   269

16.3   Writing a Professional Report   269

     16.3.1   Using visual material   270

16.4   An Oral Presentation   271

     16.4.1   Presentation structure   272
     16.4.2   Presentation rules   274
     16.4.3   Unforgivable sins made during presentations   274
     16.4.4   Using visuals during a presentation   275

Bibliography   280

Index   288

PART 1

Introduction to Uses and Methods of Marketing Research

Introduction to Marketing Research

Learning Objectives

1 Recognize that research is an integral component of marketing strategy
2 Define marketing research
3 Describe the development of marketing research as a profession
4 Explain how marketing research is incorporated into the marketing plan
5 Discuss the importance of conducting ethical research

WHAT MOTIVATES YOUNG PEOPLE TO BUY? AUTOMAKERS NEED TO KNOW!

Surprisingly 6 per cent of all US car sales are made to people 16 to 24 years old. Because this is a sizeable target market segment, automobile companies have spent millions on design and advertising trying to win this segment's brand loyalty. However, the distinctive stylish designs created for the Pontiac Aztek, Chrysler PT Cruiser and Toyota Echo failed to interest young potential auto buyers.

Why did the cars fail to attract buyers? CNW Marketing Research studied young auto buyers to learn what really motivates them to purchase. They found that the average price of autos purchased by this group was only $15,000. The research found that young people were interested in style, but first wanted low price, good value and long warranties.

Was the research correct? The South Korean company Hyundai Motors produced two cars that offered these benefits. When the automaker introduced the Accent (priced at $10,000) and the Elantra (priced at $13,000) they were immediately popular with young people. In fact they were so popular with the target market segment of young consumers that the overall average age of all buyers was only 24. Hyundai was successful in reaching the target market of young consumers because not only were the cars relatively inexpensive compared with other vehicles, they also came with long warranties – and they looked good.

1.1 Research and Marketing Strategy

Marketing is a new field of academic study in comparison to subjects such as chemistry or philosophy. However, marketing is not a new human activity. People have always produced goods that they wished to barter or sell for either another needed product or money. To do so they need to find buyers. The field of marketing simply takes this basic human behavior and plans its strategic implementation.

While there are many definitions of marketing, the definition used by the American Marketing Association on their website (www.marketingpower.com) describes marketing as:

> Marketing is an organizational function and a set of processes for creating, communicating, and delivering value to customers and for managing customer relationships in ways that benefit the organization and its stakeholders.

The definition describes marketing as an exchange that satisfies both the seller (organization) and the individual (buyer). Marketing is sometimes misunderstood as only selling, with the organization convincing the buyer to purchase something they don't want or need. While selling is an important part of promotion, there would be no long-term gain for any organization to focus only on selling their product. Even if they could use high pressure sales techniques to convince buyers to purchase, business success relies on repeat customers. Such customers would most likely feel manipulated and be unlikely to purchase again. The definition also states that an organization should only provide products that fulfill its goals. Thus the organization has a mission and a strategic plan and marketing exists to help the organization meet both, while at the same time meeting the needs of customers.

Therefore, marketing is much more than just the promotion of a product. The field can be described as a circle with the customer in the middle surrounded by the four 'Ps' of promotion, price, product and place. All four of these components of marketing must provide the customer with a wanted or needed product at an acceptable price, in an appropriate place, and with effective promotion. However, to accomplish this goal the organization must first listen to the customer's wants and needs.

1.1.1 Stages of marketing development

Marketing has developed and evolved as social and business conditions have changed. An early approach to marketing was focused only on the production of goods. When consumer goods became more plentiful, the approach changed to selling as a means of convincing consumers to buy. Although these two approaches still exist in some industries, the current recommended approach is the marketing concept that instructs companies to first focus on consumer wants or needs.

Companies using the production concept will emphasize the most efficient way to produce products that provide high quality and low price. When using this approach companies see the marketplace of consumers as a single group with similar needs who will purchase any well made, reasonably priced product. When Isaac Singer invented the home sewing machine there was a great need for his product. Its successful introduction to the marketplace is an example of the production approach (see the case study below). The problem with this approach today is that people can choose from so many products with high quality and low price. Therefore, consumers also want the products they purchase to provide additional benefits. The production approach does not address this issue. To determine what additional benefits are desired, it is necessary to conduct product research.

THE PRODUCTION CONCEPT AND THE INVENTION OF THE SEWING MACHINE

It is easy to take for granted that in the present day people have the availability to purchase more products then they can possibly need or use. This has not always been true as there was a time when mass produced goods were uncommon. For example, in the first half of the nineteenth century all of a family's clothing had to be handmade. Unless wealthy enough to employ a seamstress, a woman would arduously produce all her family's clothes by hand using a needle and thread. This task was in addition to all her other household chores.

The Singer Company's introduction in 1858 of the first lightweight home sewing machine, the 'Grasshopper', changed the way clothing was produced. The machine was inexpensive and allowed women to greatly lighten their workload. For this reason the machine was immediately popular. Within five years sales had reached 20,000 machines annually.

Source: Singerco.com, 2007

The sales concept focuses on using the right sales technique. When companies were able to produce more mass-produced goods than were immediately needed by consumers, they started to focus on how to sell products. A company using this approach will assume that customers will not purchase their product without considerable persuasion. This approach is still used today in certain industries. For example, life insurance is a product that is needed but that consumers do not usually enjoy buying. A salesperson needs considerable skill in sales techniques to overcome this resistance. If the sales concept is used consumer research is still needed to determine which approach will be most successful. Even with research, the sales concept usually does not lead to repeat purchases and therefore is generally not recommended for consumer goods.

The marketing concept, which starts by taking into consideration what benefits consumers desire, is the approach recommended by most marketing experts. This approach is recommended because there are now so many products available in the marketplace that only those products that provide consumers with the benefits they desire will be purchased.

For example, the Toyota Sienna minivan is one of many minivans on the market targeted at families. To differentiate their vehicle from the competition's, Toyota conducted research to find what features would make traveling with children easier. As a result they included such features as a passenger-side power sliding door and a rear seat DVD entertainment system. The research succeeded, as *Consumer Reports* rates the Sienna as having the most family-friendly features (CR Quick Take, 2004).

The marketing concept, where the needs and desires of the consumer are taken into consideration when the product is designed, is considered the best approach to marketing. However, in order to follow this concept an organization must know what consumers need and desire. In fact marketing research is needed equally by both those businesses that sell tangible goods and those companies that sell intangible services. An example of how a financial institution can use research is given in the box below. Once again, the only way for companies to know what consumers desire is through marketing research. For this reason research can no longer be considered an optional activity in which the organization engages if it has the time and money. If research is not conducted, there is a good possibility that the time and money an organization does have will be wasted.

SERVICE BUSINESSES CAN ALSO USE MARKETING RESEARCH

Companies that provide services can also use marketing research to provide information on consumer wants and needs. Research can provide organizations with information on the consumer segments to target with their services and also their competitors' actions. Credit unions are financial institutions that find new customers by offering membership to employees of other companies or organizations. The following research questions were suggested as ways that credit unions could use research to increase membership:

Who are our potential members and where do they work?
What products do they need that they are not getting from their current financial institution?
What potential companies could we target for membership?
What products are offered by those competing credit unions that are successful in recruiting new members?

Source: Freeborn, 2004

1.2 Defining Marketing Research

The official definition of marketing research, according to the American Marketing Association, can be found on the website www.marketingpower.com.

> Marketing research is the function which links the consumer, customer, and public to the marketer through information – information used to identify and define marketing opportunities and problems; generate, refine and evaluate marketing actions; monitor marketing performance; and improve our understanding of marketing as a process.

> Marketing research specifies the information required to address these issues, designs the method for collecting information, manages and implements the data collection process, analyzes the results, and communicates the findings and their implications.

This definition may be meaningful to a marketing professional but may be difficult for someone studying marketing to understand. The definition is easier to comprehend if the four ways research can be used are explained individually:

1. 'Identify and define marketing opportunities and problems' means using research to explore the external environment.
2. 'Generate, refine and evaluate marketing actions' means using research to determine whether the company is meeting consumer needs.
3. 'Monitor marketing performance' means using research to confirm whether the company is meeting the goals it has set.
4. 'Understanding marketing as a process' means using research to learn to market more effectively.

Although the AMA definition is a useful summary of all that marketing research can accomplish, a simpler definition can be constructed. According to the dictionary, the word 'research' means to search or investigate exhaustively or in detail. The thesaurus gives as a synonym for 'research' the word 'inquiry', which means the act of seeking truth, information or knowledge. So market research can be defined as a detailed search for the truth. Marketing has always had the function of connecting the internal structure of the organization with the external world. Marketing research is a formalization of this role.

Research that is conducted can be divided into two types. Basic, or pure research, is conducted to discover new knowledge. When the research is planned and conducted, its application or how the knowledge might be used is not of major importance. What is important is that new information is discovered. After the research has been conducted, how the information can be used is then considered. Universities or very large corporations conduct most basic marketing research.

In applied research, the research is planned so that the findings can be used to solve a specific problem. This is the type of research conducted by marketing professionals working either within an organization or for an external marketing research provider. After all, if a business is paying for research to be conducted, it needs results that will show how to solve a problem. Most businesses do not have the time or money to pay for basic research. The box below provides additional information on the differences between basic and applied research.

The important fact to remember about applied research is that the information gathered will be used to assist in making decisions. The decision might be critical and costly, such as which new product to introduce. Or the decision might be of lesser importance, such as what color should be used in a brochure. Whatever the decision, the rationale of all applied marketing research is to help organizations to limit risk, because making mistakes is expensive.

Decisions that carry a great deal of risk, such as new product introductions, will require a great deal of research. In fact a full-scale research project combining more than one research method and a large number of participants may be needed. Conducting the research will be costly but the expense is acceptable because making the wrong decision will result in a very expensive mistake. A small decision, such as what color to use in a brochure, still needs marketing research to eliminate risk – but the research can be on a much smaller scale because the risk, which here is only the cost of reprinting the brochures, is less.

1.3 The Development of Marketing Research as a Profession

At the beginning of the twentieth century there was a growth both in the number of universities and also in the number of academic fields being taught. These new academic subjects, including psychology and sociology, were interested in applying scientific methods to social problems in ways that would help to explain human behavior. However, this interest in applying scientific methods did not apply to purchase behavior and there was, as yet, no academic area of study called 'marketing' or 'marketing research'.

Yet during the same time span, in the business world marketing research became a recognized professional field. Throughout this period of economic history businesses were starting to grow from small local or regional companies to larger national companies. Since they were now selling their products over a wider geographic area it became more difficult for companies to identify and understand their customers.

Such an early marketing problem was faced by auto manufactures. Once people who had the desire and money to purchase cars had done so, the manufacturers needed to know how to use advertising to reach additional consumers. As a result, the research method of surveying was borrowed from the social sciences. However, early research survey studies confronted the key problem of identifying the appropriate consumers to include as participants. So once again researchers turned to scientific methods and adopted sampling to identify the appropriate consumers to include in studies. This new method was useful when the potential consumer group was large in number, which was indeed the case for auto manufacturers. However, the research conducted was limited to focusing on finding customers for existing products rather than finding out about consumer desire to improve products.

Market researchers soon discovered that besides surveying and sampling, they could also borrow additional techniques from the social sciences. In 1931 a manual for marketers, *Marketing Research Technique*, described not only how to use surveys but also discussed interviewing and focus groups as ways of conducting marketing research. Because of the successful use of these new techniques, interest in marketing research continued to grow during the 1930s.

After the end of World War II, there was a pent-up demand from people for the consumer goods they could not purchase during the war years. However, once production caught up with demand, companies realized their need to learn sales techniques. When such sales techniques did not sell enough products, they then tried to find additional customers and so started to focus on meeting consumer desires for products. Marketing research was now needed to determine these desires and specialized marketing firms developed to provide marketing research services to companies. As a result, universities started to teach marketing research as an academic field to provide the necessary professionals.

Academic research continues to play a role in the development of marketing science to solve management problems. In fact as marketing, including marketing research, is becoming more common in emerging markets, academic researchers have proposed new models that will help businesses gain needed information (Burgess and Steenhamp, 2006).

1.3.1 Marketing research today

Students who have studied marketing research are often employed in the marketing departments of large companies. Specialized marketing research firms also employ marketing research professionals. These firms contract to provide market research for businesses and nonprofit organizations that do not have the employees to conduct their own. The box below shows two job advertisements and what qualifications are needed.

I WANT THE JOB!

Below are two job descriptions that give some idea of the range of duties and responsibilities that a market researcher may perform:

Marketing Research Professional within a Corporate Marketing Department

The person will design and execute project plans for market research studies, including customer satisfaction and market awareness, design surveys, analyze results and prepare concise reports that communicate research findings. They must also be able to conduct analyses, trending, and interpretation of data for use by the sales division. He or she will work closely with the sales force to communicate critical market research findings. The person hired must have strong analytical and communications skills, and be skilled in quantitative and qualitative research methods, survey design, statistical analysis, and data collection techniques.

Marketing Research Planner in a Specialized Market Research Firm

The person hired will assume responsibility for managing all aspects of client research projects. This will include designing and managing focus groups and surveys, analyzing the resulting data, presenting results, and making recommendations to the client to help them make critical decisions. The person will also work in cooperation with other staff members in marketing research projects to new clients. Thorough knowledge of marketing research methods is essential along with excellent leadership, analytical, and presentation skills. The ability to independently manage marketing research projects is a must.

Marketing research responsibilities with corporate marketing departments or with specialized firms include conducting studies using methods that gather statistical information (quantitative studies). Other professionals conduct studies that gather verbal and other types of data (qualitative). Most marketing research jobs require skills in conducting both types of research.

Job responsibilities within a marketing research firm or department at the lowest level will include tabulating results and assisting in preparing final reports. Positions with more authority would include analysts who plan research projects, analyze data and write the reports. Specialized responsibilities would include people trained to conduct the research, such as focus group moderators and statisticians who can use computers to work with large volumes of data. Above everyone would be a research director who would report to the client who hired the research firm or, if the research department is in a large firm, to upper management. However, today all business people should learn marketing research skills because they are critical to successfully managing a business.

1.4 Marketing Research and the Development of the Marketing Plan

Research is too often thought of as only being useful in answering specific marketing questions. It is true that research is needed to answer such questions as what types of new products

Table 1.1 Components of a marketing plan

Traditional	*New*
Statement of Organizational Mission	Statement of Organizational Mission
↓	↓
Environmental Analysis	Environmental Analysis – **Research**
↓	↓
Competitor Analysis	Competitor Analysis – **Research**
↓	↓
Buyer Motivation	Buyer Motivation – **Research**
↓	↓
Segmentation	Segmentation – **Research**
↓	↓
Research Plan	Product Analysis – **Research**
↓	↓
Product Analysis	Distribution Analysis – **Research**
↓	↓
Distribution Analysis	Pricing Options – **Research**
↓	↓
Pricing Options	Promotional Plan – **Research**
↓	↓
Promotional Plan	

consumers might want or what new market segments to target for an existing product. However, it is better to conceptualize marketing research as a tool that should be used on a continual basis for finding new opportunities and solving problems. In fact marketing research needs to be regarded as an ongoing marketing activity.

Research plays a critical role in the development of a marketing plan for all types of businesses and organizations, both large and small and for profit and nonprofit. Marketing research has traditionally been seen as just one component in the marketing plan, but it is better to consider research as part of the entire process of developing the marketing plan and not as a single step (see Table 1.1). In fact the field of marketing research is being changed by new technologies. The marketing researcher is now seen as a consultant who can either conduct the research themselves or help organizations learn how to use the new online tools so they can conduct their own research (Siesfeld, 2005).

Rather than see research as only one step in the process of developing a marketing plan, it should be seen as essential to the entire process. After all, research is the only way a company can conduct environmental and competitor analysis. The research conducted may involve a large-scale study or be as simple as visiting a competitor's store and reading the local business news. Research is also the only means marketers can use to understand buyer motivation. This research may consist of a large formal survey, informal interviews, or both. First, the proper target market segment cannot be chosen without researching the demographics of the consumer marketplace. Next, additional consumer research will be needed to determine what a target segment needs and wants. Finally, decisions about product, distribution, pricing and promotion can only be successfully answered after conducting marketing research. The researchers may find that there is a need for a new product category, such as sleep, that was never thought of before (see box below).

> ## CAN YOU MARKET SLEEP? CERTAINLY!
>
> Not too long ago the idea of selling water to people who already had healthy water coming out of their kitchen taps might have seemed far fetched. Of course, today many people take the idea of buying bottled water for granted.
>
> Well, sleep is now being marketed to busy professionals and students at new sleep salons. If you get too tired, and can't make it home for a nap, at these salons you can rent an hexagonal pod with a leather recliner, a relaxing soundtrack and a cashmere blanket. Who will want to sleep at home anymore?
>
> *Source*: Singer, 2007

1.4.1 The relationship between data, information and knowledge

The purpose of research is to provide the knowledge needed to solve a problem and not just to answer a question as to the cause of the problem. Too often researchers lose sight of this simple fact. Instead they view research simply as a means of collecting data. As a result a complex research study is designed that gathers a great amount of data about a problem. These data are then bound with a strikingly designed cover and given to management – along with a large bill for the service. It is then assumed that management will be able to turn such data into the answer they need to solve their problem.

While the research process might have been rewarding for researchers, those managing the organization will be left dissatisfied. Managers need more than raw data. They need information that explains the causes of a problem and then the knowledge that provides answers to the problem. The analysis of the data is just as important as its collection. This relationship is demonstrated in Figure 1.1 below.

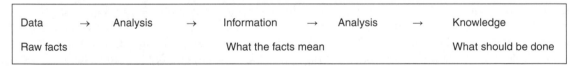

Figure 1.1   The relationship between data and knowledge

It might be helpful to use physical illness and the patient-doctor relationship as an example in explaining the relationship between data, information and knowledge. For example, a patient may go to the doctor because they are having a problem sleeping at night. After questioning the patient, the doctor will order tests (research) to confirm the diagnosis. The doctor could then hand over the test results to the patient in raw data form as they were received from the lab, but this would be totally confusing to most patients and therefore of little assistance.

The doctor could go one step further and provide information to their patient by explaining the cause and diagnosis of the problem. The patient now has information and a name for what is wrong. However, what the patient really needs is the knowledge of how to solve the problem. The patient needs to know more than what is wrong – he or she wants the answer to the question 'How can I get to sleep?' Researchers should use their skill and experience to analyze the data to provide understandable information and then use the information to provide knowledge about the solution to the problem.

Marketing Research

1.5 Ethics in Marketing Research

Ethics provide a system that helps a person to determine what is right and good from what is wrong and bad. Ethics also provide an individual with guidelines that will help in making decisions. The ethical system a person uses for making decisions in his or her personal life most likely is the result of family or educational influence, or both of these. However, the ethical behavior of people continues to be shaped by their environment, even as adults. This includes the environment in which they work (Barnett and Valentine, 2004).

An ethical system for employees of an organization is often called a code of conduct. If a company employs a researcher and does not have a code of ethical conduct, the researcher can use a code produced by a research association or society. A code of conduct is important because research is the search for true information. To knowingly conduct research that is biased is harmful to both the individual researcher and the field of research as a whole. With the renewed emphasis on corporate ethics (or the lack of them), marketing research ethical issues should not be taken lightly. It is sometimes said that any actions internal to a company that are not against the law should be allowed. However, just because something is legal this does not make it ethical.

1.5.1 Ethical research issues

The first issue where a researcher may encounter an ethical dilemma is if the purpose of the research itself is unethical. It is the researcher's responsibility to ensure that the research study is not designed to obtain predetermined results. After all, by manipulating who is asked and the way questions are phrased, it is possible to design a study so that it will obtain predetermined answers. Sometimes the organization commissioning the research may have the desire to reach a particular outcome. This can be communicated to the researchers by stressing that obtaining the contract for research may hinge on ensuring the desired research findings. It is better for the reputation of a researcher if the research is never undertaken than to report results that are knowingly misleading. By participating in this study, not only is a researcher acting unethically, they are making all future research efforts suspect. Sometimes researchers will work with groups that are particularly vulnerable, such as children. Extra care must be taken that they are not harmed during the research process (see box below).

PROTECTING CHILDREN

Special care needs to be taken when conducting marketing research with children. Parents, research organizations and the general public all have a stake in ensuring the protection of children. Below are three of the suggested guidelines from The World Association of Opinion and Marketing Research Professionals (ESOMAR):

The welfare of the children and young people must always come first. They should experience no harmful effects from participating in research.
The researcher should communicate to the parents or guardians the safeguards that are in place.
The general public must be confident that the children will be protected and there is no possibility of abuse.

Source: World Association of Research Professionals, 2006

Another guideline in conducting research ethically is always to be honest with the participants. For this reason, research participants should always be told who is conducting the research, what methods will be used and the amount of the time that will be necessary. Participants should also be informed of how the data collected will be used. Finally, if deception is necessary as part of the study, the participants should be informed that the true topic of the research will not be revealed until after the research is conducted. After providing this information, the researcher should answer any questions the participants may have.

In qualitative research indirect methods are often used to obtain information, for example perhaps when conducting observational research at an airport, researchers may appear to be fellow travelers. In focus groups, the clients commissioning the research may watch the participants from behind a screen or one-way window. Sometimes participants in an interview may be told that the subject to be discussed is different from the real topic. Although some of this deception is necessary in the research process, nevertheless this does not mean that the researcher does not need to consider ethical issues.

If at all possible, researchers should present themselves accurately and be honest with participants as to the purposes and methods of the research. If this is not possible because of the research design, the participants should be informed at the start of the research that they are not being provided with all the relevant information. This information should then be provided at the conclusion of the research.

A third ethical issue relevant to market researchers is to avoid any harm to the participants. Market researchers may borrow research tools from the social sciences, such as the field of psychology, but are not trained as social scientists or psychologists. Therefore, marketing researchers must be very careful not to cause participants any emotional distress. A researcher for a product such as intruder alarms may legitimately want to know about how safe people feel in their own homes and what would make them feel safer. Factual questions such as 'Has your home ever been broken into?' are therefore a necessary part of finding and interviewing a potential target market segment. However, market researchers must be extremely careful to avoid such questions as 'Will you tell me how your felt when you were attacked?' These questions can open a floodgate of emotions to which the researcher is not trained to respond.

The emotional wellbeing of participants in focus groups and interviews should also be respected. While follow-up questions are a legitimate part of the process, participants should not be pushed to respond to questions when they feel uncomfortable or evidence distress with the topic. Researchers cannot know the personal history of participants. A question about flashlight or torch use may ask 'How do you feel when the power fails and you are left in the dark?' This might trigger an unpleasant or troubling memory for participants. A better question, which is designed to elicit facts and not emotions, would be 'What do you do when the power fails?'

1.5.2 Guidelines for conducting ethical research

- Never conduct research where the search for truth is compromised
- Always be honest with research participants
- At all times protect participants from harm

Below is an example showing the statement of ethical principles for the Marketing Research Society. Even for someone who does not belong to the Society these are still excellent principles to follow.

MARKETING RESEARCH SOCIETY: ETHICAL PRINCIPLES

The Market Research Society, with over 8,000 members in more than 50 countries, is the world's largest international membership organization for professional researchers and others engaged or interested in market, social and opinion research. The Society's Code of Conduct starts with a statement of general principles:

Market researchers will conform to all relevant national and international laws.

Market researchers will behave ethically and will not do anything which might damage the reputation of market research.

Market researchers will take special care when carrying out research among children and other vulnerable groups of the population.

Respondents' cooperation must be voluntary and must be based on adequate, and not misleading, information about the general purpose and nature of the project.

The rights of respondents as private individuals will be respected by market researchers and they will not be harmed or disadvantaged as the result of cooperating in a marketing research project.

Market researchers will never allow personal data they collect for a research project to be used for any purpose other than market research.

Market researchers will ensure that projects and activities are designed, carried out, reported and documented accurately, transparently, objectively and to the appropriate quality.

Market researchers will conform to the accepted principles of fair competition.

The Society then provides a list of participants' rights which can be summarized as follows:

Participation must be voluntary.

Participants' anonymity must be protected.

Participants, especially children and young people, must be protected from harm.

Participants must be told of any duplicitous methods that will be used.

Participants should be able to easily verify the researcher's identity and credentials.

Source: Market Research Society, 2006

Summary

1 Marketing research is the planned and systematic search for the truth on how to meet consumer desires and needs. Marketing started with a production concept where the goal was to make goods cheap and easy to purchase. Once a sufficient flow of consumer goods was being produced the emphasis switched to a sales approach. Today research is necessary if any type of organization is going to follow the marketing concept of putting consumer needs and desires first.

2　Marketing research can be defined as a means of gaining information on marketing problems and opportunities. Marketing research is used to answer organizational questions in an effort to reduce risk and therefore reduce expensive mistakes. Research can be used by large corporations, but also by small businesses and community organizations.

3　Marketing research developed as a separate professional field when businesses started to grow from local to national companies. Owners of larger businesses could no longer know their customers personally. These business owners needed to use research to discover their customers' needs and desires. Today marketing research professionals can work in the marketing departments of large companies or specialized research firms.

4　The traditional process for developing a marketing plan lists marketing research as a distinct step. It is better to think of marketing research as a tool that is helpful in every step of the marketing process. The research process creates data. It is the researcher's responsibility to turn these data into useful information that provides the knowledge to solve problems.

5　Ethics form a system that helps to determine what is right and good from what is wrong and bad. When ethics are applied to daily life they can be used as guidelines on how to act. A code of conduct is a formal statement by an organization of which actions are allowed and which are prohibited. Ethical standards are important in marketing research to protect the integrity of the field and also to protect participants, especially children, from harm.

Key Terms

applied research　research conducted to solve an immediate problem

code of conduct　official list of standards of what is acceptable and unacceptable behavior

ethics　set of beliefs used to distinguish what is right and good from wrong and bad and that result in a duty or obligation to act in a certain way

marketing concept　philosophy that states the purpose of marketing is to provide consumers with products they either need or desire

marketing plan　description of how a company plans to meet consumer needs by targeting a specific market segment with a needed product at the right price, sold at the correct place and promoted effectively

marketing research　ongoing process of gathering accurate information from the external environment and consumers to assist the company in implementing the marketing concept

observational research　methodology where information is gathered by watching participants and recording their actions

production concept marketing philosophy that states that the company's decision on what to produce should be determined by what product can be produced best at the lowest price

qualitative research research based on social science principles used when the problem is still vague or when information is sought on feelings, beliefs and attitudes

quantitative research research based on scientific principles used when proof of a fact is needed or when the research question deals in descriptive facts such as who or how many

research proposal written plan of action that describes why and how the research will be conducted and also how the resulting information will be analyzed and reported

sales concept philosophy that states the most important function of marketing is sales and that consumers can be convinced to buy a product if the right sales strategy is followed

---

Discussion Questions

1 Why is research considered an integral part of the marketing department's responsibility without which the company cannot succeed?
2 Why is marketing research necessary for a company that is planning to open a retail shoe store and wants to implement the marketing concept?
3 Provide your own definition for marketing research.
4 What is the difference between pure and applied research? Can you give an example?
5 Why should even nonprofit community organizations use marketing research?
6 Can you provide an example of an organization at your school that could use marketing research?
7 Why did marketing research develop as a profession just when businesses grew and had customers nationwide?
8 What type of marketing research job would you find interesting? Why?
9 Why is it important to understand the distinction between data, information and knowledge?
10 What ethical issues should be of concern to researchers?

Recommended Reading

Andreasen, Alan R. (2002) *Marketing Research that Won't Break the Bank: A Practical Guide to Getting the Information You Need.* San Francisco, CA: Jossey-Bass. An easy to read book aimed at the owners and managers of small businesses. This book has examples of how research techniques can be used easily and inexpensively.

Bartels, Robert (1988) *The History of Marketing Thought.* Columbus, OH: Publishing Horizons. While currently out of print, this book is worth finding in the library for the information it provides on the early development of marketing as a business and academic discipline.

Hunt, Shelby D. (1993) *Controversy in Marketing Theory: For Reason, Realism, Truth, and Objectivity.* Armonk, NY: Sharpe, M.E. Inc. A book that covers marketing theory as compared to other theories, beginning with Plato and to scientific realism. Specifically discusses arguments on the effectiveness of marketing research.

Malhotra, Naresh K. (ed.) (2007) *Review of Marketing Research, Volume Three.* Armonk, NY: Sharpe, M.E. Inc. Seven long articles by leading experts on the latest issues in marketing research, including searching for information via the internet and the adoption of other technologies.

Murphy, Patrick (ed.) (2005) *Ethical Marketing.* Upper Saddle River, NJ: Pearson Prentice Hall. The book first covers all major ethical theories and then applies them to the field of marketing. Ethical issues when conducting marketing research are specifically addressed.

2 Research as a Process

Learning Objectives

1   Understand the varying reasons for conducting research
2   Describe the steps in the research process
3   Examine the three unique approaches to conducting research
4   Briefly describe the different marketing research methods

IT MAY BE PINK FOR GIRLS AND BLUE FOR BOYS, BUT IT'S GREEN FOR WOMEN

A recent British survey by Emap Advertising found that women are more concerned about environmental issues than men. The survey, which polled 10,000 consumers, found that women are more likely to recycle than men. It also found that, when purchase decisions are made, women were more likely to consider a company's environmental policies. Women even based their grocery purchases on environmental issues. When men do recycle or base purchases on environmental issues, it is often because a woman influenced them to do so.

The growth of the environmental movement has even resulted in the publication of a new magazine, *Green*, which is available at Tesco stores. The magazine is targeted at the market segment of environmentally-aware individuals.

Questions: What use would it be to the publishers of *Green* to learn more about men's attitudes toward the environment? What are some examples of research questions that need to be asked by management to assist *Green* in becoming a successful publication?

Source: Grande, 2007a

2.1 The Uses of marketing research

Marketing research is used to answer fundamental questions that affect the future of an organization. Therefore marketing research is a skill needed by all types of organizations, both large and small. Small businesses as well as large corporations can benefit from the knowledge that research provides. In addition, community, arts and other nonprofit organizations can also benefit (see box below).

EVEN ARTS ORGANIZATIONS NEED RESEARCH!

Here are some issues for which an arts organization needs research:

Problem: 'The 30 and 40 something market segments are conspicuous by their absence in our audience and among our membership'.

Research Question: 'What should we begin to do in terms of core and extended offerings to attract and maintain the patronage of these hard-to-reach segments'?

Solution: Consumer research

Problem: 'Attendance for the organization has been flat for the past three years while regional leisure and cultural patronage have been increasing at an annual rate of low single digits'.

Research Question: 'What is causing our relative market share to shrink'?

Solution: Competitor research

Problem: 'Management is planning a very innovative program series for the upcoming season. The associated investment and risks are considerable'.

Research Question: 'What do we need to do to find out if the box office will respond favorably before making the investment plunge'?

Solution: Product research

Source: Chen-Courtin, 1998

Small businesses may believe that they do not have the resources to conduct marketing research. However, a small business usually operates on a narrow profit margin leaving it particularly vulnerable to competition. Even losing a small percentage of customers can mean potential bankruptcy. Therefore, small businesses need to research what products and services customers want and need. In addition, it is essential that they conduct research on a continual basis as to what products and services are being offered by competing businesses.

Nonprofit organizations may also feel that they do not have the time or money necessary to conduct research. Yet all types of nonprofit organizations can benefit from conducting research.

For example, community-based social service nonprofits could use research to determine what services are needed by the people they serve. Other nonprofits, such as arts organizations, face the challenge of finding audiences and can use research to help with segmentation and promotion decisions.

Large corporations often have internal marketing research departments. Even so, they sometimes hire specialized external marketing research firms to conduct research. Marketing research is especially necessary when corporations develop new products or reposition current products. Research is needed to thoroughly analyze consumer needs, as a failed introduction or repositioning of a product can be a very costly mistake.

2.1.1 Marketing research and the organization

A marketing department provides an organization's connection between its internal structure and the external environment in which it exists. A company's internal structure will consist of such departments as operations, human resources, production, finance and purchasing, while the external environment will consist of larger societal forces. Research is the tool by which a marketing department can understand how the external environment will affect an organization's strategy. A marketing department will also provide needed information to other company departments.

The external environment can be pictured as a sphere surrounding an organization. The components of the external environment include the economic, competitive, legal/political, social and technological. It is the role of marketing departments to explore these environments and to look for problems and opportunities of which companies should be aware.

For example, marketing research can assist purchasing departments in answering the political question as to whether a government crisis in another country will affect the price of raw materials. Sales departments may need assistance in answering the economic question of how a decline in income will affect consumers' purchasing habits. Production departments may need help in answering legal questions, such as whether new governmental environmental regulations mean the redesign of product packaging. Marketing research should be used on an ongoing basis to answer these types of questions.

Aside from the external environment, a marketing department also needs to communicate between an organization and their consumers. A marketing department needs to supply the organization with the information to help determine the right product, price, place and promotion that will motivate consumers to purchase. Unfortunately some companies assume they know what consumers want. At the beginning of Chapter 1 was the example of how US automakers assumed that young people were only interested in purchasing cars with cutting edge style. Automakers may have been right that young people were 'interested' in style, yet when research was conducted it was found that price and value were the main motivations to purchase a specific car.

2.1.2 Research issues

There are a number of different issues that an organization can chose to research (see Table 2.1). Research on the consumer marketplace can be used to determine who is buying a specfic product. Companies should also consider conducting research regarding competitors' products and services as it can provide valuable information on how a business can improve. For example,

Table 2.1   Research issues

Issue	Purpose	Research question
Market	Composition of customer market segment	Who is in our customer market segment?
Competitor	Consumers' perception of competition	What else do they buy and why?
Consumer	Motivation for purchase	What is the motivation for buying our product?
Product	Improvement of product	Does our product provide the desired benefits?
Promotional	Effectiveness of different messages and media	What and where do our customers hear about us?
Distribution	Ease of purchase	Is our product available at the right locations?
Pricing	Choosing pricing levels	What do our customers think of our price?

organizations should analyze their customers' perception of competitors, as such research helps to determine whether companies should add to their own products any of the benefits provided by competing products.

Market research can determine the composition of the current customer segment. Consumer research can examine customers' reasons for purchasing and is critical to both increasing the current market segment and finding new target markets. Distribution research is conducted to determine if the product is being sold at the right locations. Organizations also need to use research to determine if a specific product has the benefits that consumers desire. Even watermelons can be changed to meet consumer needs (as explained in the box below). Another important area of research is determining if a product is being effectively promoted. Lastly, determining the correct price for a product can make the difference between a successful and unsuccessful product launch. Information gathered on all of these issues will help businesses to learn where and how they need to improve.

WHAT'S THE PROBLEM WITH A WATERMELON?

Consumer research at Syngenta and Seminins, both large seed companies, found that for single people, couples and small families, watermelons are just too big. Even for larger families there was an objection both to the way watermelons take up too much space in the refrigerator and the fact that they are too heavy to take on picnics.

The result of this consumer research was the development of 'personal' or 'mini' watermelons. They weigh only three to five pounds and are seedless and sweeter than traditional melons. However, they cost two to three times per pound more than traditional melons.

Has this stopped consumers from purchasing? No – in fact when the mini-melons were introduced, demand exceeded supply. Consumers were willing to pay more for the benefits they desired. Yet no one would have known about these consumer desires without first conducting marketing research.

Source: Auchmutey, 2004

Table 2.2 Steps in the research process

1. Determine the research question
↓
2. Decide on the sources of information and sample profile
↓
3. Choose the research approach
↓
4. Plan the research method
↓
5. Conduct the research
↓
6. Analyze and report the findings and recommendations

2.2 The Research Process

Too often, when a company conducts research it begins without proper planning. However, the chances of finding the correct answer to a research question are greatly increased by following a specific six-step process (see Table 2.2 above). The process starts with determining what the organization needs to know and where it can find the information. In addition, researchers must determine who will participate in the research and the number of participants that will be needed. Researchers must then decide what research approach is appropriate for the research question and must choose the most suitable research method. They must then plan the process of conducting the research. After the research is conducted, the final step will be to analyze and report the findings and recommendations.

2.2.1 Determine the research question

The first step, designing the research question, is generally difficult and time consuming. Because organizations are often in a hurry for answers, the temptation is to start the research process before determining what they really need to know. As a result, they may either ask a poorly-defined research question or even the wrong question entirely. To be effective, a research study must be both well designed and narrowly focused. If the research question is too broad, too much information will be obtained. In addition, the large amount of resulting data will be difficult to analyze and, therefore, of little use to an organization. Even worse, if the wrong question is asked, the wrong information will be obtained and all the research effort will be wasted.

2.2.2 Sources of information

Researchers need to put considerable thought into planning the sources from which information can be obtained. The different sources for data are categorized as secondary (data that already exist) and primary (data that the researcher collects). In addition, secondary data can be categorized as internal (which the company already has) and external (which must be gathered from other sources). Sometimes, an organization may even have already collected enough data to answer their question. In other cases, the answer to a research question might already be available as a result of research conducted by other organizations. However, even if a research question is not answered, collecting secondary data can help with the design of a primary research method.

A researcher will collect primary data directly from participants to answer a specific research question. Primary data are usually collected from a group of participants called a 'sample'. This sample consists of selected members from an entire group of individuals, which is called a 'population'. These selected members can be defined by demographic characteristics such as age, gender, or occupation. They also might be defined by psychographic characteristics such as lifestyle or opinions. In addition, they can be defined by their geographic location or product usage levels. A description of the individuals in the sample is called the 'participant profile'.

The method that will be used to choose the individuals that will be included in a sample will differ depending on what type of research methodology will be used. Probability sampling is used to randomly select the people in a sample. Nonprobability sampling is utilised when the judgment of a researcher is used to make the selection.

The population being studied could be current customers who frequently purchase a product with the purpose of determining how a company can improve that product's design. Past customers could be included in the sample to find sources of consumer dissatisfaction or to determine what other competing products they also purchase. Rather than current or past customers, potential market segments of interest to that company can also be studied. For example, research can be conducted to determine what type of promotion might motivate older consumers to purchase. Another purpose of researching a sample of potential consumers is to determine how a product needs to be adapted to offer the features and benefits they desire. For example, a company that produces camping equipment might include in their sample individuals who are interested in extreme sports in order to learn how to adapt their product to meet these consumers' preferences.

2.2.3 Choose the research approach

The next step is to choose a research approach. The process of conducting primary research starts with deciding whether the research question calls for descriptive, exploratory or causal research. The choice will depend on whether or not a research question needs to be answered with quantifiable facts. If a research question asks 'How many?' or 'Which one?', descriptive or causal research will probably be used. If a research question asks the question 'Why?', then exploratory research will probably be used.

Understanding how an organization plans to use the information will also help in making an appropriate decision. If an organization wishes to prove a fact about the demographic composition of its customers, such as how many females as compared to males purchase a product, then a descriptive study would be appropriate. If, on the other hand, an organization wishes to discover why sales are falling, it will need to conduct exploratory research. Causal research will help determine the effect of a proposed change.

2.2.4 Planning the research method

After choosing the research approach, researchers must design the research method. This will include the details of how the research will be conducted, including when, where and by whom. The available research methods will include surveys, focus groups, interviews, projective techniques, observation, ethnography, and grounded theory. A research plan will include the timeline for the research, the people needed and the budget.

For example, this step may involve writing survey questions or the script to be used in a focus group. The more detailed the planning, the more smoothly the research will proceed. Therefore everything, from how many copies of the survey form are needed to who will be responsible for ensuring that the focus group participants arrive, should be considered.

2.2.5 Conducting research and reporting findings and recommendations

Finally, researchers will be ready to conduct the research. Once done, the final task is for researchers to analyze the data and report the findings and conclusions. Analysis requires repeatedly going over the collected responses to find common themes, patterns and connections. Reporting may be in the form of a written report, a verbal presentation, or both. A written report presenting the results of a quantitative research study will usually have an introduction followed by a description of the methodology. It will also have a section with findings supported with statistics and charts. These findings will be the basis of the recommendations given in the report. With quantitative research someone who has not conducted the research can still write the report based on the findings.

A report for a qualitative research study will follow the same outline. However, because there are no statistics or charts different types of visuals will be used to help clients understand the findings. Some tools that can be used include diagrams, quotes, photos and even videos. With qualitative research, the person who conducted the research must be involved in the writing of the report.

2.3 Research Approaches

One of the questions that an organization must decide before conducting research is which research approach will be most appropriate. The approach chosen will depend on the research question and the type of information a company is seeking. There are three general research approaches; descriptive, exploratory and causal. Each can be considered as being similar to a different type of tool box. Each approach 'box' contains certain tools or methods that are most useful with that approach. After deciding the research approach, the company will choose the best method.

For example, if a car needs repair a person will open the automotive tool box and perhaps select a wrench. If a house needs repair, a carpentry tool box will be opened and a hammer may be selected as the needed tool. Each tool box will have a choice of tools that will be needed for a specific type of job. However, the first step is choosing the right tool box, not the specific tool (see Table 2.3).

2.3.1 Descriptive research

A company will perform descriptive research when it needs to obtain specific details on its consumers and their purchasing behavior. Descriptive research is used when statistical data are needed on a fact. The tool used to conduct descriptive research is almost always surveys. The advantage of a survey is that, if the number of people surveyed (the sample) is large enough, it can be said that a fact has been proved and is true of the entire group. Descriptive survey data can give answers such as '37 per cent of our customers are over the age of 55' or '52 per cent of our customers purchase four times a year'. If the number of people asked to complete the survey is large enough compared to the total population under study, the answer can even be said to have been proven.

Table 2.3 Research studies and their use

Method	When to Use	How to Use
Descriptive	Use when details and numbers are needed	Research on customer demographics or purchase frequency
Exploratory	Use when seeking insights on motivation/behavior	Research on purchase motivation or attitude toward the company
Causal	Use when needing to determine effect of change	Research on effect of product of promotion change on purchase

Conducting descriptive research can be expensive and time-consuming. However, it is necessary if a company wants to prove a guess or hypothesis about consumers or their behavior. For example, a descriptive study can be designed to prove that '10 per cent of all current consumers will purchase the more expensive new product model'. This guess or hypothesis can be proved within a certain level of confidence that the answer obtained from the descriptive survey sample is true of the entire population. However, descriptive research can also be used to obtain details without relying on statistical proof. Descriptive research is sometimes used to address issues that are just beginning to be explored, such as the integration of the attitudes of consumers across the European Union (Lemmens et al., 2007). In the case of this study a survey was used without any attempt to prove a hypothesis.

Many organizations have relied heavily on surveys as their only means of market research. This is unfortunate as the type of information that surveys can provide is limited. Yet another reason for rethinking this dependence on descriptive surveys is that it is increasingly difficult to find a sufficient number of people who are willing to respond. Because people are often pressed for time, and also because of privacy issues, it is difficult to motivate people to respond to a survey in person, over the phone or by mail. In an effort to make participating in a survey more convenient, the internet is increasingly being used. However, conducting surveys online also produces problems in that this is limited to obtaining responses from only those people who find participating online both convenient and attractive.

2.3.2 Exploratory research

Companies should use exploratory research when a research question deals with finding information on consumer attitudes, opinions and beliefs. Such exploratory research can be useful even when there is no specific problem to investigate. For example, a company might use exploratory research to look for marketing opportunities by researching trends or changes in consumer behavior. The research methods available to conduct exploratory studies include focus groups, interviews, projective techniques, observation, ethnography and grounded theory.

All of these methods use a qualitative research approach. Exploratory research is designed to let participants provide their own answers. The research question, rather than asking for facts, focuses on a consumer's needs, desires, preferences and values. Because so many different answers will result, statistically provable answers cannot be generated, but exploratory qualitative studies, if designed with considerable thought as to what information is wanted and how it is to be obtained, can provide invaluable information to a company. Such a study may be large and complex or it can be conducted on a small scale. Either way, the consumer information received will provide details and insights that will help an organization adapt its product, price, promotion and distribution to meet consumer desires.

When using exploratory research tools, the emphasis is not on the size of a sample. Instead it is on choosing the correct participants and the analysis of the information they provide. For example, if asked why they purchase a company's product, even if each individual has a unique answer, common themes will almost always appear. A researcher will analyze the responses and then group them by these common themes. One advantage of qualitative research is that it can also be approached in low-cost ways that are available to smaller businesses. The importance of research to small businesses is addressed in the box below.

EVERYONE NEEDS RESEARCH!

Why do small businesses and organizations believe that marketing research is only for large corporations? Here are some myths and responses:

'I'm already doing enough research' – but are the data the right data?
'Research is only for big decisions' – but research for small decisions is still useful.
'Losing control'– but research does not need to be turned over to specialists.
'Market research is survey research' – but there is much more to research than surveys.
'Market research is too expensive' – not necessarily.
'Most research is a waste' – this can be avoided.

Source: Andreasen, 2002

2.3.3 Causal research

If a company wants to study the effect a change in its product will have on consumer purchasing or the possible success of a new promotional campaign, it should use causal research. Causal research is conducted to discover whether the change a company is planning to make will have a positive or negative effect on consumers. Research questions that require causal research have a cause and effect – for example, such questions as 'Will a new promotion campaign using a celebrity increase purchases of books among young people'? or 'Will customers at the cinema purchase more refreshments if we have a new menu'? These issues can also be explored using qualitative techniques. Even the effect of intangible factors, such as smell and sound, on sales can be researched (Spangenberg et al., 2005).

If the change has already happened, internal quantitative data might already exist to answer the question. For example, if a company wants to know whether their new menu has increased sales, it can look at the sales figures. However, this is an expensive way to learn whether a new menu has proved successful. A better use of research would be to use qualitative research tools before implementing the change. For example, by trying the new menu on a small-scale first, the menu items might be discussed in a focus group to see whether customer reaction will be positive or negative. Then for further confirmation, a survey could be conducted.

2.4 Research Methods

Once the general approach is understood, the next step will involve choosing a research method and then planning the research. Marketing research methods can be divided into two different types – quantitative and qualitative. For a small study, research methods of only one type might be used. However, for some large-scale studies both types of research may be needed. Quantitative research uses mathematical analysis to provide proof of a fact or a hypothesis (guess or assumption). When properly implemented, quantitative research can answer questions such as 'How many consumers prefer our new product?' or 'Which of these three packaging designs is most attractive to consumers?'

The standard tool used when conducting quantitative research is the survey. Survey questions give participants a selected number of responses such as yes/no or frequently/sometimes/never. The responses are then entered into a computer using a statistical software package. The software will tabulate if there are enough responses to support a 'proved' fact. This proved fact is then said to be true of the group of consumers as a whole (population) even though only a selected number (sample) were asked.

Of course it is impossible to ask all consumers. Therefore, it is necessary to determine how many people should participate in the quantitative survey to support this proof. To determine the correct number, researchers use their knowledge of sampling and statistics to construct a sample that contains the required number and type of participants.

This proof of consumer behavior is important when a company is planning a major expenditure, such as the introduction of a new product or a new promotional campaign (see box below). While quantitative studies can be expensive, because they must be conducted with a large enough sample, in some situations they are worth the cost. The cost is acceptable because if the wrong decision is made, even more money could be lost.

WHY BOTHER WITH RESEARCH? TO MAKE SURE YOUR MONEY IS SPENT WISELY!

Producing a television commercial is an expensive undertaking. Below are some figures on the costs of making a 30-second TV 'Got Milk' commercial. The commercial was designed to increase the consumption of milk by adults. With this level of expense any company would be wise to use research first to make sure that the final commercial will indeed motivate consumers to buy milk.

Television production	$281,000
Postproduction editing	45,000
Music	6,000
Sound effects/narration	1,000
Actors	11,000
Tapes and dubs	1,000
Legal	1,000
Shipping	1,000
Agency travel, casting	16,000
Total	$363,000

Source: Berger, 2004

2.4.1 Quantitative vs. qualitative research

While quantitative studies are useful for answering questions such as 'How many?' and 'What?', they are not as useful when answering questions such as 'Why?' or 'What if?' A qualitative study is designed to uncover consumer attitudes, beliefs and opinions rather than facts. Because it is difficult to know consumer preferences before the study is conducted, a quantitative survey form with predetermined answers can result in misleading results. Instead, a wider variety of qualitative research tools, including interviews, focus groups, observation and projective techniques, is available. These tools, when used by trained researchers, allow participants to fully express their opinions and beliefs. Another unique aspect of qualitative research is that new techniques are continuing to be developed by researchers (Shakar and Goulding, 2001).

Qualitative research uses fewer participants who are not necessarily representative of all consumers in the population. In fact sometimes they are chosen because they belong to a distinct segment, such as older or ethnic consumers. The data that result from using a qualitative approach are not in the form of statistics but rather in ideas and quotes expressed by participants and researchers' notes. Interpretation of the data requires special skills, but correctly analyzed qualitative data can provide a rich source of information for marketing ideas including new concepts for segmentation. For example, one British study used qualitative methods to examine the UK debate on the nature of childhood (O'Sullivan, 2005).

2.4.2 Research methodologies

Once a research question has been decided upon and the research approach has been chosen, the next step is to choose a research method (see Table 2.4). Methods can include the traditional quantitative marketing survey used in descriptive research. There are more research tools available for conducting qualitative exploratory research including focus groups, interviews, projective techniques, observation, ethnography and grounded theory. (These methods will be described in more detail in later chapters.)

Table 2.4 Research methods

Method	Description
Survey	Set of pre-determined questions
Focus groups	Group dynamics to draw out responses
Interviews	One-to-one in-depth discussion
Intercept interviews	Two to three short questions asked
Projective techniques	Creative techniques to get emotional responses
Observation	Watching people's behavior and actions
Ethnography	Studying people in an everyday context
Grounded theory	Refining the questioning while the research is conducted

Surveys

Surveys are written instruments that ask a series of predetermined questions. These questions can be answered by checking one of several suggested answers, or the questions might be open-ended and will allow participants to answer in their own words. Surveys can be administered in several ways including in person, over the phone, by mail or online. The benefit of conducting a survey is that a researcher can tabulate and compare responses as the same questions are asked of each participant. Because the questions and answers are standardized, if enough survey responses are collected, it can be said the response is true of an entire group. Technology has changed the way surveys are conducted and many are now completed online. Even the administration of in-person surveys has changed, as hand-held devices rather than the traditional paper forms can be used to enter responses (McGorry, 2006).

There are disadvantages to the survey method. A well written survey will take time to develop as the questions must be carefully written so that there is no ambiguity as to what they mean. To ensure this is true, a survey form must be tested on sample participants before it is widely distributed. If a large number of responses are received it will be necessary to use a computer database program to record the answers. In addition, it is becoming more difficult to motivate participants to complete a survey form.

Focus group

A focus group brings together a group of individuals, who are then encouraged to share their opinions and concerns. By putting people together in a focus group, they can be encouraged to respond to each other's comments and go beyond their initial response to a question. It is the focus group moderator's responsibility to keep the discussion on track and encourage responses. A formal focus group is usually conducted by an outside professional moderator. Using researchers who work for the organization as moderators is not considered a good idea, as they might introduce preconceived ideas into the focus group process.

Focus groups are a method that can be successfully used even by small businesses and nonprofit organizations. Even if they cannot afford a focus group that is planned and conducted by a professional researcher, an organization will still obtain valuable information by asking a few of its customers to participate in an informal focus group. The person moderating the focus group does not need to be a professional marketing researcher, but does need basic skills in listening and human relations. Often graduate students from a nearby university can be used for this purpose. The role of the moderator is to be noncommittal and objective and to listen and record what the participants say. What is critical is that the moderator guides the conversation by encouraging the participants to keep their comments focused on the subject, while not guiding the opinions expressed.

Interviews

Interviews can be one of three types – in-depth, intercept or expert. In-depth interviews are used to obtain information on how a participant feels about an issue. The advantage of this method is that the interviewer has time to explore an individual's first response to a question with additional, probing, follow-up questions. These allow the researcher to obtain more in-depth information. The follow-up questioning is necessary because when first asked a question many people will respond with what they believe to be the correct, or appropriate, answer. Also, most people want to be polite by answering in the affirmative and with positive praise whenever possible. The disadvantage is that interviews take considerable time, and therefore money, to conduct. Also, since each interview takes time fewer can be conducted.

Intercept interviews are often called 'person-on-the-street' interviews. They are designed to be short, taking only three to five minutes, and are limited to a specific topic. To conduct the interviews a researcher will go to a location where participants can be found. The advantage of intercept interviews is that many responses can be collected in a short period of time. The disadvantage is that the method leaves no time for probing follow-up questions.

In addition, a researcher can conduct expert interviews. The participants in these interviews are not potential or current consumers but rather individuals who have specific knowledge. This knowledge will involve the industry as a whole or knowledge about a company's target market segment.

Projective techniques

Projective techniques can be incorporated in both interviews and focus groups to encourage communication or they can be used on their own. These are techniques that obtain information in ways other than verbal response. The technique is borrowed from psychology and is gaining increased use in consumer marketing. Some simple projective techniques include word association, sentence completion, and cartoon tests. These are also tools that creative people working in marketing should enjoy using.

Word association is simply asking for a participant's first response to a name, photo or event. The idea is to get emotional responses, rather than intellectual thoughts, about a company, brand name or product. Word association can be used in focus groups or interviews to get respondents to communicate on an emotional rather than intellectual level.

Cartoons can also be implemented. The cartoon will usually consist of two characters with speech bubbles over their heads similar to comic books. For example, one character might be saying, 'Hi Ahmad, I was thinking of shopping at Sam's. Want to go?' Survey participants will then put their own answers into the second character's speech bubble.

Observation

Another research method that can be used by all types of organizations is observation. This is an inexpensive qualitative method that can be easily adopted by small businesses and community nonprofits. If a business wants to know how its customer service desk is being used, it can station researchers to watch and then note the behavior of customers as they seek assistance. A museum can use observational research to track the actions of specific groups of visitors. For example, families or single people can be observed to help the museum to determine which galleries are most visited, the length of a stay and what displays attract the most attention. This method will often give more accurate information than surveying, as most people do not keep track of what they do while shopping in a store or when visiting a museum. The example below shows how observational research can even be conducted on the way to work.

OBSERVATIONAL RESEARCH CAN BE CONDUCTED ANYWHERE!

African-Americans' share of book buying is increasing in the USA while the market for books as a whole is stagnant. In fact, African-Americans spent $300 million on books in 2003. To meet this demand, publishers are hurrying to sign up new authors – and African-American writers are responding by sending their manuscripts to publishers.

But how do publishers decide what books to publish? According to Malaika Adero, an editor at Atria (which is part of Simon & Schuster), one tool she uses to get ideas for what new books to publish is to watch what people are reading on the subway. While on her way to the office, she is already at work conducting consumer observational research.

Source: Collier, 2004

Ethnography

Ethnographic research studies the daily lives of participants. The research can be conducted where participants live, where they shop and where they work. Ethnographic research does not rely on people's responses and instead studies what they actually do. Ethnography requires researchers skilled in observing and interacting with people on a participant, rather than a research, level. Often such researchers have a background in anthropology which helps them to understand and adapt to various cultures.

The ethnographic research study is designed to study actual product purchase or use experience. To do so, researchers will use photos, videos, journals or participant observation. For example, they may record the actions of families as they prepare dinner. One insight that might be discovered is that some children may want to be involved in food preparation. From this insight might come a new promotional campaign showing children and adults cooking together.

Grounded theory

Most research studies start with analyzing the cause of a problem. A researcher will have a theory on why consumers are behaving in the way that they do in regard to a purchase or the use of a product. There is no hypothesis, rather a research methodology is designed to study this behavior. Instead of a researcher first establishing a theory and an hypothesis and then asking questions to determine if they are correct, a researcher will observe this behavior to determine a theory.

What is also different about grounded theory is the way that methodology evolves during the research process. The research will take place where consumers normally conduct the behavior being studied, and will also use both observation and interviewing. As the research is conducted who is interviewed and the questions they ask will be changed, based on the previous observations and interview question answers.

Summary

1 Research can answer fundamental questions that affect the future of any organization. For this reason, even small businesses and nonprofit organizations should conduct research. It can answer questions about the external environment including consumer segments and competitors. Of course an organization should always research a consumer's motivation for purchasing a product. The organization may also need to research the components making up the marketing mix which includes product, promotion, price and distribution.
2 Research is most successful when it is planned using the six steps in the research process. The process starts with determining the research question and deciding on the source of information and the sample. Next a researcher will choose the research approach and plan the research method. Finally, they will conduct the research and analyze and report the findings.
3 The research methods of descriptive, exploratory and causal each have specialized uses. Descriptive is best when details are needed, exploratory when seeking insight, and causal when it is important to understand the effect of a change.

4   Quantitative and qualitative research approaches each have their uses. Quantitative research is based on scientific methods and can provide proof, while qualitative is based on social science methods and provides in-depth information on attitudes and beliefs. The standard research tools are surveys, interviews, focus groups, projective techniques, observation, ethnography and grounded theory. This chapter has given a brief description of each of these, although in future chapters more details will be provided.

Key Terms

causal research   research designed to determine how one action will affect consumers and their behavior

data   all the relevant raw facts regarding a problem

descriptive research   research that is designed to be used when it is important to obtain numbers or facts

ethnography   research study where the researcher participates in the same behavior as the research subjects

exploratory research   research used when the research question is still not clear or when few facts are yet known about the problem

external environment   economic, competitive, legal/political, social and technological forces that affect organizations

grounded theory   researchers observe consumer behavior in order to develop a theory

hypothesis   statement that makes an assumption about the cause of a problem

information   relevant data that have been analyzed to diagnosis the cause of a problem

knowledge   information that has been analyzed to find a solution to a problem

observation   research method where information is gathered by watching participants and recording their actions

projective techniques   set of research tools that are used to obtain information indirectly rather than through verbal response

research question   what a company needs to know to solve a problem and provide the basis for a research study

sample   a group of individuals chosen to participate in a research study because they are representative of a larger population

secondary data   data that already exist in a useable form because they have been collected by others

1 Why do small businesses and nonprofit organizations often believe they can-not conduct marketing research?
2 What are some of the issues that a large multinational corporation might research?
3 How does marketing research provide the link between the internal and exter-nal environments in which a company operates?
4 How does qualitative research lead to better company performance?
5 You are conducting research for a grocery store on why consumers buy organic produce. Do you recommend quantitative or qualitative research and for what reason(s)?
6 Sales and revenue are falling at the university's bookstore but no one knows the reason for this. Would you suggest conducting descriptive, exploratory or causal research? Why?
7 If a market researcher approaches you while walking home after class to ask if you will take five minutes to complete a survey about your shopping habits, what would you say? Why?
8 Give an example of both qualitative and quantitative data that could be gath-ered on your class.
9 What are the differences and similarities between the three research approaches?
10 Give three research methods that could be used to ascertain students' satisfac-tion with this class.

Recommended Reading

Abrams, Rhonda (2006) *Successful Business Research: Straight to the Numbers – Fast!* The Plan-ning Shop. Not many books focus on how to find numerical data that researchers need when conducting secondary research on competitors. Using this book will help researchers find sales figures for competitors and the market share for products.

Carson, David, Gronhaug, Kjell, Perry, Chad and Gilmore, Audrey (2001) *Qualitative Market-ing Research.* London: SAGE. This book explains how statistical information can be enriched through the use of qualitative research findings. While discussing the methods, it also explains the theories on which these are based.

Daymon, Christine and Holloway, Immy (2002) *Qualitative Research Methods in Public Rela-tions and Marketing Communications.* London: Routledge. A basic text that covers all the steps involved in conducting qualitative research. It includes information on interviews, focus groups, grounded theory and ethnography.

Franses, Philip Hans and Paap, Richard (2001) *Quantitative Models in Marketing Research.* Cambridge: Cambridge University Press. A review of different quantitative models that is written for readers with differing levels of numerical ability.

3 Determining the Research Question

Learning Objectives

1   Explain the importance of critical thinking when making assumptions
2   Describe the critical thinking process
3   Understand the process of obtaining internal secondary data
4   Appreciate the importance of writing a clear research question

ONE LOOK AND THEY KNEW THEY WERE MEANT FOR EACH OTHER!

If it sounds like a line from a romance novel, it could be. But it could also be what a publisher says to a new romance novel author. Publishers love romance, as no other type of book has a higher profit margin than romance novels. This fact is attributed to the knowledge publishers have of romance novel readers. Publishers will have researched everything – from where romance novel readers buy their books to what type of book cover they find attractive. And having this knowledge means fewer books that don't sell and happy readers who keep buying more books that do sell. In fact, romance novels bring in twice as much revenue as either science fiction or mysteries.

How do publishers get this information? By obtaining qualitative information from bookstore staff about what customers want and quantitative data from their own research on sales figures. In contrast publishers of other types of fiction simply publish lots of books in the hope that some will sell well.

Questions: How would you convince publishers of mysteries, science fiction and novels to follow the example of romance publishers? What type of arguments do you feel these publishers would make in return?

Source: Andriani, 2007

3.1 Critical Thinking

A problem can be described as a question for which there is currently no answer. When faced with a problem, it is tempting for an organization to start researching the answer immediately. The temptation to begin researching right away results from the belief that an organization both understands the source of the problem and that the answer is self-evident. However, time will not be saved if a company starts to research immediately. Instead, both time – and money – will be wasted, as the first analysis of a problem is rarely correct (see box below).

WRONG ASSUMPTIONS CAN RESULT IN EXPENSIVE MISTAKES AND UPSET CUSTOMERS

The combination football and baseball stadium became a popular idea during the 1970s as a way for cities in the USA to save money. Cities were fighting to attract more sports teams to their areas and building new stadiums is expensive. So why have two stadiums when one will be sitting empty so much of the year?

It was assumed that it would make no difference to sports fans what the stadium looked like and where the teams played. It was also assumed that all sports attracted an undifferentiated mass of sports fans.

Did fans accept the combination stadium? No, they cried 'Foul!' While many people certainly attend more than one sport, football and baseball are different products that provide different benefits and need to be packaged and sold separately.

What city officials found was that sports fans have an emotional connection to where a sport is played. They prefer a football stadium and a baseball stadium to be just that. As a result, San Francisco invested in building a new baseball stadium downtown rather than play baseball at the football stadium. Three Rivers Stadium in Pittsburgh and Veterans Stadium in Philadelphia, both of which were combination stadiums, have been demolished and replaced with separate sports facilities for baseball and football. In Pittsburgh, the Three River Stadium was replaced with the Heinz Stadium for the Pittsburg Steelers and PNC, a classic style baseball park for the Pirates. Somebody should have asked the fans!

Source: Ries and Ries, 2004

This decision to start research without proper planning is a common mistake made by all types of organizations. Unfortunately, a company that starts to research prematurely has probably not even correctly identified the source of a problem. This failure will lead to one of the most frequent mistakes in marketing research, which is to base the research study on the wrong research question. If this is done, the original problem will remain even if the research is conducted correctly because the researchers asked the wrong question. In the example regarding combination football and baseball stadiums, the question asked was how to save money. The question that was not asked – and should have been – was how the fans might react to the change.

3.1.1 Critical thinking and faulty assumptions

The most common difficulty faced by organizations when starting the research process is making a faulty assumption about the cause of a problem. Assumptions can be thought of as facts that are believed to be correct without proof. Faulty assumptions are often based exclusively on personal experience, rather than on objective fact. This rush to judge why a problem exists is naturally simpler and quicker than searching for facts, as it takes little critical analysis. Yet just because the cause of a problem seems self-evident, this does not make it true. An assumption about a new product opportunity that is acted upon without questioning can lead to expensive failures. Therefore, instead of making assumptions, researchers need to take the time to think critically about what the true nature of a problem or opportunity.

A classic example of starting a business without first conducting research is the dot com company Webvan. This online grocery purchase and delivery service was started with the mission that it would revolutionize the way people purchased groceries. The founder of the company was so convinced of the success of his idea that he managed to persuade others to invest $1 billion. And yet, Webvan declared bankruptcy in 2001 having lost $830 million. As the founder said later, 'Retail 101 is "Prove the market and then grow"'. The way to prove that there is a market available is first to do your research in order to make sure your original assumption is correct (Swartz, 2001; Fost, 2003).

If a wrong assumption about the cause of a problem or the potential success of an idea is made, the wrong research question will be asked. The company will then design and conduct research which will result in the wrong answer. As a result of the wrong assumption a great deal of research time, money and effort will be wasted. One way for market researchers to avoid this situation is to use critical thinking, which is a process of questioning and evaluating assumptions. Critical thinking is a difficult skill that requires effort and a creative imagination. However, research results will improve by applying critical thinking to the research process.

Sometimes a company can find that the change required can be as easy as packaging the product in a different size (see box below).

AMERICANS ARE GETTING BIGGER – SO NABISCO IS REPACKAGING THEIR SNACKS

It may seem as though everyone is trying to lose weight, but obviously not everyone is succeeding. The amount of food Americans have available to eat has increased by 18 per cent since the last generation, and Americans have taken advantage of this increase by consuming 23 per cent more in calories. Societal concern about obesity is serious and, of course, everyone knows that cookies, crackers and chips are not diet food. Marketers at Nabisco, part of Kraft Foods, took note of this change in the external environment and decided to react. The problem was that although consumption of products such as Oreo cookies, Chips Ahoy, Wheat Thins and Cheese Nips can add to weight gain because of the calories and carbohydrates they contain, the company still wanted consumers to purchase.

(Continued)

A first response to this problem might have to change the recipe of the snacks to lower the calories. This is the route the company could have taken, however they knew from research that it was the taste of the treats that made them popular. Therefore, they tested another solution to the problem – packaging the treats in 100-calorie servings. Kraft had also noticed the popularity of certain diets, such as the South Beach Diet expounded upon in a bestselling book. The packaging of smaller portions has become so popular that Kraft is now repackaging new foods that will meet specific diet requirements. Consumers can now enjoy their snacks – while still following their favorite diet and controlling their waistlines.

Source: Kraft Foods, 2004, 2006

3.2 The Critical Thinking Process

Critical thinking can be thought of as a three-step process. The first step is identifying the pre-existing assumptions held by company employees regarding the cause of a problem or a potential opportunity. The second step is to use internal research data to challenge whether these same assumptions are accurate and based on fact. The third step is to explore new ideas about the actual source of a problem and its possible solution.

3.2.1 Challenging assumptions

Unfortunately the second step in challenging assumptions about the cause of a problem is where the critical thinking process often stops. As a result assumptions are accepted without being questioned. The reasons for this automatic acceptance include common patterns of thought among company employees and the natural desire most people feel to conform.

If everyone in a company tends to view that company's product, their consumers and the external world in the same way, it is difficult for researchers to argue against these beliefs. However, it is these common patterns of thought that can cause a company's problem and its solution to seem self-evident. These common thought patterns can also keep companies from seeing opportunities that can be explored by using research. If everyone thought the same, who would think of flavored bananas (see box below)?

HOW MUCH WOULD YOU PAY FOR A BANANA?

In pre-Starbucks' times, coffee could be purchased inexpensively at many types of establishments. Consumers didn't expect the coffee to taste great, or the coffee shop to look good. After all, at least the coffee was cheap – so who could complain?

(Continued)

Then along came Starbucks. In 1983 Howard Schultz, who had joined Starbucks the previous year, was visiting Milan, Italy, were he was impressed with the popularity of espresso bars serving high quality coffee drinks in a relaxed atmosphere. He convinced the owners of Starbucks to use research to test his assumption that Americans would be willing to pay much more for a quality coffee product. The idea was successful and today there are 7,569 Starbucks around the world. People are willing to pay much more than 50 cents for a Starbucks' coffee because they consider Starbucks' products to be better.

Bananas are another inexpensive and common product. Can this same quality and price transformation happen to the banana? Chiquita International Brands Inc. would like to increase revenue by having people not only eat more bananas, they would also like them to pay more for their bananas. To make this happen, the research labs at Chiquita are working on developing flavored bananas with a hint of another fruit flavor. Eight different flavors have been developed thus far. Is their assumption that people would pay much more for a unique banana correct? Consumer research to test this assumption will have to take place before large-scale planting of the banana varieties begins.

Source: Cornwell, 2004; Starbucks, 2007

The more prevalent these common patterns of thinking are, the more important it is to challenge such assumptions. And yet if everyone else is sure of the problem and wants to move forward with corrective action, there is a natural desire to conform to their opinion. Nevertheless, it is the responsibility of market researchers to ask questions about whether such assumptions are based on fact, even when this is unpopular. Only after false assumptions have been eliminated can new ideas based on true facts be proposed.

For example, a company that produces bulletin boards targeted at university students for use in dorm rooms might be faced with the dilemma of declining sales. In an initial marketing meeting about the problem, the sales department might suggest that the problem is caused because the product is too expensive for students to purchase. This answer is based on the assumption that all students are on limited budgets and would purchase this item if they could afford to do so. Therefore the sales department may recommend the product price be lowered. The production department staff might assume that bulletin boards are at the end of the product life cycle and no longer needed. Therefore they may recommend that the bulletin boards be dropped from the product line. This answer is based on the assumption that students keep all their information on their computers and have 'paper-free' dorm rooms. Both answers seem to be based on true assumptions – students do lack significant financial resources and they do use computers.

3.2.2 Using internal data to challenge assumptions

However, in this case market researchers should challenge the assumption that sales are down because students cannot afford this product – by asking if students' limited budgets keep them from purchasing other products. The answer can be found by analyzing internal company data on student spending. The data might demonstrate that students are still spending money on this company's other product offerings and therefore are able to make such a purchase. The second assumption (that dorms are now paper-free and therefore bulletin boards are obsolete) could be checked by interviewing the company's sales staff who will be familiar with student dorm rooms. Here evidence would be found that bulletin boards were still needed for a variety of uses, such as posting photos or menus from pizza restaurants that deliver. Internal data found through this process may be sufficient to prove or disprove assumptions at this stage of the research process. While this may seem to slow the process down, time will be saved in the long run because the correct research question will be the end result.

Even large, successful, businesses must routinely go through this process. When Disney first introduced its films into the Indian market they were not a hit with audiences. They realized that their assumptions of what people wanted in a film were based on their American model. After researching consumer assumptions they made the decision to produce films locally, in India, so that the content better reflected the local culture. This same model is now being used in China, Russia, Latin America and South Korea (Marr and Fowler, 2007).

3.2.3 Generating new ideas

With the initial assumptions dealt with and any wrong assumptions discarded, it is time for the final step in the critical thinking process. This is to explore new ideas regarding the problem or potential opportunity. This step in the process demonstrates why market researchers' knowledge of a product and target market is essential. Using this product and consumer knowledge shortens the process of generating and developing new ideas. This is because a researcher will have already challenged many of the assumptions and will have a knowledge base about the product and consumers on which to form new ideas. This is one reason why market researchers will often specialize in conducting research on a product category or specific market segment. If a market researcher does not have this information, additional external secondary research will be needed.

In the example above of why students were not buying bulletin boards, a researcher might check sales figures from the finance office for other products aimed at the university market to see if they have also suffered a decline. In addition, they might interview employees in the sales department who are knowledgeable about the university's student market segment. By doing so they might obtain information that students are in fact buying bulletin boards – they are just buying a competitor's model!

A research question can now be asked as to how to improve the product. The question might be phrased as 'What additional product features and benefits need to be added to meet the competitive threat?' A company will now be ready to invest time and money in designing research to find the correct answer (see Figure 3.1).

3.2.4 Making a correct assumption

Not every problem requires extensive critical thinking. Sometimes the assumptions made about the cause of a problem are clear to everyone in a company, including the researchers. For example, if the owners of a local coffee shop see customers' cars across the street in the parking lot of the recently opened Starbucks, the problem is clear. Little questioning is needed to challenge the assumption that the customers left because they are buying that competitor's product. However, if the coffee shop's owners who take pride in their product conducted additional research, they might find that customers want more than a cup of coffee.

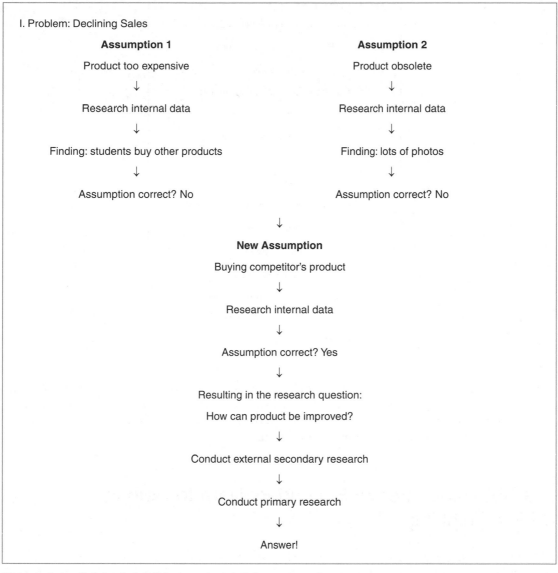

Figure 3.1 Critical thinking as part of the research process

Yet even when assumptions as to the cause of a problem are correct, critical thinking skills must still be used when deciding what research is needed. The next step for the coffee shop owners here would be to plan research to decide what action to take to counter the competitive threat.

For example, the owners might have a number of ideas on how to counter the threat, which could include lowering prices or increased promotion. The problem is that the owners will not know which idea might work. In this case, research on how other coffee shops have responded to competition should be conducted before a plan of action is devised.

```
┌─────────────────────────────────────────────┐
│                                             │
│         Information from Existing Data        │
│                                             │
│            Previous research results          │
│                                             │
│                Sales receipts                 │
│                                             │
│         Customer complaint information        │
│                                             │
│             Customer databases                │
│                                             │
│            Product service requests           │
│                                             │
│               Catalogue orders                │
│                                             │
│                Website hits                   │
│                                             │
│        Information from Company Personnel      │
│                                             │
│                 Sales force                   │
│                                             │
│             Production managers               │
│                                             │
│              Financial analysts               │
│                                             │
│          Human resources professionals        │
│                                             │
└─────────────────────────────────────────────┘
```

Figure 3.2   Sources of Internal Secondary Data

After checking with other local coffee shops, the owners may find that more than one idea can be used to successfully regain customers. However, the owners may only have enough resources to implement one idea. If this is so research would be needed to confirm which approach would motivate the most consumers to return from Starbucks.

3.3 Obtaining Internal Secondary Data to Help in Critical Thinking

Information which is internal to a company will be needed during the critical thinking process to challenge assumptions and to help define problems. Figure 3.2 above provides a summary of sources of internal data. Rather than searching for the 'right' answer to a question, at this point in the process a researcher should realize that there may be several right answers, parts of which must be integrated into the final answer (Martin, 2007).

Researchers can obtain existing information by analyzing internal company data. In addition, they can interview company personnel who have relevant information about the problem. All companies have at least some available data that can be used by researchers. For example, data gathered together in useable form as the result of previous research may already exist. The marketing department in a larger company usually routinely conducts consumer research when developing new products or new promotion campaigns. These research data would be kept in a marketing information database in order that they would then be available to assist in answering future research questions.

Also available to the researcher are raw data that come from other departments in a company. For example, even small companies have sales receipts that researchers can use to learn where their customers live. In addition, customer complaint forms will provide useful information on product improvement ideas. A company's financial records will also give information on sales activity by time period and region. If a company is large enough to have a customer database, the data it contains will provide information on customers' purchase habits. Data on product service requests can provide insights as to possible design problems, while catalogue orders display information on customers' geographic location. Finally, website hits will let a company know how many people are accessing the information. In fact, companies may have a significant amount of internal data already that could be analyzed as discussed in the box below.

COLLECT YOUR OWN INTERNAL DATA!

Of course, a marketing department can find out how satisfied customers are with a company and its employees by looking at the customer complaints that have been logged. However, these are only the customers who have bothered to complain. There are additional ways that could be recommended to collect data.

Market researchers can call this company's own 800-number line and ask for assistance. Are they greeted warmly? Could the employee answer their question? Did they hang up satisfied with the help they received?

Another way to collect internal data is for the marketing department to regularly check this company's website. Is it well designed? Does it provide the needed information or are the information and links out-dated?

These actions will provide researchers with a bit more internal data that could help determine the cause of such problems as declining sales.

Source: Donath, 2004

3.3.1 Obtaining existing internal data from people

There will also be company employees with information that will be useful to researchers. Which employees researchers speak with is partly determined by the nature of the problem. If a company is faced with the problem of falling sales revenue, there may be a variety of departments within that company that will have employees who should be interviewed. For example, interviewing someone in the finance department to provide an analysis of revenue figures may answer the question of whether the decline in sales has been a reoccurring phenomenon or is a surprising event after years of increased sales.

The production department may be able to provide information on any changes in a product's quality. Staff should be able to answer questions such as if they believe any changes in the production process have affected sales. The human resources department might not be the first port of call for researchers, but they also might be able to provide necessary information. Their staff should be able to answer questions such as whether the increasing difficulty of hiring good sales personnel has negatively affected sales. The sales force can be a wonderful source

Table 3.1 Information from company employees

Department	Possible question
Finance	Has sales revenue fluctuated seasonally or yearly in the past?
Purchasing	Has there been any change in the raw materials used in production that has affected quality?
Production	Have new manufacturing procedures affected product quality?
Human Resources	Has there been a difference in the education level and abilities of company personnel hired?
Salespeople	Have any new market segments been purchasing the product and if so why?

of information. They can be asked if they have noticed any changes in the purchasing habits of the consumer segment that usually purchases the product. Table 3.1 above provides examples of possible questions that could be asked.

3.3.2 Conducting internal interviews

Gathering information from internal sources should be handled in the same professional manner as conducting research outside of an organization. The researcher who is conducting interviews should prepare beforehand a set of questions that need to be asked. The answers should be carefully noted during the interview for later analysis and reference. To prevent any confusion if it is necessary to go back for additional information, the researcher should record the name and title of the interviewee and also the date and time of the interview.

Besides gathering facts, the researcher should also use the interview questions to learn more about what the company employee feels is the reason for the problem. If an employee gives more than one reason, they should be asked to prioritize these as to importance. Once the most important problem has been decided upon, the researcher should then ask the employee why they believe this is true and what evidence or insight led them to this conclusion. Asking for concrete examples of the problem that they have experienced in their department will also help to clarify the issue at hand. Finally, asking the interviewee if they would recommend anyone else that should be spoken with could assist in uncovering additional useful information.

3.3.3 Deciding not to conduct additional research

Conducting market research takes time, costs money and uses staff resources. There are occasions when a marketing researcher will recommend that research is not conducted. It may be that initial discussions with internal personnel regarding an issue have provided enough information to correct a problem. Perhaps such a problem resulted merely from a breakdown in communication flow within an organization. While this is certainly a problem that must be addressed, it is not one that needs research to be undertaken by a marketing department.

Another reason for research not being conducted is when answering the question will cost more than the problem. A company that produces backpacks in black only might plan a $5,000 research project on what other colors consumers might prefer. However, the sales department may estimate that offering the product in various colors will result in an increase in sales of only $3,000. In this case the additional revenue exceeds the cost, and the study should not be conducted.

3.4 Determining the Research Question

Writing a research question that clearly states the problem to be researched takes considerable thought. Since this question is the rationale for the all research that will be conducted, it is well worth the effort to make sure that this question is focused on the correct problem. In addition, a research question will need to address what current or potential consumers will need to be asked to learn more about a problem. A well written research question will make planning the remainder of the research study much easier. Table 3.2 below provides examples of the relationship between type of organization, specific problems and the resulting research questions.

Table 3.2   Examples of problems and research questions

Organization	Problem	Question
Large corporation	Declining market share	What new product should we introduce to motivate purchases by older consumers?
Small business	Reduced marketing budget	What is the best way to communicate our marketing message to college students?
Government	Increased demand for recreational facilities	Who are the users of our parks and playgrounds?
Non-profit organization	Decline in funding	Who are our contributors and why do they donate?
Business start-up	Determining location	Who are our customers and where do they live and shop?

3.4.1 Decision-making process

When conducting internal research, researchers may uncover many different possible research questions that could be asked. The following three-step decision-making process of writing, prioritizing and choosing based on cost/benefit analysis can help to clarify which research questions should be asked. To begin with, after gathering information from internal data and people, a marketing researcher will state the general problem that needs to be addressed. Researchers will then write down possible research questions that address the issue.

After this has been done, a researcher will prioritize the relevant possible research questions that have been discovered through internal research. Nearly all problems are complex and there will be more than one insight that could be researched. For example, the problem of declining purchases of carbonated soft drinks by young consumers could give rise to a research question addressing the effectiveness of a company's current promotion campaign. Another suggested research question might address the packaging of a product, while a third might suggest that price is the issue a research question should focus upon.

Researchers now analyze the potential benefits of the data that would be obtained from those questions that have been prioritized as most important versus the cost of the research. The cost of conducting a research study includes not only financial costs but also staff resources and time. Some of the financial costs of research will include the money spent on determining appropriate participants and designing a research instrument. Actually conducting the research will involve such financial costs as distributing survey forms, making phone calls, hiring specialized staff, paying participants and conducting focus groups. In addition, if staff do not have the specialized skills required, they will face the expense of hiring extra staff.

All this activity also takes up staff time which in turn cannot be devoted to other marketing tasks and responsibilities. A research project can take a significant time commitment – anywhere from weeks to months to complete. Only after taking all these financial and staff factors into consideration, are researchers ready to decide which research question an organization should address.

3.4.2 Purpose of the research question

Good research starts with data, which are turned into information to provide companies with the knowledge they need to solve problems. Researchers must always remember that research is conducted for the purpose of solving a company's problems. For research to be useful researchers must have an understanding of companies needs, and not just a knowledge of research methodology (see box below).

IT'S ALL ABOUT THE COMPANY

'The thing is, practically everybody who's not actually in research and of research is talking about how research is broken'. This quote was the result of a reporter's attendance at the 2004 American Association of Advertising Agencies Media Conference. What did he mean by broken? The consumer marketplace is increasingly complex because of the many means of reaching consumers. How and where consumers receive marketing messages has become extremely fragmented. Because of this it is difficult for researchers to track where consumers have heard a particular marketing message.

Researchers, therefore, are not able to provide the knowledge that companies need to understand the effectiveness of their promotional campaigns. The reporter argued that many research companies are so busy competing with each other by touting their own specialties that they do not take the time to understand what companies need.

Source: McManus, 2004

To provide the necessary information it is important to have the right research question stated correctly. The research question may be stated in either an interrogative or declarative style. An interrogative research question identifies the information needed in question form: for example 'What type of media is the best means to communicate promotions to college age males?' A declarative research question identifies the information needed as a statement: for example 'The purpose of this research is to determine the best media to use when communicating promotions to college age males'. Either form can be used as the start of a research proposal.

3.4.3 Research questions and research approaches

Research issues may be expressed with questions that start with 'Why?' or 'How?', such as 'Why have young people stopped purchasing our soft drinks?' or 'How can we use online promotion to regain our market share of young soft drink consumers?'. These will most likely result in an exploratory research approach that is qualitative. This is because researchers do not have enough information to state the question more narrowly. Therefore, they may anticipate that many different answers from participants will result and that the answers may vary greatly.

Research issues may also be expressed with questions that start with 'What?', 'Who?' or 'How many?'. Questions such as 'What is the most popular sport among university students?', 'Who is the purchase decision maker in families when a new auto is bought?' and 'How many consumers will prefer to have our product sold online?' are all questions that will result in descriptive, quantitative research. Researchers should never first decide the type of research methodology and then phrase the question to justify its use. Instead, the research methodology should be determined by the type of question.

3.4.4 Writing the question

For both quantitative and qualitative studies, the question itself needs to be as narrowly defined as possible. To do so, researchers must define who, where, what, when and how as will be used in the question (shown in Table 3.3 below).

Table 3.3 Defining the research question

Who?	Describe the participants who will take part in the research by demographic, psychographic and usage characteristics
Where?	The geographic location of current or potential consumers or the area of product sales
When?	The time frame of the behavior under study
What?	A specific description of the product
Why?	The attitude or motivation of concern to researchers
How?	The proposed actions that could be undertaken by the company

This includes whose behavior is of concern to the researchers. For example, the question as to why young consumers are purchasing less soft drinks could be improved by defining what age group is meant by 'young' consumers. They also must decide if they want this information on all young consumers or only those from a certain income level.

Researchers should also be concerned about where the behavior under study is taking place. For example, they must decide if they mean all young consumers nationally or only those living in urban areas. The geographic area might also be defined by where the product is sold. In the case of company expansion, the area might also be where a product will be sold in the future.

Researchers must also establish the time frame for the behavior that is being studied. For example, the research question might ask about changes in behavior in the last month, year or longer. In addition, researchers must define what products they are studying. For example, are they interested in sales of all of a company's soft drink products, or only a certain brand, package style or size? The question could be rephrased as, 'Why are sales of our fruit flavored soft drinks declining among young, single females, aged 18–24, living in metropolitan areas, and who are financially independent from their families?' The question could be further improved by more clearly defining the 'Why?' in the above question. It could be clearly stated as 'due to increased concern about healthy eating'. Of course, this may not be possible if the researchers have not been able to come to this conclusion before the start of the research process.

The question of 'How can we regain our market share of young soft drink consumers?' also needs to be stated more specifically because there can be so many possible means to regain market share. The means could include price decreases, packaging changes, product enhancements or new promotional campaigns. Most companies will not have the resources to plan and conduct primary research to answer all of these questions. The final decision on which question to research will be based on analyzing the benefits of the research versus the cost. After considering these factors, the final question could be restated as 'What type of promotional message will motivate purchase of our fruit flavored soft drink by health conscious females, aged 14–18, living at home in suburban areas, over the next year?' Sometimes who should be the focus of the question will change over time (see box below).

MOMS RESEARCH WHAT MOMS WANT

Marta Loeb started Silver Stork Consultancy because there was little market research on moms. Loeb, a mom herself, believed that since the US birthrate was at a 30–year high in the 2000 census, it was time for companies to pay attention to what moms need in products, by using what she calls 'mom intelligence'.

She finds this information by employing 12 independent researchers and consultants, most of whom are also mothers. In addition, a network of 3,000 working and non-working moms is paid to hold focus groups in their homes.

The approach works because moms speak the same language and can emotionally connect. This helps provide better information on what moms want to companies who produce products aimed at the mom market.

Interestingly, moms have found that dads are just as involved in family life, with 80 per cent stating they are involved in purchasing the items used daily in the homes. So Silver Stork now calls itself a 'family-focused' research company.

Source: Sutherland, 2004; Frukhtbeyn, 2005

There are general rules that should be remembered when a research question is written. First, the question should be an assertion of fact on which the researcher takes a side. It should not be stated in vague terms such as 'The reason for declining sales may be a lack of promotion'. The purpose of the research will be to determine if it is, or if it isn't. Therefore the researcher must decide which way to state the question – but it can't be both ways.

In addition, the researcher must state the question so that it argues only one point of fact. The question 'Are sales declining because of a lack of promotion or because of increased competition?' is actually two research questions. Different methodologies and different research participants may be needed for each. Thus if the researcher tries to combine them, the research may answer neither question.

Lastly, a research question must pass the 'So what?' test. Does the question generate enough interest from management that they will be willing to approve the research? The answer must lead to a recommendation that will either significantly increase revenue or decrease expenses, or it will not be approved.

Research questions can be developed for any component of the marketing mix and, also, the target market segment and consumer behavior. Table 3.4 below provides examples of research questions that could be asked for each component of the marketing mix.

Table 3.4 Sample research questions

Target market	What is the consumer demographic profile most likely to purchase our product?
	What target market segments are aware of our brand name?
	Should we expand internationally by selling in Europe?
Buyer behavior	What is the frequency of purchase of our shampoo for sports enthusiasts?
	Do our teenage customers show brand preference or purchase based on price?
	What uses do women with families have for baking soda?
Pricing	Will raising the price of our basic product 5 per cent negatively affect sales?
	Are younger consumers aged 14–18 less sensitive to price changes?
	Will parents aged 25–40 prefer lower quality if it means lower prices?
Product	What new design features do our older consumers want on sinks and lavatories?
	Should the company produce a pocket-size version of our product aimed at the 'tween market?
	Will demand among children for our toy trucks increase more than 10 per cent over the next year?
Promotion	What automotive sales approach results in the most repeat sales to single women aged 20–25?
	Are purchases by rural consumers with medium income affected by positive company publicity?
	What advertising media reaches our suburban male target market segment?
Distribution	What is the best location in Williamsport for our new store?
	Will importing our product, rather than using local production, hurt sales among families?
	What is the optimal shelf location in the supermarket for our new breakfast product?

Summary

1 Too often organizations will start research without critically thinking through the problem that they are confronting. As a result an organization will make a faulty assumption about the cause of a problem and the wrong research question will be asked. If the wrong question is asked the data will not be helpful to the company. The time and expense of conducting research will have been wasted. Therefore marketing researchers must carefully think through all possible causes of a problem.

2 Following the three-step critical thinking process will help researchers challenge commonly held assumptions to ensure that when the research question is written it will focus on finding an answer to the appropriate problem. The first step is to identify such commonly held assumptions. These should then be challenged on the basis of internally obtained data. Finally, if the assumptions are proved false, new ideas as to the cause of the problem should be generated.

3 To be able to challenge assumptions, the researchers need to gather as much internal company information from the data and people as possible. They can obtain this data from sources such as sales receipts, databases and service requests. They can also interview company personnel in production, sales, and human resources to better understand how each department views the problem.

4 After gathering internal information the researchers will be ready to write the research question. Because the process of gathering internal information may result in more than one research question, the researchers should use the decision-making process to assist in deciding which of these to pursue. The research question that will be used to obtain this knowledge can be written as a question or as a statement, but should be as clear as possible as to what data are needed. It must also clearly define the research problem.

Key Terms

assumption   fact that is believed to be correct without outside proof

critical thinking   process of identifying pre-existing assumptions, challenging these assumptions and exploring new ideas

decision-making process   method of prioritizing when there is more than one solution to a problem by obtaining information, stating the general problem, prioritizing possible research questions, and analyzing the benefits versus the costs of each

internal secondary information   data that the company already possesses that can help define the research problem

research question   what the company needs to know to solve a problem and the basis for a research study

Discussion Questions

1 You are presented with the general problem of declining sales at a small company manufacturing gourmet cookware. What are the steps you would take in the process of trying to determine the research question?
2 Why is the critical thinking process when developing in the research question so important?
3 Why might a researcher face opposition when she or he challenges assumptions that are held by most company employees?
4 Why is developing the research question the most important step in the research process?
5 When might it be acceptable not to proceed to primary research after conducting internal secondary research?
6 If you were working for a community organization that sponsors basketball leagues for youth and were presented with the problem of decreased participation, what types of internal information should you analyze?
7 How would you describe the difference between internal and external secondary data?
8 What would be an appropriate research question to use to determine which sports should be offered by your school?
9 Give an example of a research question that the local Red Cross organization could use to determine why blood donations are declining. Now state the research question in both an interrogative or declarative style.
10 Under what circumstances is not conducting research the right decision?

Recommended Reading

Dewey, John (2007) *How We Think*. Mineola, NY: Dover Publications. This reprint of a classic book addresses the issue of how people use information to solve problems.

Fitzgerald, Stephen P. (2002) *Decision Making*. Oxford: ExpressExec. This is an interesting book that covers the various ways that a business can make decisions. The steps from contemplation to implementation are discussed.

Lewis, H.W. (2003) *Why Flip a Coin? The Art and Science of Good Decisions*. New York: Barnes and Noble. The book explains the various ways that decisions can be made scientifically and does so without using mathematics.

Robinson, W.P. (2006) *Arguing to Better Conclusions: A Human Odyssey*. Lawrence Erlbaum. Why do people stick to false assumptions when the evidence is contrary to their belief? This book will explain the reasons using communication, language and thinking.

Thayer-Bacon, Barbara (2000) *Transforming Critical Thinking: Thinking Constructively*. Columbia: Teachers College Press, Columbia University. While mainly written for those in education, this book's examination of the thinking and decision-making process is useful for any reader.

4 The Research Proposal

Learning Objectives

1   Understand the three reasons for writing a research proposal
2   Describe the components of a well written research proposal
3   Explore the types of external companies that conduct marketing research

TESCO KNOWS US SHOPPERS

Tesco have already expanded their successful grocery store model across Europe and into Asia. The next stop for their expansion plans is in the United States just outside of Los Angeles, California. Will Tesco be successful? After all, both Sainsbury's and Marks & Spencer have entered the US market only to retreat. Tesco believe they will be successful because of their emphasis on marketing research. The company spent three years researching Japanese consumers before they successfully entered the Japanese market. Tesco researchers lived with Japanese families where they learned to think small – small stores and small package sizes.

To research the grocery needs of US consumers, Tesco researchers again lived with local families. While in their homes, researchers tracked what was in the refrigerator and kept diaries of families' everyday activities. Tesco went so far as to set up a 'practice' grocery store in a warehouse and then invited groups of people to shop. Tesco researchers watched the consumers' shopping behavior and then asked for feedback on the reasons for their purchases. The research findings showed that Americans have plenty of space since Americans have lots of room. However, Tesco also found that Americans have little time for food preparation so preprepared food should sell well.

Question: While not all companies have the financial ability to duplicate Tesco's research effort, how can companies be more creative with research methodology?

Source: Miller and Olson, 2007

4.1 The Research Proposal

The research process starts when management become aware of a general problem. The problem almost always appears through having a potential negative impact on revenue. After all, companies do not conduct pure research just for the sake of 'knowing'. Instead, the problem is usually tied to a decrease in revenue due to falling sales. On the positive side, a problem might involve the need to research if a new product will lead to increased profit. After management, along with researchers, have defined the general problem the research objective will be stated. Finally, a more specific research question will be asked.

Any organization contemplating conducting research should start by analyzing internal data to help clarify the issue that is causing concern and then should formulate a research question. Once the decision has been made that primary research needs to be conducted to answer the research question, the organization should write a research proposal. Writing such a proposal would be a requirement for someone working in a marketing research company. In this case, the proposal will be a formal document that includes all details of the proposed research, along with staff assignments, a time line for completion and a budget with cost estimates. A marketing research firm should spend considerable effort in writing such proposals as they form the basis for contracts between marketing research firms and client companies. For large corporations, a research proposal will be written internally and then sent to management for approval.

However, it is also recommended that small businesses and nonprofit organizations planning to conduct research should first write a proposal as well. In this case the document is for internal use as an informal contract and planning guide. If there is a concern raised during the research process regarding the cost of conducting research, this proposal will remind everyone concerned of the commitment agreed upon. The proposal also serves as a basis for allocating tasks and assigning responsibility within organizations. The time that is spent on writing a proposal will be saved later when there is no need to renegotiate resources.

A well written research proposal will answer any questions that management, other employees, or board members might have about the research that is to be conducted. These questions would include

- Why?   The subject of the research
- How?   Which research method will be used
- When?   The time the research will take
- Where?   The place or contact method
- What?   The documentation that will be presented at the end of the research

4.1.1 Reasons for writing a research proposal

In summary, there are important reasons why the research proposal should always be written before research starts. First, it is the plan of action or the 'map' of what is to be accomplished. Just as it is a good idea to have a road map before beginning a journey to make sure that the desired destination is reached, a research proposal will ensure that researchers end up with the desired information. Second, it is the basis of a contract. A research proposal ensures that everyone agrees on what is to be accomplished, at an estimated cost, and with the necessary resources. Third, it is a method of accountability that can be used to keep research on track.

Too often managers use research to find data to support a decision they have already made, rather than finding information to help make a decision (Shapiro, 2004). The process of writing a research proposal will help clarify management's thinking. Another reason is that the proposal might be required by the company commissioning the research (see box below).

REQUESTING A RESEARCH PROPOSAL

When the Robben Island Museum in Cape Town, South Africa, wanted to have research conducted on their visitors, management was quite specific on what they wanted to know. The museum requested proposals from market research companies in which they carefully explained their need to know more about who visited and how satisfied visitors were with the visit experience. The four objectives of the research were:

- To identify and understand the profiles of different market segments
- To identify key suppliers of customers in terms of country of origin, province, institution, and so on
- To identify future market segments
- To determine how satisfied current market segments were with the current offerings, ways to improve and the identification of any other needs

Interested marketing research firms were asked to write a proposal that would detail the methodologies they would use to meet these objectives.

Source: Robben-Island, 2006

4.2 Components of a Research Proposal

A research proposal is essentially a 'game plan' of what will be done. It can vary in length from a single page to as many as 20 pages, depending on the size and complexity of a research project. Regardless of the length, a proposal should at least consist of three sections and an appendices (see Figure 4.1).

The first section describes a problem by providing an introduction and stating the research objective and research question. The second section describes the methodology including the research approach, method and data collection plan. The section on analysis and findings will contain information on how the data will be analyzed and how the findings will be reported. The appendices will contain detailed information on the budget, personnel needs, timeline and other relevant information.

4.2.1 Components of a research proposal – the problem

The first section of the plan, 'The Problem', describes the background to a problem and the rationale for undertaking research. The information used to define this problem will have already

```
               The Problem
            Introduction
         Research objective
         Research question

              The Methodology
          Research approach
           Research method
          Data collection plan

            Analysis and Findings
              Data analysis
      Methods of reporting of findings

                 Appendices
           Budget and timeline
      Examples of possible research tools
          Confidentiality statement
          Other relevant information
```

Figure 4.1   Proposal outline

been obtained through internal secondary research and also through interviewing relevant company personnel. The first section of the proposal will also describe the research objective and research question.

The introduction will include information on who is the author of the proposal and who will be conducting the research. It will also state under whose authority the proposal is being submitted. The proposal starts with this information to provide legitimacy to its contents. It is especially important to inform the readers of the department, or official who has requested or who will benefit from the research. After all, if the research proposal is approved, time and money will need to be spent. It is much more likely that the research proposal will be approved if it is explained how an organization will benefit from the research.

If this is not done, management may believe that a marketing department wants to do the research because of their own interests, rather than any larger organizational need. However, rather than initiate action on their own, marketing departments will usually view research of such issues as potential product improvement ideas and potential consumer market segments to target, as a result of a request from management or from another department in a company. The research request is usually initiated because of a change in the external environment, such as a threat from a new competitor, or in the internal environment, such as declining revenue.

Once the request to conduct research has been made, it is not uncommon for company personnel to be unable to state the exact cause of a problem. It is the responsibility of marketing researchers to conduct the internal research to clarify a problem so that the right research objective is undertaken. For example, a department may be facing decreased sales revenue. Management's first guess as to the reason for this problem may be ineffective advertising. As a result of this belief management may state the research objective as 'to determine new, more effective promotional ideas'. However, after meeting with management and conducting internal research it may become apparent to marketing researchers that the real reason for the decline in revenue

Table 4.1 Research problems, objectives and questions

Problem	Objective	Question
Our bakery is located in a deteriorating neighborhood	To determine if the bakery should relocate	What percentage of current and potential customers is lost because of the bakery's location?
Our bank has new competition opening in town	To determine how to keep existing market share	What kind of promotion would be effective in communicating the bank's unique products to current customers?
Our furniture company needs a new source of revenue	To determine if there is a potential market segment for a new line of furniture aimed at the 'tween' market	What is the right marketing mix that will motivate parents to purchase new furniture for their 'tweens'?

is that a competitor is offering a new product that is stealing away customers. The marketing department might then recommend that a better research objective might be 'to determine what product improvements are needed to meet the competitive threat'. This new objective will result in a very different research question.

Such information on the objective of the research and the research question is included after the introduction to a report to help readers understand the overall reason for a proposal. The research objective would be the facts or information that researchers hope to find, while the research question would detail the specific data that are needed.

It is important to understand the difference between a general problem, a research objective, and a research question (see Table 4.1). Management will usually state the problem to the marketing department in very general terms. However, the research objective and question must be narrower in scope. Marketing researchers may want to examine examples of academic research proposals to learn more about how these are written for basic research. The proposal should make clear that the researchers understand the research process (Schultz, 2005a).

The research objective section will start with a description of what is currently known about the problem under consideration. This description would result from information obtained through internal secondary research that was conducted by researchers before writing a research proposal. Internal information, such as financial and sales data (along with opinions from internal experts), would assure readers the research question was based on accurate assumptions. This section provides the justification for the research.

Once a research objective has been clarified it is the responsibility of marketing researchers to suggest potential research questions. Using the research objective of the feasibility of introducing a new line of furniture for 'tweens', the research question might be to determine the marketing mix for a new line of furniture aimed at the 'tween' market. A researcher might then rewrite the general research question to be more specific. Potential research questions might focus on the consumer, product, promotion, price or place.

Examples of research questions are

- *Consumer* Who exactly is the target market segment for the product?
- *Product* What type of style and features should the furniture have?
- *Promotion* Who should the promotion be aimed at – kids or their parents?

- *Price*   What price is the target market willing to pay?
- *Place*   Where should the product be sold?

At this point in the process, there may be more than one research question. A proposal should state which of the research questions are of primary importance and which are secondary. After all, at the proposal stage there is no guarantee that an organization will fully fund any research. If necessary, researchers can scale back research by eliminating the research to answer the secondary question. This will then decrease the cost of the research and lower the budget.

It is also important in a proposal for researchers to clarify what will not be researched. For example, research on the feasibility of introducing a new line of furniture will not take into consideration current product improvement ideas. There is often a desire by management to attempt to save money by asking too many research questions at one time. However, if too many subjects are attempted at one time, the research findings will become confused.

4.2.2 Components of a research proposal – the methodology

The second section of the proposal, 'The Methodology', would explain the research methodology including the approach and method that will be used to answer the research question and the data collection plan. It should not be assumed that those reading the proposal are familiar with research terms and methods. Therefore, when discussing the methodology it is important that a proposal both explains and clarifies the meaning of such terms as 'descriptive', 'exploratory' and 'causal', as these words might be used differently by managers. If researchers suggest that research should be conducted with more than one approach and method, it is especially important for a proposal to explain the reasons for doing so.

For example, a research problem might state the need to determine why consumers do not subscribe to satellite radio. The proposed methodology might include both exploratory qualitative research to obtain information on the reasons, followed by descriptive survey research to confirm the focus group findings. Consumer research might start with exploratory focus group research. The data from this research might suggest that people are unaware of the service and may also provide a number of promotional ideas that would build awareness and encourage subscription. The next step in the plan might be to conduct descriptive research using a survey to determine which specific promotional ideas will result in the most subscribers. It would be important to explain why both approaches were needed to meet the objectives of the research and answer the research question.

Once an approach has been explained a proposal should provide as much information as possible about the method. The more thoroughly a research method is detailed, the more management will feel confident in approving a proposal. In addition, the more planning that is done before the start of the research, the easier this research will be to conduct.

If a company needs to conduct research in another country, a proposal should also address how the methodology will need to be adapted. This would include the need to partner with local firms to gain access to cultural knowledge. In addition, the timeline will need to be adjusted to allow more time for project completion (Young and Javalgi, 2007).

For example, if a proposal suggests focus groups be conducted, the proposal should state the number of focus groups, who the participants will be and the topics to be discussed. In addition, it should also explain how many people will participate and how they will be chosen. Logistical details such as dates, times and locations should be given. Finally, the choice of moderator for the focus group will be should be discussed.

Thus the proposal information on focus groups encompasses

- Number of groups
- Number of participants in each group
- How participants will be chosen
- Length of time for focus groups
- Names of moderators
- Locations where focus groups will be held
- Starting date for focus groups
- Date when focus groups will be completed

When research involves conducting descriptive quantitative research such as surveys, proposals should include information on both their method and the participants. This would include information on the length of the survey and the type of questions to be asked. Proposals should also describe the procedure for testing questionnaires. Information on sampling plans and how participants will be chosen should also be included. Finally, how researchers will analyze the data should be discussed.

The proposal information for a survey should encompass

- When that survey will be conducted
- The length of the survey form
- The type of questions to be asked
- An example of a survey question
- A testing plan for the survey questions
- A sampling plan for choosing the participants
- A contact method for the survey form
- The number of forms that should be completed
- The analysis method for the data collected

What a proposal does not need to include is a finished research methodology. At this point in the process, researchers cannot prepare a final focus group script or survey questionnaire as this will need additional research time and money. If possible, examples of methodologies from previously conducted research should be included. These would give management an idea of the type of research instruments that will be used without committing researchers to exact questions. If the methodology is new, such as online research, researchers will need to supply additional information, such as cost savings, as to why the method is being proposed (see box below).

ONLINE RESEARCH IS GROWING

Online research is gaining in popularity because it is cheaper and faster than traditional delivery methods. The amount of money spent on online research has grown in the USA from $3.8 million in 1996 to $1.35 billion in 2006. Yet this growth might not be surprising considering the growth in online use during the same ten years. What is surprising is the fact that one-third of all US spending on market research surveys is now spent on online surveys. The reason for this change is that conducting a survey online has cost savings of 15–20 per cent over mail surveys and 30 per cent over phone surveys.

While a quantitative research method such as a survey can be done online, qualitative methods are more difficult to adapt. Qualitative research conducted online is only 1 per cent of all spending. Qualitative research is still heavily dependent on face-to-face contact.

Source: Johnson, 2006

4.2.3 Components of a research proposal – analysis and findings

The final section, 'Analysis and Findings', describes how the data will be analyzed and reported. This section would include information on how the coding of transcripts or notes from focus groups will be used to find common responses and themes. It would also include how survey data will be analyzed, including any software packages that will be used.

A proposal should be very specific on what information will be provided to management and in what format. The research deliverables might include not just a final report but also ongoing feedback. This might be done informally through phone calls and email. Management may be offered regularly scheduled meetings and weekly reports during the research process. The more research is costing, the more management will want to be kept abreast of progress. This is also helpful for researchers as any misunderstandings can be clarified and rectified immediately, rather than having disappointed clients at the end of the process when it is too late to make changes to the methodology.

In addition to ongoing feedback, the research deliverables will include written documentation such as a formal report and verbal presentation. Sometimes the final report may be provided in an alternative format, such as video. Management may also be provided with completed survey forms, tape recordings or videos of focus groups, and survey data files. For this reason it is important that researchers be careful to keep all documentation during the research process.

Researchers will also need to make a formal presentation of their findings to management. This will allow management to ask questions regarding the impact the research findings may have on strategy. While it is management's decision what action to take as a result of the research, researchers can help to clarify the meaning of their findings.

4.2.4 Appendices

Any final material contained in the appendices of a research proposal could include a breakdown of costs, personnel needs, a time schedule for completion, examples of the research methods and any technical details of the data analysis technique. It is important that a detailed timeline be provided in the research proposal, as it is not unusual for management to not understand that good research takes time. For this reason just giving a start and end date should be avoided. A proposal should also provide a breakdown on when each task will be completed.

A sample proposal timeline for a survey could be as follows:

Week One:	Preliminary secondary research on problem
Week Two:	Write questionnaire
	Meet with management to review
Week Four:	Choose sample
	Meet with management to review
Week Five:	Test questionnaire
Week Seven:	Conduct survey
Week Eleven:	Analyze data
Week Fourteen:	Write report
Week Sixteen:	Present findings

In addition to the timeline, a proposal should contain a budget for expenses. It is not necessary to provide a breakdown of all expenses. What should be laid out clearly is the breakdown between general labor and overhead expenses and expenses specific to the research. Such expenses would include survey form reproduction, the hourly rate for a call center if a phone survey is to be conducted, the room rental for focus groups and any travel expenses for attendance at meetings.

If the expenses seem higher than management is willing to pay, researchers might wish to present two research scenarios at different cost levels. However, a proposal should also explain how the research will be impacted if the research proposal with the smaller budget is chosen.

It is also important that a proposal provides details in the appendices on the personnel that will be needed to conduct research. Not only the number of people, but also the number of hours they will be working on the research, need to be explained. Labor costs are often a large component of a marketing research budget. This may be due to the number of people who will be needed to conduct a survey, or it may be the cost of hiring a professional moderator for focus groups. If specific personnel will be needed they should be mentioned by name to ensure their availability for the research project.

The appendices should contain a statement of confidentiality. This statement would explain that any information about a company discussed during meetings with researchers will be kept confidential. In addition, a proposal must state whether the research methodology created to conduct the research belongs to the marketing research firm concerned or the company commissioning the research. Lastly, what will happen to all resulting documentation will be explained. A proposal may state that all documentation such as completed survey forms, tapes, or notes may be returned to the company commissioning the research or may be destroyed. The issue of confidentially is especially important when the research involves new product development and other strategic issues. The time an outside marketing research company spends on a proposal should be seen as a necessary investment to get the job (see box below).

A well written research proposal may make the difference between a marketing firm receiving a research contract or not. According to market researcher Matthew Singer, to help increase the chances that a firm will be successful in obtaining a contract, the writer of the proposal should ask themselves the following questions:

What are the key questions/information needs that research must address?
What are the vital business decisions that the research findings will affect?
How will the results be used?
What other marketing factors are contributing to the need for research?
Has previous research been conducted on related topics?
Are there secondary objectives that also need to be addressed?

The research proposal will only be accepted if an organization believes that the cost of doing the research is more than covered by the value of the information received.

Writing a winning research proposal is a skill that can be learned. An organization needing research will first issue a request for a proposal or RFP. When writing a research proposal in response to an RFP the following steps are suggested:

Reflect on the client – include any unique perspectives
Read and decipher – write a checklist of conclusions based on the RFP
Make preliminary contact – build interest and gather information
Use your checklist as a guide – don't overlook any important issues
Draft and proof – mistakes undercut credibility
Submit in a timely fashion – proof of an ability to meet deadlines
Follow up on receipt – call and make sure it arrived
Track acceptance/rejection factors – live and learn!

Source: Singer, 2006

4.3 The Research Industry

Marketing research can be conducted internally by company employees or a company may hire an external firm to conduct research. During the process of writing a research proposal, a company must make the decision whether to conduct the research themselves or to hire an external market research firm. The decision to hire an external firm could be based on the fact that that company does not have the staff, expertise or time to conduct the research internally. If the decision is made to hire an external research provider, it is important to understand the composition of the marketing research industry. It is also important for those making the choice of which firm to hire to understand the general guidelines in choosing a research supplier. Choosing a research supplier is an important decision that should be given adequate time and attention (see the box below).

4.3.1 Structure of internal marketing research departments

The marketing research needed to answer a research question can, of course, be conducted by company employees. Who is involved in conducting the research depends on the size of the company. A large corporation, such as Coca-Cola or Proctor & Gamble, has the financial resources to have a specialized consumer research department within their general marketing department. The box below provides information on positions at General Mills.

Marketing Research

(Continued)

If you worked for General Mills some of your responsibilities would include:

- Managing all the stages of research projects
- Developing new products
- Improving product quality
- Developing advertising
- Evaluating the results of consumer promotions

General Mills considers the following as 'Success Factors' for marketing researchers:

- Proven analytical skills
- Outstanding communication skills
- A high level of motivation
- Good business knowledge
- Excellent interpersonal skills

Source: General Mills, 2004

The place of a marketing research department in an organization chart varies. It may be a centralized department reporting directly to top management. Or it may be decentralized with separate marketing research divisions for different product lines, consumer market segments, or countries or regions in which a company operates. Employees who work in these specialized consumer research departments are usually highly skilled with degrees in marketing. In fact many of these positions require a researcher to have an advanced degree in business or statistics. Even entry level positions will at minimum require a Bachelor's degree.

While this is the type of research department of which people may be most aware, marketing research is also conducted in small corporations, small businesses and sole proprietorships. Small corporations without national or global reach will have a marketing department where employees are expected to handle a number of different marketing functions, including research. If a company has specialized research needs the employees feel they cannot handle, jobs will be contracted to external marketing research firms.

Small businesses may not even have a separate marketing department; a single employee may be responsible for all the marketing functions. This employee may have a degree in business but may or may not have taken a marketing research class.

Many people are the sole proprietors of their own business. These business people will perform all the management and marketing functions. These include informal marketing research, although these people may not always think of it in these terms. They might just call it 'keeping on top of what my customers want'. Table 4.2 below shows the level of responsibility in different sizes of organizations.

4.3.2 External providers of marketing research

The decision to hire an external firm may be made even when a company has a research department. This occurs when an organization feels they do not have the staff available to conduct

Table 4.2 Different levels of internal marketing research capabilities

Organization	Capabilities
Large corporation	Specialized marketing research department
Small corporation	Marketing department also responsible for research
Small business	Marketing employee responsible for all marketing functions
Sole proprietorship	Marketing, including research, one of many functions performed by owner

research or they need expertise that they simply do not have. This expertise might be in research with a specific target market segment, such as young ethnic males, or may require a specialized research tool, such as observational research. External marketing research providers can be categorized as advertising agencies, syndicated firms, and custom marketing research firms.

Marketing research firms

- Advertising agencies – research is one of many services offered
- Syndicated firms – they sell data they have collected
- Custom research firms – they design research studies to meet client needs

Advertising agencies
Advertising agencies have internal research departments that deal with such issues as finding the correct marketing message and the best image to represent a client company. They also research the best media to use to reach a specific target market.

Syndicated research firms
These companies are in business to collect data on a continuing basis regarding the consumption of a specific product or products or the purchasing behavior of a specific target market segment. These data are then sold to companies, which specify how much data they want and the analysis they require. The more data and analysis that are requested, the higher the price. What a syndicated research firm does not do is conduct research specifically designed for a single company. For example, ACNielson collects information on TV and media viewing and also on ad recognition on the internet. Anyone, including the public, can buy the products they sell by visiting their website.

Custom research firms
Custom research firms will design a unique research project to answer a company's research question. They will then conduct the research and analyze the findings. These firms can be further divided into specialized and full service custom research providers. Research conducted by a custom marketing research firm usually starts with a call from a client. This client company will have a specific problem which requires research that the firm will design and conduct. For a custom research firm there is no reason to conduct research if they are without a client with a problem.

Specialized custom market research firms conduct specialized research on a specific product category or market segment. These marketing research firms can be grouped by their area of specialization. For example, they may specialize in consumer food products or in young people as a market segment. Some firms, such as IMS Health Inc, specialize in designing research for the pharmaceutical industry. Johnson Controls does research only on automotive interiors. Other

Table 4.3 Questions to ask when hiring an external research firm

Business practices	What guarantee do I have that you will deliver the completed research product on the specified date?
	Will you provide a detailed estimate of the prices you will charge for the research?
Skills and expertise	What are the qualifications of your staff?
	What research techniques do you use?
	What market segments do you research?
Reputation and ethics	Can I ask previous clients about the quality of your work?
	Do you have a professional code of conduct for your company?
	Have you ever turned down a potential client?

firms specialize in researching the target market segment of the young, urban male. These firms focus on a specific market segment, but research many different products. For example, they will have contracts with companies that produce clothing apparel, or soft drinks, or are media and telecommunication companies.

On the other hand, full service custom research firms will take on any project no matter what the target market segment or the product line is. These full service companies are able to offer a wide range of expertise and services. They are in effect 'one-stop' research firms. However, they may lack the depth of knowledge that has been acquired by specialized custom firms.

4.3.3 Guidelines for choosing a research company

When choosing an external research company, there are general guidelines that should be followed. A company should examine a research firm's business practices, skills and expertise, and their reputation for quality and ethical conduct.

It is important to interview not just those representing the research firm, but also, if possible, the researchers themselves. In addition, asking for references from other companies who have hired a particular firm can provide information as to their reputation. Hiring a research firm is expensive, so the decision should be made as carefully as when buying an expensive piece of equipment. Table 4.3 above gives examples of those questions that should be asked.

4.3.4 The global research industry

Marketing research has become increasingly global. In fact, marketing research is now a $21.5 billion global industry (ESOMAR, 2006). To be one of the largest marketing research firms now requires global reach. This is demonstrated in Table 4.4 by examining the number of countries in which the largest firms have offices. This is proved by the fact that the top five research companies in the world have an average of offices in 58 countries. The largest, VNU NU (whose company slogan is, 'We measure. We analyze. We inform. We know. We answer.'), has offices in 81 different countries. Often this global expansion is through the acquisition of smaller, local research companies in specific countries. For example, in June 2004 IMS Health acquired United Research China, which specialized in researching the consumer health market in China (IMS Health, 2004).

4.3.5 Marketing research associations

There are numerous marketing research organizations that provide an opportunity for those involved in the research industry to both network and learn from others working in the research

Table 4.4   Top five global research organizations

Firm	Website	Revenue (millions)	% Revenue outside country
1 VNU NU, Netherlands	www.vnu.cm	3538	99
2 Taylor Nelson Sofres, UK	www.tns-global.com	1803	84
3 IMS Health, USA	www.imshealth.com	1755	64
4 Gfx AG, Germany	www.gfk.com	1311	73
5 The Kantor Group, USA	www.kantargroup.com	1237	65

Source: Honomichl, 2006

industry. Some of the organizations are specific to a region or country. The Council for American Survey Research Organizations represents research firms in the USA, Canada and Mexico. Other organizations, such as the Market Research Society with 8,000 members in more than 50 countries, are global in reach. Organizations such as the Advertising Research Foundation focus on a specific area of marketing research. Others, such as the Qualitative Research Consultants Association, focus on a specific type of research.

Marketing research associations

- Advertising Research Foundation (ARF) (www.aftsite.org)
- American Association for Public Opinion Research (www.aapor.org)
- American Statistical Association (ASA) (www.amstat.org)
- Council for American Survey Research Organizations (CASRO) (www.casro.org)
- Council for Marketing and Opinion Research (CMOR) (www.cmor.org)
- Market Research Society (www.marketresearch.org.uk)
- Marketing Research Association (MRA) (www.mra-net.org)
- Pharmaceutical Marketing Research Group (PMRG) (www.pmrg.org)
- Qualitative Research Consultants Association (QRCA) (www.qrca.com)
- Research Industry Coalition (RIC) (www.researchindustry.org)
- World Association of Opinion and Marketing Research Professionals (ESOMAR) (www.esomar.org)

Summary

1   A research proposal should explain the 'why, what, when, where and how' of the research. It is necessary because research takes resources including money, people and time. Although the proposal will take time to write, it is necessary for three reasons. First, it is a plan of action that keeps research on track. Second, it is the basis of the contract on what resources will be needed. Third, because it has described the tasks to be completed and those responsible, it is a way to ensure accountability.

2   The research proposal has three main sections; the plan, the methodology and the analysis and findings. The plan will include an introduction and will also state the research objective and research question. The methodology section will include information on the research approach, the methodology and the data collection plan. The analysis and findings section will describe how the data will be analyzed and how the data will be presented once the research is completed. The proposal concludes with appendices that provide details on the timeline, budget and personnel needs.

3   Who conducts marketing research will vary depending on the size of the organization. A large company may have a specialized research department while a sole proprietor may need to conduct all the research personally. If an outside research firm is hired the choice is between using an advertising agency, a syndicated firm or a custom research firm. Advertising agencies provide research along with many other marketing services. Syndicated research firms collect information on an ongoing basis which they then sell. Custom research firms work with client companies to design proposals that meet their specific needs.

Key Terms

advertising agency   company that offers a variety of services, of which one may be research, to assist firms with promoting their products

custom research firm   company that will design a research project for a company that will specifically address their research question

marketing research association   membership organization of companies that conduct marketing research

research proposal   document that describes the purpose of the research, the methodology and the sample

syndicated research firm   company that sells research data that have already been collected

---

Discussion Questions

1   Why should a research proposal be written before starting research?
2   What is the relationship between a research problem, objective and question?
3   Why should the research proposal be careful to explain marketing research terms?

4 How does the research proposal form the basis of a contract even when the research is conducted internally?
5 What is the purpose of providing detailed budget information?
6 Why would a company commissioning research be concerned about confidentiality?
7 Why would a company with an internal consumer research department sometimes commission research from an outside firm?
8 Why does the industry contain companies that specialize in providing different types of research services?
9 What is the difference between a syndicated and specialized custom research firm?
10 Why is it important for a company to be careful when choosing an external research provider?

Recommended Reading

Brace, Ian and Adams, Karen (2006) *Introduction to Market and Social Research: Planning and Using Research Tools and Techniques.* London: Kogan Page. A book that asks the reader to answer basic questions, such as why research is needed, and then takes the reader through the process step by step.

Crouch, Sunny and Housden, Matthew (2003) *Marketing Research for Managers.* Boston, MA: Butterworth-Heinemann. Besides describing the research process, this book addresses specific issues in using research in online, industrial, and international markets.

McQuarrie, Edward R. (2003) *The Marketing Research Toolbox: A Concise Guide for Beginners.* London: SAGE. Describes the marketing research process in terms of business decision making. Also discusses how correctly planned research should provide businesses with direct benefits.

5 Cultural Considerations for Marketing Research

Learning Objectives

1 Introduce unique international marketing research challenges
2 Examine the importance of language translation
3 Understand how Hofstede's cultural dimensions affect conducting research
4 Appreciate the unique ethical issues when conducting cross cultural research

GLOBAL BUSINESS NEEDS GLOBAL RESEARCH

Looking for investment opportunities? How about a shopping mall in Cambodia?

Here's proof this is a global marketplace. An American is using the AIM market, part of the London Stock Exchange, to raise funds to build an 'American-style' shopping mall in Pnom-Penh, Cambodia. Parkson, a Malaysian department store, has already signed on as an anchor tenant. The planned project will include a 600-space car park and 100 serviced apartments.

The developer of the project is an American married to a Cambodian woman. Asked why he chose to raise the funds for the project in the UK, the developer stated that the project's investor base is global and London is the center of global finance. While the developer has a global outlook on finance, the development plans were born in the USA.

Questions: Will the average Cambodian shopper want an 'American-style' mall? Who is the 'average' Cambodian shopper? What other research questions would you recommend be answered before the project is built?

Source: Rossiter, 2007

5.1 International Marketing Research Challenges

International marketing research can be defined as research that is conducted in one or more countries other than the country of the company commissioning the research. This international research may be conducted because this company already sells products in more than one country, or because they hope to do so in the future. If more than one country is involved in the research project, the company may decide to conduct the research either simultaneously or sequentially, country by country.

When researching the introduction of an existing product into a new country, any company needs to understand the unique needs, wants and desires of foreign consumers. Companies will use this information to adjust the products, prices, distribution and promotion to make their products more attractive to local consumers. Rather than adapt a current product companies may also use marketing research because they want to develop new products that uniquely meet the needs of consumers in other countries. In this case, research is even more important.

Almost all international marketing research is also cross-cultural research. This is true because national boundaries are usually also cultural boundaries. Marketing researchers need to be aware that within any foreign country there may be more than one cultural group. Therefore marketing research designed for a foreign country may need to be adjusted for more than one culture. Below is some advice that should be considered before any cross-cultural research is conducted.

CONDUCTING GLOBAL QUALITATIVE RESEARCH

Global corporations often have global brands, whether they are Starbucks, McDonalds or IBM. However, even if the brand name remains the same the marketing mix offered will differ across borders and cultures. Qualitative research can be used to determine how product, price, promotion and distribution will need to be changed. However, before research can be conducted there are changes to the research process that need to be made if research is to be successful. These changes can be summarized as:

- *Integrate local knowledge*   Hire local researchers to help and then make the necessary changes to the research method they recommend.
- *Form global teams*   Before the research starts, use meetings between marketers in the home country and local researchers to share cultural knowledge.
- *Translate carefully*   Before starting research, it is not only the words in any research instruments but also their meanings that need to be translated and, if necessary, the language should continue to be adjusted during the research process.
- *Understand the culture*   Explore the country using an interpreter to engage consumers in conversation.
- *Find common themes for the final report*   Rather than merely listing findings by country, in the final report find common themes before differences are discussed.

Source: Seidler, 2003

5.1.1 Cross-cultural research at home

Cross-cultural research may also need to be conducted in a company's own country. This will be the case if the country where a company is based is home to more than one cultural group. These different cultural groups may have existed together in the same country for centuries. For example, a country such as Romania has been home to culturally unique groups throughout its history. Alternatively, different cultural groups may result from recent immigration. For some countries, such as the USA, immigration was how such nations were formed.

Unfortunately, just because there is more than one cultural group living in a country does not mean that market researchers are adept or even aware of the need to adjust their methodology. This lack of awareness may result because the newest immigrant groups are usually not represented in the ranks of marketing professionals. In the USA Hispanics now account for 14 per cent of the population, but only 62 per cent of US Hispanic Americans have finished high school (SRBI, 2005). Of course, this fact will change over time as Hispanic Americans take advantage of the educational opportunities available to their families. However, the lower education level that exists now explains why there are few Hispanic marketing professionals. As a result this population might be ignored when conducting marketing research. Unfortunately, by not adapting marketing research techniques to better assess the wants and needs of Hispanic Americans marketers are ignoring a potential consumer segment of 41.3 million people.

5.1.2 Unique research questions

The marketing research process does not change because it is being conducted across cultures. What does change is the choice of methodology and how that methodology is implemented. In addition, marketing across cultures may result in unique research questions. For example, aspects of consumer behavior that researchers take for granted in their own culture may need to be researched in another culture. Design preferences such as color, style and package size may also change from culture to culture. The preferred brand name may vary as well. In addition, where a product is purchased and how that product is used may differ. These variations will result in the need to ask additional research questions.

Examples of research questions which address cultural differences

- What are the design preferences for color and style?
- In which retail outlets would our ethnic target market segment be looking for our products?
- Who makes purchase decisions in these families?
- What type of media does the culturally distinct target market segment use?
- Do consumers want different packaging of products?
- In what language should products' instructions be written?
- How much disposable income does the average consumer have?
- How are our products used?

5.1.3 Availability and comparability of secondary data

Much of the secondary data that a marketing researcher might find available in the USA or Europe may not be available in other countries. The availability of information on demographics and consumer behavior depends on having an institution gathering and maintaining the data over a period of time. This continuity in turn depends on having a stable government or non-governmental bureaucracy to support that institution.

Another issue when conducting international secondary research is that many researchers have become dependent on using online sources of data. However, these sources may be absent in other countries because the relevant information has not been computerized due to the cost. In this case, researchers will need to find and analyze original documents and sources, but even then they may experience problems because the data may not be accurate. In some countries the purpose of collecting data may not have been to provide an objective source of information for researchers. Rather, the purpose may have been to only collect data that supported government policy.

5.1.4 Level of cultural difference

When developing a research plan for conducting international research marketing researchers should consider the level of cultural dissimilarity between a company's home country and the new geographic area in which it plans to market. These differences could include both language differences and cultural values or dimensions. Sometimes research conducted in the same country as where a company is located might still be faced with language and cultural values issues when researching consumers from a minority cultural group. While the considerations of language and cultural values must still be taken into account, this research will be easier to undertake. This is because even if they are not members of a culture, researchers will probably have been exposed to that culture through personal relationships or through the media. In addition, finding assistance in obtaining cultural information will be easier as local experts can be found to assist with research.

It is important for marketing researchers to remember that even if the minority culture uses the same language as the majority culture, there will still be differing cultural values that must be considered when designing the research methodology. Below is an example of research that was conducted on international students studying in the UK.

HOW DO INTERNATIONAL STUDENTS VIEW STUDYING IN THE UK? A SURVEY CAN ANSWER THE QUESTION

Ipsos MORI, based in the UK, is a research company that conducts both quantitative and qualitative research. Not only do they meet the research needs of UK companies, through their links with Ipsos companies located around the world, they also serve the research needs of companies world-wide.

To learn about the motivation and attitudes of international students studying in the UK, Ipsos MORI conducted in-person interviews with 1,025 undergraduate and postgraduate students at 20 UK universities. The sample was constructed so that the students' areas of study were proportional to the number of full-time students studying in the field across the UK. The resulting report, 'The International Student Experience Report 2006', contained facts about international students studying in the UK such as the following:

Why do they come? Because the education will help them find a job.
How do they choose? Academic reputation is the reason for their choice of university.
How do they pay? Money is less of an issue than for UK students as families help financially.
Who are their friends? They mostly make friends with students from other countries.

All of this information could be used by UK universities in developing a promotional campaign targeted at potential international students.

Source: Ipsos MORI, 2006

When research is conducted in another country that shares the same language, it is easy for researchers to assume that the values are the same. However, a shared language does not mean that the cultural dimensions are similar. Americans, Australians, Canadians and British people may all speak English, but a marketing research plan will still need to be adjusted for cultural differences.

Research is most challenging when both the language and cultural dimensions are different. In this case, researchers must use local expertise to ensure that their research design will obtain the needed information. Even when using local research firms companies must be aware of communication difficulties that might arise from language and cultural differences between management teams and foreign marketing researchers.

5.2 Language Issues

Differences in languages between the country where management is located and the country where the research is being conducted will result in additional steps in the research process, including research questions and translation needs.

5.2.1 Translation needs

The first issue here is that additional research will need to be conducted to determine the correct wording for brand names and promotional material (see the box below). The wording used in advertisements (including written ads, brochures, billboards, posters and also broadcast messages) must be researched. It is not enough to simply translate a message. While factual information can be translated and still be understood, promotional material often conveys an emotional rather than a purely factual message. Emotional messages are difficult to communicate, even between people sharing the same culture and language. Therefore additional research will need to be conducted in order to choose how a message should be conveyed, even before the translation issue is faced.

A ROSE BY ANY OTHER NAME MIGHT NOT BE A ROSE!

When a company markets internationally, they must conduct additional research to ensure that their marketing message is translated and communicated correctly. Language is especially important when choosing brand names. Sometimes companies may decide that they want a name that is recognized globally. Therefore they may choose to keep the sound of the brand name similar, even if the meaning to the local language-speaking group may change. However, while this technique might make sense to the company trying to build global awareness, it might be ineffective in attracting foreign local consumers to the product. Even so, most companies try for a similar sounding name believing it builds on their global presence. Yet conducting research on this issue may show it is best that a company sacrifices global branding and finds a name that will more effectively build a local market share.

Source: Francis et al., 2002

5.2.2 Translation during the research process

The second issue is that companies must translate all research material. Translation of both verbal and written information may be needed during several steps in the research process. This includes the planning phase, when preparing research materials and putting together a final report.

Planning phase

If possible, companies undertaking international marketing research should do so by partnering with a research firm in the country where the research will be conducted. This would be advisable because a commissioning company will lack both the language and cultural knowledge needed to conduct effective research in a foreign country. However, this partnership does not mean that translation will not be needed. While all the marketing researchers in a foreign research firm may speak the language spoken by the local consumers, not everyone in a foreign research company will speak the same language as the management in the commissioning company.

If everyone does not speak a language at the same level, a translator should be employed at the research planning meetings. After all, it is difficult enough to communicate effectively about research goals and objectives when everyone speaks the same language. In addition, communication in planning meetings is generally difficult as people start with generalities as research ideas are sorted through and then a meeting will build in complexity as various needs are prioritized. If the added difficulty of language misunderstandings is present, there is an even greater likelihood that miscommunication will take place. If there is any confusion about the purpose of research and the research question it will result in designing a study that will not provide the needed information in any language.

Research material

Translation of questionnaires, interview questions and focus group scripts is more involved than simply having an adequate word for word translation. There are many important cultural issues that will affect word choice. For example, when writing questions, researchers should be aware of wording issues involving ethnicity. There may be many names for the same ethnic group. There may be an official government designation, a commonly used name by other members of that society, and a name that is used within a group itself. Researchers should always use the term that an ethnic community prefers to have used when addressed by those people who are not members of their group. The term that members use among themselves may not always be the term that they prefer others to use, and in fact they may even find it offensive. Besides the research instruments, researchers should not forget that any participant instructions will also need to be translated.

In addition to translating all written material, oral translation will be needed when conducting interviews and focus groups. Of course interviewers and moderators must speak the same language as research subjects as this is the only way to ensure that effective communication can take place. They will therefore need to be bilingual so that a written and oral report can be prepared for management.

Another translation issue arises if someone from the company commissioning the research wishes to observe a focus group or interview. It will then be necessary to provide for simultaneous translation while the research is being conducted. This translation should take place in a separate area designed for viewing and listening to the research while it is being conducted so that the translation will not disrupt the research. For example, if a German automotive company has commissioned research regarding the auto preferences of Romanians, they will observe the research while the translator repeats in German what both the moderator and the participants are saying in Romanian. When simultaneous translation is to be used, the translator should be briefed about the purpose of the research so that they can be ready to translate any industry-specific jargon.

Research findings reporting

Of course, the final written report will need to be translated. The company commissioning the research should request a copy of the research in both the language in which the research was conducted and the language of management. In addition, any research instruments and research notes should be translated even if originally written in another language. If there are any difficulties with the research recommendations, the research instruments can be checked to discover if the problem was as a result of language misunderstandings. Finally, a researcher who is bilingual should give the oral presentation. If this is not possible an oral translation may be needed at the presentation of the report.

5.2.3 Back translation

To ensure that the translation of all written material is correct, researchers may want to use back translation. When using this translation method the written material is first translated from the home into the foreign language. For example, a questionnaire written by researchers in French will be translated into German. Then another translator will translate the same questionnaire from German back into French. If the translation has been correct, the meaning should still be the same to the French researchers who originally designed the questionnaire.

Back translation is useful for both technical documents and research material. A research proposal and contract will contain technical and business jargon that has a very specific and legal meaning. It is very important that these documents be translated correctly. Research materials, such as questionnaires, will often use terms such as idioms and clichés which are common in everyday life and are therefore culturally specific. Not all translators are comfortable with translating all types of language. After all, many people would have difficulty explaining the exact meaning of legal jargon or idioms in their own language. While the use of back translation is the norm when a company needs to conduct a survey in another language, another proposed method involves researchers and translators working as a collaborative team to establish equivalency (Douglas and Craig, 2007).

5.3 Hofstede's Dimensions of Culture

Many of the decisions people make each day as they go about living their lives are made at an unconscious level. After all, life would be much too difficult if every decision had to be carefully considered. So people get up in the morning and eat what they consider to be 'normal' breakfast food. They commute to work in a normal fashion, work at normal occupations, and have normal family living arrangements. Of course, a 'normal' breakfast meal of cornflakes for one person may be fish soup for another – and meanwhile, each may consider the other's choice 'strange'.

Self-reference is a term used to describe the fact that everyone believes his or her way of life is the 'norm'. This is not necessarily a problem unless a person comes into contact with other people who have different ideas of what constitutes a 'normal' life. This person then has the choice of feeling threatened and reacting negatively or reacting with interest and exploring the cultural difference. Below is an example of how one company approached consumer research in the People's Republic of China.

USING RESEARCH TO GAIN INSIGHT INTO CHINESE CONSUMERS

Lenovo, a producer of PCs and other technological products, wanted to sell products to the Chinese consumer. However, so did Hewlett-Packard, Dell and IBM. Lenovo knew that to successfully compete they would have to understand what benefits Chinese consumers wanted in technological products. Discovering consumer preferences is difficult enough when you are familiar with the consumer culture. Therfore, Lenovo established a team to undertake marketing research to discover more about the needs, wants and desires of the Chinese consumer.

This process involved inventive secondary research before they went to China and observation, ethnography and projective techniques once in the country. The research started even before the Lenovo team left for China. Researchers studied photos of Chinese billboards while listening to all types of Chinese music. The team also examined Chinese consumer products. A professor was asked to teach them Chinese history and cultural differences. A Chinese exchange student was asked to describe the Chinese lifestyle and their use of technology. All of this was done so that the team would be better able to conduct research when they went to China.

The next step in the research was to directly experience Chinese culture. The team members lived in China – commuted to work on bicycles, ate in dining halls, sang in kara-oke bars. While they did so, they conducted observational research by noting how people used technology in their everyday life.

The researchers then conducted ethnographic research in consumers' homes. They not only observed the use of technology, they also analyzed the fashion tastes of consumers by examining their clothing and furnishings. Although an interpreter was used on these home visits, the researchers also broke down communication barriers by using projective techniques. Research participants were each given a camera, a glue stick and a poster board, and asked to record their actions during a typical day.

Once the research was done, the information was compiled onto 'Ethnography Inspiration Sheets'. These sheets were used to position Chinese consumers within five segments and products were designed to meet the needs of each. The research was so successful in predicting Chinese preferences it won a gold medal in the 2006 Industrial Design Excellence Award.

Source: ZIBA Design, 2006

When researching marketing issues across cultures it is imperative for researchers to remember that the self-reference criterion is unacceptable. Instead, researchers must remain aware that all consumers have their behavior and desires shaped by their national and ethnic culture. Even within a single country several different ethnic and cultural differences may exist among people who belong to different groups.

Of course, on a basic human level people have the same emotional makeup. Everyone feels pride, humility, anger, love, anxiety and courage. What differs in cultures is which emotions are encouraged and which are suppressed. One model of trying to understand the similarities and differences across cultures was developed by Geert Hofstede. He argued that everyone carries mental programs that shape their actions and values (Hofstede, 2001). These mental programs are the result of socialization from within families, schools and other organizations to which a person is exposed while young. Of course even in the same country the values and behaviors of individuals, families, schools and organizations may vary. However, there will also be striking similarities that will distinguish one country's culture from another's.

Hofstede's model is based on research conducted on the characteristics and values of IBM employees in many different countries. The research revealed that human behavior is not random. Statistical analysis revealed four main characteristics where differences were shaped by an individual's cultural environment. These dimensions of predictable behavior are termed power distance, uncertainty avoidance, individualism/collectivism, and masculinity/femininity.

5.3.1 Power distance

Power distance describes how individuals react to authority. No society exists where everyone has equal power. For example, within an organization a boss has more power than a subordinate. Because of this power difference, the boss can determine the behavior of the subordinate much more than the subordinate can determine the behavior of the boss. This would also be true between those in political power and ordinary citizens. The same could be said between family members, although who holds the power in a family may differ between cultures.

This situation of inequality, where one person has the power to determine the behavior of another, holds true across all cultures. What differs is the acceptance of such inequality or power distance. Do those without power try to reduce the control that the powerful have over their lives? Or is there an acceptance that such a difference in power levels is 'normal' and therefore acceptable?

People in a country with high power distance will believe that decisions made by those in power should be accepted. There is a belief that those with power will make rules that will lead to the happiness of most people and therefore these rules should be followed. However, in an organization in a country with low power distance there will be the belief that people at all levels have the ability to make the decisions that are best for them. Because everyone has the ability to make good decisions, subordinates will expect to have an input into decision making. Therefore, if more people from every level are involved in the decision making, the better the decision will be. Some examples of power distance and specific countries are:

Lowest power distance countries	*Highest power distance countries*
Austria	Malaysia
Israel	Romania
Denmark	Guatemala
New Zealand	Panama
Sweden	Philippines
Ireland	Russia

Relation to marketing research

The dimension of power distance has a direct application to marketing research. For example, the USA is a country that ranks low on power distance. Therefore, a marketing researcher should expect that the average consumer will have insights that they believe will be valuable to those making product decisions in the company. Based on this assumption, a researcher will plan a focus group or interviews to gather opinions on management's decision to introduce a new product.

In a high power distance country research participants might find this idea rather ridiculous. Those in a focus group will see the researcher as someone in a position of power and not to be challenged. Interview subjects will believe that the management of the company includes the best people to make the decision as to what to produce. If those in power have both the authority and the responsibility to make decisions, why are consumers being asked what should be produced?

5.3.2 Uncertainty avoidance

Part of being human involves being conscious of time and therefore being aware that we are constantly confronted with an unknown future. However, it is psychologically impossible to live in a state whereby a person must acknowledge that at any moment the future could radically change. To lessen this anxiety regarding this unknown future, countries create laws, perform religious rituals and use technology. Such laws govern people's behavior so that it can be more predictable and this therefore results in less anxiety. Religious rituals are used to provide comfort and also a belief in a knowable future that will occur after the present uncertain reality. In addition, countries will use technology to protect against the randomness of Nature.

How accepting people are of the ambiguity of the future differs between cultures. Families, schools and governments transmit this level of acceptance through their use of laws, religion and technology. Avoidance of uncertainty will lead to behavior that is considered rational, such as keeping the same job for a lifetime. In contrast, this same behavior in a country with less uncertainty avoidance will be seen as irrational.

Organizations cope with uncertainty avoidance by creating rules and organizational rituals. An organization in a high uncertainty avoidance country will have many rules that govern behavior. People who live in a high uncertainty avoidance culture will find these rules comforting rather than restrictive. They will know that if they follow the rules the future should hold few surprises. Employees in these countries will also tend to stay with the same employer to avoid the implied threat that a new employment situation would present.

Lowest uncertainty avoidance countries	*Highest uncertainty avoidance countries*
Singapore	Greece
Jamaica	Portugal
Denmark	Guatemala
Sweden	Uruguay
Hong Kong	Belgium
Vietnam	Malta

Relation to marketing research

People from countries with high uncertainty avoidance cultures will find novelty a threat rather than exciting. They will fear failure more than they will anticipate success. Therefore a task with no rules and without any definition of what is to be expected would not be welcomed. However, people from low uncertainly avoidance cultures will find new challenges and unfamiliar situations exciting. Rather than worry about failure, they will focus on the possibility of success.

Research techniques that require participants to take risks based on little information would make individuals in high uncertainty avoidance cultures uneasy. Creative projective techniques, such as asking participants to draw a visual ad for a product based on their opinions, provide little guidance as to what is expected. Such techniques would not work well in a high uncertainty avoidance culture. Even open-ended questions in a survey form may go unanswered as there is too much risk of giving an answer that might be perceived as wrong.

5.3.3 Individualism versus collectivism

All human beings are social animals with a need to belong. However, whether this desire to bond is encouraged varies between cultures. The issue of individualism versus collectivism affects social and living arrangements both at home and at work. This cultural dimension will shape the decision of who people will choose to live with, whether alone or with family members, and will even shape who is considered 'family'. In individualistic cultures, 'family' often means the nuclear family only. Even within the nuclear family children will move away as soon as they can be self-sufficient. An adult child still living at home will need to be explained to other family and friends, as it seems somehow 'unnatural'. In collectivist cultures the concept of family is extended much more broadly to include those who may be distantly related. In these cultures adult children who choose to move away from the family may be seen as 'unnatural'.

However, the concept has a broader implication than just where people live and who they consider relatives, it also impacts on how people think and work in organizations. In an individualistic society people are expected to have their own unique thoughts and ideas and are rewarded for doing so. In collectivist societies, people will tend to think the way others do so and group decisions will be respected.

Highest individualism countries	Highest collectivism countries
USA	Guatemala
Australia	Ecuador
UK	Panama
Canada	Venezuela
Netherlands	Columbia
New Zealand	Indonesia

Relation to marketing research

The marketing concept puts the individual needs and wants of the consumer at the heart of the marketing mix. The purpose of marketing research is to uncover these needs and wants. While it is true that individuals differ because of their genetic makeup, their family experiences and their external environment, in collectivist cultures it will be much harder to prompt individuals to express these differences.

Particularly in focus group situations, research subjects from collectivist cultures will be more likely to agree with other group members rather than explore the differences that might cause disagreements. Also, when answering survey questions, people from collectivist cultures are likely to respond to questions based on the views of their families and friends rather than on their own opinions.

5.3.4 Masculinity versus femininity

Biological differences between the genders are the same everywhere, but the importance of these differences and how they are reinforced differ across cultures. Differences involved in child bearing are biologically determined. However, while not absolutely determined by biology other behaviors are statistically more common in males or females. This is because every society has ideas of what behaviors are considered appropriate for males or females.

While these ideas of gender specific appropriate behavior vary between cultures, there are similarities. In most cultures men are expected to be more aggressive and concerned with status while women are expected to be more nurturing and concerned with the family. However, how these roles are applied may differ. For example, in Russia the occupation of doctor has been seen as one that is natural for women because it involves caring for people. In the USA the occupation of doctor has been seen as natural for men because the power of being able to heal gives status (Hofstede and Hofstede, 2005).

A culture is referred to as 'masculine' when the difference between gender specific behaviors is reinforced. In a highly masculine country, men are expected to be aggressive, tough and driven by the need for status, while women are expected to be modest, to nurture the family and maintain social relationships. The difference in a highly feminine country is that there is more leeway for these roles to overlap. Women are allowed to be more aggressive and it is socially acceptable for men to be more caring.

Highest masculinity countries	Highest femininity countries
Slovakia	Sweden
Japan	Norway
Hungary	Netherlands
Austria	Denmark
Venezuela	Costa Rica
Switzerland	Estonia

Relation to marketing research

Masculine versus feminine behavior has a direct implication for consumer research as it affects who is considered as a consumer. In a high masculine country, men make the major shopping decisions involving expensive products while women will shop for food and everyday items. Therefore men will be asked to participate in research that asks for opinions on expensive products such as automobiles. In feminine countries, men would feel free to involve their wives in making this decision. As a result, women will have an impact on the purchase decision and should be included in the research. Likewise, in a highly feminine country, men may equally take on the task of food shopping. Research on household products, such as laundry soap, will also want to gather male opinions. Table 5.1 below summarizes the effects and the necessary adjustments.

5.4 Marketing Ethics and Cultural Values

Ethics are socially based ideas of what is correct behavior versus wrong behavior. Ethical rules are learned while young from family, the educational system and religious institutions. If ethics

Table 5. 1 Hofstede's Cultural Dimensions

Dimension	Effect on research	Needed adjustments
Power distance	Participants in focus groups and interviews from high power distance countries will defer to a researcher as the person with a position of authority.	Use techniques that will allow participants to provide information anonymously.
Uncertainty avoidance	Participants from high uncertainty avoidance countries will find techniques that provide little direction threatening.	When using such techniques more information on expectations needs to be provided.
Individualism vs. Collectivism	Participants from collectivist cultures in focus groups will not want to disagree with other participants. Survey questions may be answered based on the opinions of the group rather than the individual.	In-depth individual interviews may be needed so that sufficient time is available to convince participants that their views are valid and necessary.
Femininity vs. Masculinity	Who makes the purchase decision varies based on the cost of a product and its perception as something that is used by only men or women.	The research sample will need to be adjusted to adapt for gender differences in product purchasing.

are the result of socialization it can be assumed that they may differ from culture to culture. This leaves marketing researchers with a dilemma. When market researchers are in 'Rome' should they 'do as the Romans do' even if it conflicts with their own ethical principles? One theory that can help clarify the issue is contextualism (Hooker, 2003).

Contextualism argues that while the rules of conduct may vary in different cultures, they may still spring from the same universal principle. A universal principle is one that is true across cultural boundaries. An example of such a principle is that the strong should protect the weak from harm. However, the application of a rule can vary depending on who it is that a culture defines as being in need of protection. A culture that sees women as being in need of protection will seek to protect women from strangers, particularly men. Therefore they will not be open to the idea of a male researcher interviewing a female participant without a male family member present.

The researcher may come from a culture that does not believe women need this type of protection. Therefore this refusal to allow women to participate in research if the moderator or interviewer is male may be difficult to accept. However, it may help if the researcher remembers that the behavior is the result of a universal belief that both cultures share. Rather than waste time in disagreement, it might be better spent on adapting the research methodology to ensure that the cultural value of the protection of women is respected.

5.4.1 Stereotyping

Everyone constructs stereotypes of groups of people different from themselves. These stereotypes take the qualities of a few members of a group and project them onto all members of that group. People construct stereotypes, either positive or negative, in an effort to make sense of the world.

A researcher may have a positive stereotype of groups based on perceived personality traits. For example, Americans may be seen as friendly, Germans as hard working, and the French as romantic. However, some stereotypes held by researchers may be negative. While stereotypes can be used as a 'shorthand' method of understanding the world, the problem is that they may blind researchers to reality. If a researcher holds the stereotypes mentioned above they are much less likely to note that Americans can be unfriendly, Germans can be laidback, and the French can be unromantic. Researchers will only notice these traits if they are very extreme because they conflict with their stereotypes.

It is impossible for researchers to be free of all stereotypes. Researchers are naturally more likely to feel positively about groups that they associate with positive personal qualities and to feel negatively about a group that they associate with negative qualities. Rather than be free of all stereotypes, the goal is for researchers to be aware of their stereotypes and to make the necessary adjustments in their attitudes. For example, a researcher working with a group of Japanese focus group participants may believe that the Japanese are hard working with little preference for leisure time. As a result this researcher is less likely to see the variation in the group members. Therefore, they are less likely to notice the focus group member who is unhappy with his or her job and dreams of living on a beach somewhere.

5.4.2 Prejudice

Prejudice is always a negative phenomenon. It can be based on age, gender, nationality, ethnicity, occupation and sexual orientation. This type of attitude engenders negative attributes which may have no basis in reality to all the members of a specific group. Prejudice is usually learned early as a result of family, school and social experience. However, it can also be developed later in life as the result of associating with others who share a common prejudice. It can make a person so uneasy that they will avoid contact with members of a group he or she views negatively. Prejudice can even lead some people to actively seek out members of a group so that they can express their hostility.

Because prejudice is usually learned early in life, it can be difficult to overcome. If researchers realize that they have a problem with prejudice they should avoid working with groups they view negatively. Even if researchers feel they can hide their feelings, their attitudes may still show. For example, a researcher may have learned a very negative view of an ethnic group. Even if the researcher is now aware that this prejudice is incorrect, part of their feelings may still show in a focus group setting. Because members of the ethnic group have probably all experienced discrimination based on their ethnicity, they will be quick to pick up on this prejudice and the focus group will not be effective as a result.

Summary

1 A company may need to conduct marketing research across cultural boundaries whether on a unique cultural group in the same country or a different country. There are a number of unique challenges a company may face when it conducts marketing research across cultural boundaries, including the need to research consumer preference questions that would normally not require research.

The amount of research challenge will depend on the level of cultural difference between the marketing researchers' own culture and the culture that is being researched.

2   Marketing in other countries where a different language is spoken will require translation. Translation issues the company will face include the need to translate meetings, research materials and the final written and oral report. To ensure accuracy, back translation, where the language is translated from the home to the foreign language and then back again, is recommended.

3   The self-reference criterion refers to the fact that most people assume their own behavior is the normal standard against which other behaviors should be judged. While all people have the same range of emotions their behavior is shaped by culture. An international marketing researcher must be able to understand the validity of the choices made by members of other cultures. These cultural differences can be explained using the dimensions of power distance, uncertainty avoidance, individualism versus collectivism, and masculinity versus femininity. Each of these will affect the choice of research subjects, research methodology and the way that methodology is implemented.

4   Contextualism is a theory that explains that although behaviors may vary across cultures they may still be the expression of the same underlying value. Rather than focusing on the disagreement regarding this behavior, it is better for marketing researchers to understand what value the behavior expresses. Marketing researchers must also be aware of their own stereotypes and prejudices. Stereotypes, either positive or negative, occur when the actions of a few are believed to be true of everyone in a group. Prejudices are always negative and are based on preconceived ideas rather than reality.

Key Terms

back translation   translation of a document from the original to another language and back to the original language to determine if the first translation was correct

contextualism   different behaviors may arise from the same underlying ethical principle

cross cultural research   research where the marketing researchers are of a different cultural background than research participants

cultural dimensions   classification of cultural characteristics and behavior

power distance   cultural dimension that describes the level of acceptance of power and status differences

prejudice   dislike of all members of a group based on a preconceived idea which may have no basis in reality

self-reference criterion   judging the values and actions of other cultures by the standards of the home culture

stereotyping   believing the actions or values of a few members of a group must be true of all members of that group

uncertainty avoidance   level of acceptance of the ambiguity of the future

---

Discussion Questions

1 What are some of the reasons why organizations may be unwilling to undertake international marketing research?
2 What different cultural groups could be researched in the country where you live?
3 Can you think of some consumer preference questions you would need to ask because you currently do not have the necessary information?
4 What country would be very dissimilar from your own in terms of culture and language?
5 Why is it more difficult to conduct secondary research in other countries?
6 How do Hofstede's cultural dimensions affect marketing research?
7 Give an example of how power distance is exhibited in the classrooms of your country.
8 How would uncertainty avoidance affect how individuals in different countries approach an open-ended question on a survey or participate in a focus group?
9 Can you think of an example from your culture that explains the difference between masculine versus feminine behavior?
10 Why is it important that researchers understand their own stereotypical beliefs and prejudices about people?

Recommended Reading

Brewer, Thomas L. (ed.) (2003) *Oxford Handbook of International Business*. Oxford: Oxford University Press. Twenty eight chapters on different aspects of international business written by leading experts comprise the contents of this book. It also contains an interesting chapter on research trends in international marketing.

Edmunds, Holly G. (2006) *The AMA Guide to the Globe: Managing the International Marketing Research Process*. Mason, OH: Thomson/Southwestern. This book provides a step-by-step process for a marketer who is confronted with the need to conduct international consumer research.

Ember, Carol R. and Melvin Ember (2001) *Cross Cultural Research Methods*. Lanham, MD: AltaMira Press. Rather than showing how to conduct marketing research this book covers how to research cultures, a useful skill for someone responsible for international consumer research.

Gannon, Martin J. (2001) *Working Across Cultures: Applications and Exercises*. London: SAGE. Marketers who research cross-culturally not only need to know theory, they also need to understand how to interact with people from different cultures. This book uses easy exercises and questionnaires to help the reader gain insights into their ability to interact cross-culturally.

Guirdham, Maureen (2005) *Communicating Across Cultures at Work*. Lafayette, IN: Purdue University Press. Topics include how culture affects behavior, communicating interculturally and working abroad. Interesting European diversity data are included.

Harkness, Janet A., Van De Vijver, Fons J.R. and Mohler, Peter P.H. (2003) *Cross-Cultural Survey Methods*. Hoboken, NJ: Wiley-Interscience. Equivalency of method and comparability of findings are addressed in this book. Also included are 21 articles on international research.

Rugimbana, Robert and Nwankwo, Sonny (2003) *Cross-Cultural Marketing*. London: TL EMEA Higher Education. This book examines multi-culturalism from a consumer perspective rather than that of the organization. While all the information is interesting, the book also includes a chapter dedicated to conducting cross-cultural marketing research.

Cultural Considerations

6 Conducting Secondary Research

Learning Objectives

1 Define secondary data, their benefits and the criteria that determine their usability
2 Discuss how secondary data can be used to examine the external environment, the industry and consumers
3 Explore the sources of quantitative and qualitative external data
4 Describe the steps in the secondary research process

EVERYONE'S INTO HEALTHY AND NATURAL – SO NESTLÉ AND COCA-COLA LISTEN AND ADAPT

Fizzy soft drinks are not selling as well as they used to. So Nestlé, the world's largest food company, and Coke, the world's largest producer of soft drinks, have reacted to this trend. Through research they have found that not only do people want to be healthy, they want to be slimmer. So the companies developed Enviga, a 'natural' drink containing green-tea extracts, caffeine, and other natural ingredients and this comes in green-tea, peach and berry flavors. The product's claim to fame? Drinking it helps burn calories. (Although a consumer would have to drink 20 cans to rid themselves of the calories of one Big Mac.)

Question: What other products could be developed in response to current social trends?

Source: *The Economist*, 2007

6.1 External Secondary and Primary Research Data

After a researcher has defined the problem using critical thinking skills and internal data, the next step in the research process is to determine what external information is already available that could assist in answering the research question. The two types of external research data that can be obtained by market researchers are commonly called 'secondary' and 'primary'. A researcher will obtain primary data directly from research participants. In contrast, secondary data already exist as someone else has collected them as the result of previous research. Secondary data, despite the name, are the first type of data that should be used by researchers.

Why use secondary data first? Since secondary data already exist they are less costly than obtaining primary data. Not only do researchers not have to spend the money to conduct research, using secondary research data saves time. Finding information is much easier and quicker thanks to the internet, as there are a wealth of online sources of secondary data. In fact the amount of available data is so great that researchers need to develop skills in determining what information is relevant and credible.

6.1.1 Institutions that collect secondary data

Secondary data may have been collected as part of research conducted by an educational institution, a government department, a trade association or a commercial data provider. The faculties of educational institutions such as colleges and universities may conduct research that has been funded by a grant. In turn, this grant may have been received from a large corporation or government agency that needed research data on consumer preferences, or from a government agency that wanted information on social trends. If the grant was from a corporation, the data may not be available to the public. Research may also be undertaken solely as the result of professorial interest. Since the goal of professors is to publish research, this kind of data will be made available to the public.

Government agencies will conduct their own research to provide information to guide policy decisions (see box below). The information collected will include population demographics and economic detail, all of which should be available to researchers.

IF OTHER RESEARCHERS HAVE ALREADY ASKED THE QUESTION, THE ANSWER MAY BE WAITING ON A CENSUS WEBSITE

In the American fact finder section of the United States Census website (www.census.gov) there is a page that keeps track of questions that people have already used to query the huge database that results from census data. Here are some sample questions that have been asked:

What are the fastest growing counties in the US?
What is the latest estimate on the growth of the Hispanic population?
What are the home ownership rate and rental vacancy rate?
What business data are available for my area?
What are the percentages of religious affiliation?

Source: AskCensus, 2006

In addition, trade associations will conduct research on products produced by members of the association. For example, the ACEA (European Automobile Manufacturers Association) gathers information on auto industry-related statistics. Therefore primary research on the auto industry should not be conducted without first ascertaining what secondary data are already available.

Not to do so is wasteful of researchers' financial resources. Finally, commercial research companies will provide data for a fee.

6.1.2 Benefits of conducting secondary research

Once a research proposal has been approved, researchers may be tempted to immediately start conducting the primary research methodology by designing a survey or holding a focus group. However, there are many benefits to first conducting external secondary research including lower costs, research answers, assistance with the design of research methodology, and providing industry information.

Lower Costs

The costs involved in obtaining primary data include determining and obtaining a sample, designing the research methodology and analyzing the findings. Because secondary data, unlike primary data, have already been collected they can be obtained at lower cost. However, not all secondary data are free. If the data are obtained from a commercial provider there may be a cost involved. If this is the case researchers may find that the cost of the secondary data is still much lower than the cost of obtaining the data through primary research.

Research answers

There are occasions when only secondary research is conducted. By analyzing the secondary data researchers might find an answer to a research problem. This is most likely to happen if the research question is general in nature. For example, if the research question is the percentage of people in the city who are concerned about weight gain, these data might have already been collected by a local health organization. However, most research questions are more specific to a company's product or target market segment and the data collected through secondary research data will not be specific enough to provide the necessary answers.

Research methodology design

Secondary research can provide information that will help to design the primary research methodology. Data from existing sources of consumer preference can provide information on desired product benefits that will help in the design of a questionnaire or focus group script. For example, if a company is considering designing a new accessory for use with cell phones, research of articles on cell phone design might find an industry study on consumer preferences regarding features. This information could then be used to develop a questionnaire that could be used with local consumers.

Industry information

Another benefit of secondary research is that it can provide background information on an industry. Even if the secondary data that are analyzed do not directly provide the answer to the problem, their collection and analysis are still helpful in providing background information and context on the research issue. Using this knowledge can help a researcher choose the correct research method and design a better research tool.

6.1.3 Requirements of secondary data

Secondary research for existing data is always the first choice for researchers as it saves time and money. However, secondary data should only be used if the data are relevant and relate appropriately to the problem. The data should also be credible, timely, accurate and affordable. Ensuring the usability of secondary data is the responsibility of researchers.

Data used by the researcher should not only deal with the consumer market segment or the product category, they must be relevant by specifically addressing what researchers need to know. With vast amounts of information available online, it is relatively easy to find data. However, researchers must take the time and effort to verify the credibility of sources of data to ensure these come from reputable organizations or publications. If the source is a website it can be more difficult to determine creditability. Researchers must verify which individual or organization is responsible for the content of a website.

Besides the relevance and credibility of a source, researchers should determine the date when a study was published, as the data should be timely. What is considered outdated depends on the product or consumer groups being studied. Fashion and technology information becomes dated very quickly. In other fields, the opposite is true.

When evaluating the accuracy of data, a researcher should ascertain who it was who originally collected the data included in a study. It is not necessary to know researchers personally, but it is necessary to know that the specific organization for which researchers collected the data is reputable. How the data were collected should also be examined. Data that have been collected using the wrong method or a flawed sample will result in erroneous results. Finally, the cost of the data should be considered. Even the best data cannot be used if they cannot be afforded.

Secondary data requirements

- Relevant – they must address the issue being researched.
- Credible – the source is a respected provider of information.
- Timely – the data are not outdated.
- Accurate – the data are correct.
- Affordable – if not free, the company can afford the data.

6.2 Secondary Research Uses

Three major issues that a marketing researcher should use secondary research to explore are the external environment, the industry as a whole, and consumer segments. Fortunately much of this research can be conducted right from a researcher's computer. However, a visit to a public or business library to use online databases may also be necessary.

6.2.1 Secondary research on the external environment

Research on the external environment should include searching for data on social, economic, legal and technological issues that might affect the research question. When researching the external environment the secondary research might focus on social changes that could affect the benefits that consumers desire from a product. Another example of research on the external environment would be general economic news, as this would affect the pricing of a product. Researchers might examine the legal environment for changes in laws that could affect how a product may be packaged and promoted. Finally, the technological environment needs to be researched for any implications it may have on new product development. Below is an example of how Folgers used research to create a new product.

WHAT'S NEW WITH COFFEE? RESEARCH GAVE FOLGERS AN IDEA

Folgers was looking for a competitive edge for a new coffee product. Consumers were buying more upscale coffee and both gourmet and flavored coffees were selling well. But Folgers wanted a new breakthrough product rather than merely a 'me-too' product. Researching the external marketing environment they found that 35–40 million Americans had reduced their coffee consumption because drinking coffee irritated their stomachs.

As a result, Folgers is marketing the first new coffee product in 20 years (since decaffeinated coffee was introduced). Folgers 'stomach friendly' coffee is made from specially roasted beans that do not cause irritation. So coffee drinkers with delicate stomachs can now drink again!

Source: Folgers, 2006

For example, if a research question is designed to determine the reason for a decline in consumption of a company's prepreared chocolate dessert, there are probably no legal issues that need to be researched as these would not affect consumer consumption of that product. However, there may be social and economic issues. Researching the social environment might lead a researcher to articles and other information regarding the increase in obesity and the resulting popularity of low calorie diets. Researching economic issues might reveal that consumer spending has fallen. If so, it may also show that economic hard times have resulted in consumers buying less of expensive prepreared food products. Both of these facts will be worth considering when designing the research study.

There will be occasions when an organization is conducting research when there are little secondary data available. This may be particularly true when research is focused on an ethnic group with a small population. In this case little may have been written about the group and even less research conducted on the behavior of its members. However, there are qualitative techniques that can be used when the available secondary data are limited (Pires et al., 2003).

6.2.2 Secondary research on the industry

Secondary research could also gather information on an entire industry to see if there are changes that might affect a research question. These would include general data on changes and trends in that industry. In the case of the dessert product, data might reveal a trend toward smaller portion sizes or packaging that will go directly from the microwave to the table. A final issue to be researched might be of competing products. A researcher will need to know if there are new competing dessert products that consumers are purchasing. In the box below is an example of how an industry organization can provide access to secondary data.

LOOKING FOR INFORMATION ON RETAIL SPENDING? YOUR FIRST STOP MIGHT BE AT THE NATIONAL RETAIL FEDERATION WEBSITE

Consumers spent over $3.8 trillion in a single year at more than 1.4 million US retail establishments. Where is this fact found? The National Retail Federation describes itself as the world's largest retail trade association with membership including department, specialty, discount, catalog, internet and independent stores. One of the ways the organization serves its members is by conducting research. Here are two studies that anyone with an interest in retail purchasing could access:

Moms Worth More Than $10 billion This Year – Average Consumer Spent Nearly $100 on Holiday

This study provided secondary data that managers of flower shops would find helpful. The study found that Mother's Day is the second most popular flower buying holiday (Christmas is first). Of all the flowers purchased on Mothers' Day, 45 per cent of shoppers will buy cut flowers, 32 per cent will buy outdoor bedding and gardening plants, and 22 per cent will purchase houseplants.

Parents Heading to Stores Before Kids Go Back to School – Spending on Electronics up Nearly 15 Percent

This study provided secondary data that would be of interest to managers of local stores that sell school supplies. The study found that besides the usual purchase of paper and pencils, 41.7 per cent of parents will also buy electronic or computer-related equipment for their children.

Source: National Retail Federation, 2006

6.2.3 Secondary research on the consumer

One last general issue that might need to be researched would be information on consumer segments. This secondary research could be on the current market segment or on a new potential market segment. For example, the current market segment targeted by the company for the dessert product might be families. In this case research should focus on any changes in consumption patterns for families. Research might reveal that families are serving less sweet desserts because of health concerns. A researcher might also focus on new target market segments, such as young single professionals and their dessert preferences.

Research findings on new industries can quickly become available. Academic researchers are often interested in studying what is new. For example, online auction retailing as an industry segment was soon an object of study to researchers. Research findings on how consumers use these online auction websites could also help researchers to design new studies (Weinberg and Davis, 2004).

What to research using secondary data

- External environment
  - social
  - legal

- o   economic
- o   technological
- Industry
  - o   trends in consumption
  - o   competitor growth or decline
- Consumers
  - o   current customer segment preferences
  - o   potential consumer segments preferences

6.2.4 Organizing secondary data

Since there is a wealth of information available to researchers keeping track of it all is a critical issue. A means to organize data while keeping track of all the sources of the information will save time in the long run. Carefully noting the source of data will save a researcher time if they need to verify the credibility of the information. Also, any questions as to the accuracy of information can quickly be addressed, as researchers will know the exact source of any data.

To organize data, researchers should keep a log of where information was found, how it was obtained, the name of the publication, database or document and the date of the source. This information, when entered in a software database program, then forms part of a marketing information system or MIS. Even information that isn't of current interest to researchers might be of use to a marketing department in answering a future research question. Therefore maintaining relevant information can save time in future research.

This information can also be used as an example of what research can accomplish. For example, an organization may be interested in conducting research on the connection between price and perceived quality. A previously conducted study that has been presented in a journal may give marketing researchers some useful ideas for conducting their own research (Zhou et al., 2002).

6.3 Sources of Quantitative and Qualitative Secondary Data

Quantitative secondary data are numerical information on the external environment, industry and consumers that already exist. Most of this information will be from statistical studies conducted by academic institutions, trade associations, government agencies or marketing research firms. Researchers will find numerous sources of information on the external environment and consumers. However, they may also discover that finding data on competitors can be challenging. Qualitative secondary data are not statistical and will be gathered from sources such as magazines and newspapers. This type of information is very important when researching consumer preferences and competitors.

6.3.1 Quantitative secondary data

Most external quantitative secondary data result from statistical survey research that has been already conducted. Common sources of this data are academic institutions where professors conduct statistical research. In addition, trade associations will collect statistical data for their members. Local or federal government offices collect data as part of the services they provide while commercial research firms collect statistical data to sell. These organizations have the financial and staff resources to be able to conduct a survey with a large enough sample to ensure that data are statistically valid. Academic and government data are often available to a researcher at no cost. Trade association data are usually available only to member organizations and commercial research data must be purchased.

Academic researchers

The secondary data that result from studies conducted by academic researchers can most often be found published in academic journals. However, often the studies are basic and not applied research. While such data may provide the researcher with insights as to the causes of a problem, they will rarely answer a research question directly. However, examining the research of others can provide information on some basic questions. The two databases described in the box below would be helpful to those starting research for nonprofit arts organizations.

QUESTION: WHAT ARE A CPANDA AND A EUCLID?

Possible answers:

a) small furry animals
b) free databases

If you guessed the second answer, you are correct. If you work for a non-profit arts organization these databases are an excellent source of free information. CPANDA is a new interactive digital archive of secondary data on US consumer attendance at the arts. It also contains data from studies on artists, arts and cultural organizations, audiences and arts funding. The databases can answer such questions as:

How many people participate in arts and cultural activities?
How do people find out about arts events in their communities?

EUCLID has been around longer and has a database called ACRONIM that contains thousands of entries on cultural research, including government reports, and academic conference papers. The database is searchable by theme, geographic area and key words. And it's free to the public.

Source: CPANDA, 2006 and EUCLID, 2006

Trade associations

The secondary data compiled by trade associations are usually specifically focused on the consumers who purchase a product, such as orange juice or women's fashions, sold by member companies. This information can provide very specific and therefore valuable data on consumption trends and changes in consumer preferences. However, because detailed information on consumer preferences would be helpful to competitors selling substitute products, this information may only be available to those companies that belong to the association.

Less sensitive data on consumption trends may be available to the general public on the association's website (see the box below).

FACTS JUST WAITING FOR YOU TO FIND THEM

As CASRO is a trade association representing survey research companies, they do know something about collecting information. On their website they provide the following list of survey research databases:

Community Research and Development Information Service (www.cordi.lu/en/home.html) – News databases in English but also in German and French.

The Roper Center for Public Opinion Research (www.ropercenter.uconn.edu) – A collection of domestic and international survey data.

OhioLINK Database (www.ohiolink.edu/resources.cgi) – List of databases on the arts, humanities, business, law, health science, science and technology.

National Bureau of Economic Research (www.nber.org/data_index.html) – Macroeconomic data, industry statistics and demographic facts.

Industry Research Desk (www.virtualpet.com/industry/rdindex2.htm) – Practical information on researching industries.

LawRunner (www.lawrunner.com) – A comprehensive listing of legal information available on the website in both the USA and other countries.

FedStats (www.fedstats.gov) – A site that lists statistics from over 100 US government agencies that can be searched by location or by subject.

Source: CASRO, 2007

Government sources

Government departments and offices usually collect data about social trends or issues. These data are almost always available to the general public and can be accessed directly on websites or by visiting a business library. Each government office will be responsible for conducting studies in their area of concern. For example, the US Department of Commerce conducts studies on business activity in different regions of the USA. Likewise in Europe, the European Union website can be searched for industry information.

Marketing research firms

Marketing research firms are also a source of quantitative secondary data. These companies specialize in researching a certain product category or consumer market segment on a continual basis. These data are then available for purchase by any interested company or individual.

6.3.2 Types of qualitative secondary data

Secondary data, other than statistical information, are also available to researchers. Qualitative sources such as general newspapers and magazines are sometimes overlooked by market researchers as sources of information on consumer choices and competing products. These types of publications are often aimed at consumers who belong to a specific demographic group or consume specific types of products. These lifestyle publications are particularly useful for consumer marketing research.

Popular magazines

Many magazines are written to appeal to a specific demographic group. For example *Retirement Living* magazine would be read by people who are either already retired or who are still employed but planning their retirement. If marketing researchers were interested in what types of issues are of concern to this group, examining the table of contents from several issues of the magazine would help to provide this information. A travel company may also notice that many issues of the magazine had articles that addressed the new trend of grandparents traveling with grandchildren. These data could be used to develop new types of tour packages.

Other publications are aimed at groups of people who share a specific psychographic interest or lifestyle. *Car & Driver* magazine and, even more specifically, *Volkswagen Driver* would have articles focused on readers' automotive interests. Market researchers in the automotive industry should make a habit of reviewing such publications to keep abreast of consumer trends in this area. These lifestyle magazines would also provide valuable information to market researchers in related industries such as automotive supply stores. If a certain type of car accessory is being heavily promoted, such as heated cup holders, then eventually consumers will be looking for this product and stores should have them in stock.

Business and trade publications

Magazines and newspapers that cover business subjects are also a source of qualitative secondary data. They will often carry articles that relate to new consumer interests or product trends. Trade publications will also focus on a single product or industry. These business publications should be received by marketing departments and kept on file for research purposes. Likewise any trade publications pertaining to specific industry trends should be received regularly to appropriate trade association publications should be readily available in a marketing department along with competitors' catalogues and other promotional material.

Websites

Many websites also contain information that is pertinent. This includes 'zines, traditional publications that are online and websites devoted to groups that share a specific interest. Blogs, chatrooms and social networking websites are easy ways to research consumer interests, particularly those of younger consumers. Likewise websites that allow people to post reviews of products and services can provide valuable insights. An example of their use is given in the box below.

ONLINE COMMUNICATION LEADS TO NEW RESEARCH TOOLS

Traditional research tools have been adapted for use on the internet. Not only surveys, but also focus groups and interviews, are now conducted online. However, there is also research activity that has been developed specifically because of use of the internet.

(Continued)

6.3.3 Competitor secondary data

When considering the cause of a problem that is being researched, it is important to consider the actions of a company's competitors. A large corporation might have an established system for gathering information on competitors' new products, promotions or new target market segments. However, even small companies can keep abreast of competitor actions. Besides the usual sources of quantitative and qualitative data available to track competitor actions, researchers may need to take a more creative approach to finding the required information.

Marketing researchers should obviously routinely read all types of newspapers and magazines that focus on business issues to learn about competitors. However, other methods will also be needed because not all of the relevant information will be published. Here, observation of competitors should be considered. For example, the owners of a music store might note what music is being carried at other stores or played at entertainment venues. In addition, useful information can be obtained by visiting competing companies or places where competitor products are sold.

Valuable information can also be gathered through networking. If funds allow, researchers should attend trade association events so they can network and hear the latest industry news. In addition, researchers will hear all the informal gossip regarding those competitors who are thinking of introducing new products or promotions. If trade shows are out of the question all business people can afford to network in the community by attending local business meetings and events. At such events a researcher might find him or herself in conversation with a local media representative who might know about the future promotion plans of competitors or the local business reporter who should have the latest news about new products being introduced by competitors. Even real estate agents are sources of information, as they will have information on what companies are looking for new space because of expansion plans.

6.4 Steps in the Secondary Research Process

Any researcher shouldn't start the secondary research process without a plan. After determining the research objective and the research question, a researcher should then review all the available internal data including written sources and interview notes. The next step will require online access or the use of a business library, either academic or public.

Researchers should first familiarize themselves with the services such a library offers, including the use of a reference specialist. A reference librarian is familiar with all of the resources that are available and can help in guiding researchers to the best sources of information. Some libraries even offer an orientation or classes on the available resources to help business people gather market research data.

External sources of information available at a business library would include general newspapers and magazines for information on social changes. Business newspapers and journals are sources of information on industry and economic news and statistics. Government documents are sources of information on legal issues. Current information from these sources might be available in paper format, but most of the information will be contained online in specialized databases. Figure 6.1 below outlines the process.

Conduct Internal Secondary Research
Internal data
Company personnel

↓

Conduct External Secondary Research
Consumer focused magazines
Academic studies
Business magazines, journals, newspapers

Trade focused magazines, newsletters

Databases
Government sources
Trade associations

↓

If the answer is found – stop the research!

or

Write a research proposal and conduct primary research

Figure 6.1 Secondary research process

6.4.1 Finding data online

Much of the required secondary research can now be conducted online using websites and databases. This has made life simpler for researchers because much of the research can be conducted in the office environment. However, it has also made life more difficult. Because there is so much information available, it is up to researchers to plan and conduct secondary research in a manner that doesn't just obtain information, but also obtains the right information. Previously the issue facing a researcher was finding any information; now the issue is finding the correct information. Researchers will never quite know where the relevant information will be found. One example of a surprising source of data is given in the box below.

LONDON IS NUMBER ONE PLACE TO DO BUSINESS! ACCORDING TO MASTERCARD

You never know who might have the answer you need. MasterCard does more than just process credit card charges – they also conduct research. The company has constructed an index that rates cities by many factors including their legal and political systems, the stability of their economy, how easy it is to conduct business, and how easily capital can enter and leave. London is Number One with a score of 77.79 out of 100, followed by New York City with 73.80. Tokyo is third with a score of 68.09.

Secondary research is conducted because respected companies may have already found information that can provide essential background material. When conducting the research, researchers should never assume who has the information. Half the fun of research is the surprising nuggets of information from unlikely sources.

Source: CNN Online, 2007

6.4.2 Planning the search

The first step in the process of accessing online information is to decide what type of information is needed. If researchers are conducting secondary research on the external environment they may need factual information on economic news, legal issues and technological developments. If the research is on consumer preferences researchers may need information on demographic data and social trends. In addition, researchers may need information on the names and locations of competing companies.

All of these needs will have different sources of information. For example, if researchers are searching for information on trends in the sporting goods industry, there are a number of different online sources that could provide information. It would be useful in this case to analyze statistical information on what percentage of young people aged 16–22 engage in various sports activities – but such a large-scale study would be very expensive to conduct. However, if the information is already available a government agency or trade association will probably have collected it. The government agency that would collect this information might also be interested in health or tourism. The trade association might be for sporting venues, sporting good manufacturers or a league of sports teams.

Information on sports participation might also have been collected by companies that manufacture or sell sporting goods equipment. Because these companies will have collected this information for use in developing corporate strategy, it might not be in the public domain. However, the results if not the details of these types of studies may have been published in press releases that are readily available to the general public.

Table 6.1   Example of a search strategy

1	*Statistical information on sports participation among the young*	Government health or sports agency websites Trade associations Sports teams
2	*Industry information on sporting equipment manufacture and sale*	Sporting goods manufacturers and retailers websites Press releases Industry directories
3	*Lifestyle information on popularity of sports*	Books Magazines Newspapers
4	*First person online sources*	Personalized websites Blog information on sports participation Chatrooms focused on sports activities

Researchers will also want to analyze qualitative data. Books and articles on sports participation may contain statistical information on popularity that the authors were able to gather from other sources. Even if the books and articles do not provide statistical information, they will provide information on what sports are popular and also give insights into why some sports are gaining in popularity whilst other sports are declining.

Some online information exists only in the cyberworld. This type of information includes personalized webpages and blogs. Personalized webpage sites such as Facebook and MySpace are particularly popular with young people. They will use these pages to post information on their interests, including sports participation. Blogs are sites that allow for online discussion and are usually formed around a specific topic, including sports participation. Analyzing these sites can provide valuable insights into trends before they are documented in books and articles. Table 6.1 above provides an example of the process.

6.4.3 Online search strategy

Once the source of online information is decided upon, the next step is to construct a search strategy that involves identifying key words and terms to be used in searching the database. The success of accessing the correct information depends on using the correct search terms. It is rare that a researcher will identify the correct terms on the first try. For example, researchers might want to know which sports are gaining in popularity among young people. Terms such as 'sports young' might bring up too many sources of information, including data on the health benefits of sports, sports injuries, and sports for children. On the other hand, the search term of 'winter sports participation young people in Germany during 2006' would bring up few or no sources of information. Finding the correct search terms is often a matter of trial and error.

Unfortunately, researchers often have a 'microwave' mentality. They believe they should be able to put search terms and within 60 seconds they will have results, just as a microwave heats a cup of coffee. A successful online search will take time and effort because of the vast amounts of information that exist. It is unrealistic to expect that one or two tries will result in accessing relevant data.

6.4.4 Retrieving online information

Online search engines such as Yahoo! and Google are useful in looking up routine information, such as a store's opening hours or the location of the nearest hotel. These search engines are designed to help a user browse the web. The definition of 'browsing' is to look around or look through. Browsing can be an enjoyable activity as the web is full of interesting sites with fascinating details. However, these search engines are not designed for serious research.

The definition for 'search' includes the words to hunt or investigate. While browsing skims along the top of all the available information, searching explores a limited amount of information in depth. Instead of browsing the web using search engines, more specialized databases are needed to conduct research. These specialized databases are already available through public, business and academic libraries, if a company does not subscribe.

Statistical information can be obtained through official government websites or sites that access government information from many different sources. For example, demographic information on the USA can be obtained through the official US Census website of www.census.gov. However, it can also be retrieved from Ustats – a database that contains not only census but also other demographic data sources. Other statistical databases include Reference USA. British sources of demographic data are available through the Office of National Statistics website of www.statistics.gov.uk/

Corporate and trade association information would be contained in industry databases such as Edgar and ThomasNet. Other specialized databases for company information include Hoover's Online, WorldScope Global and Business Orgs. All of these contain information on businesses in many countries. There are even specialized websites that display information on business press releases, such as Business Wire.

Almost all the books in the world can be searched using WorldCat that allows searching by topic, author, title and language. Articles can be found using databases such as Business Source Premier, LexisNexis Academic, JSTOR, and Academic Search Elite. These sources are not available to the general public but are available at many libraries.

6.4.5 Combining the uses of secondary and primary data

Researchers will need to understand how to use secondary research to design primary research. For example, a researcher may be presented with the problem of declining sales of an orange juice product. One of the first questions they would want answered is whether orange juice consumption as a whole is declining or whether it is just that company's product that is not being purchased.

To conduct a statistically valid study of all orange juice drinkers in the USA would be an expensive and time-consuming effort. Fortunately, such as study is not necessary if secondary data are available. In fact the data are readily available on the US Department of Agriculture website (www.fas.usda.gov). Here researchers could find that orange juice consumption in the USA was 1.1 million tons in 2003/2004, a 9 per cent increase from 2002/2003.

A researcher will now know that people are indeed drinking orange juice. However, consumers have been shown to be buying other brands. Further external research might provide the information that orange juice is not being given as prominent a shelf space in local grocery stores because of all the new health drinks on the market. This knowledge gives the researcher a good indication of what the problem might be. However, the secondary quantitative and qualitative data do not answer the question as to whether the lack of shelf space is actually the problem for their product. A research question or hypothesis is then developed that consumers do not notice the orange juice display and therefore are not motivated to purchase. The researcher can now design a primary research study to obtain data on whether this hypothesis is true.

Summary

1 Secondary data will have already been collected by academic institutions, government offices, trade associations and research firms. The advantages of using secondary data include lower cost, the possibility of finding the research answer, assistance with methodology design and background industry information. Secondary data must be relevant, credible, timely, accurate and affordable.

2 Secondary data can be used to research the external environment including social, economic, legal, and technological issues. In addition, secondary data can be used to research industry trends and competitors. Finally, secondary data can be collected on consumers, including current and potential segments. It is important to record and organize data in a logical manner so that they can be easily retrieved when needed.

3 Secondary data can be quantitative statistical information or they can be qualitative information on lifestyle and attitudes. Quantitative data of use to the researcher may have been collected by from academic institutions, trades associations, government agencies, and marketing research firms. Qualitative data can be found in magazines, newspapers and websites. Data on competitors can be difficult to obtain and besides the usual sources, observation and networking can be used.

4 Conducting secondary research involves determining the sources of information that are available on the external environment, the industry or the consumer segment. Planning the search should include determining the key words for it. The vast amount of information available online means that the search terms may need to be modified a number of times before the relevant information is found. Such information needs to be retrieved from websites, databases, books, articles, personal websites and blogs.

Key Terms

blogs a website where a person can post thoughts and ideas, comment on other users thoughts and ideas and interact with people

credibility the level at which a source of information is seen as an authority

personalized webpages websites that are created by individuals which are then posted with other websites for mutual browsing and comment

search terms the words used to locate information online and in databases

secondary research process the process of determining the necessary information that already exists and how it will be located

trade associations organizations whose members all belong to a specific industry or business

Discussion Questions

1. What is the difference between primary and secondary data?
2. Give an example of both secondary and primary data that a researcher could compile about your class.
3. Why is credibility such an important issue when conducting secondary research?
4. What would be the benefits of conducting secondary research on why a certain group of students is not enrolling at the university?
5. For what type of research questions might government data be helpful?
6. For what type of research question would popular magazines such as *Better Homes and Gardens*, *Beautiful Home* and *Designer Today* be useful as secondary data sources?
7. Use the secondary research process to explain how you would go about researching the problem of declining enrollment at your college or university.
8. What key words would you use in searching online for information on soft drink consumption among athletes?
9. What databases would be useful for determining the demographic characteristics of the population of your home town?
10. Under what circumstances would secondary research be particularly useful?

Recommended Reading

Berkman, Robert I. (2004) *The Skeptical Business Searcher: The Information Advisor's Guide to Evaluating Web Data, Sites and Sources. Information Today.* While the book provides information on finding sources of business data, it also emphasizes how to distinguish trustworthy sources from all the others.

Dobson, Chris (2004) *An Introduction to Online Company Research.* San Francisco, CA: The Benjamin Group. The major sources of business information are critiqued by cost and rated on the value they provide to the researcher.

Grover, Rajiv (2006) *The Handbook of Marketing Research: Uses, Misuses and Future Advances.* London: SAGE. The book has excellent information on all aspects of marketing research.

Munger, Dave and Campbell, Shireen (2007) *What Every Student Should Know About Researching Online.* Upper Saddle River, NJ: Pearson Education. This book goes beyond providing the reader with information on how to research online databases by providing information on using online discussion groups, blogs and social networking sites.

Schlein, Alan M. (2004) *Find it Online: The Complete Guide to Online Research.* Tempe, AZ: BRB Publications. Besides the usual information on web sources of information, the book also tackles the subject of filtering and managing data. It also takes a global approach and is useful for researching in any discipline.

Vibert, Conor (ed.) (2004) *An Introduction to Online Competitive Intelligence Research: Search Strategies, Research Case Study, Research Problems, and Data Source Evaluations and Reviews.* Boston, MA: Thomson/Texere. Provides a guide, step-by-step, through the process of researching competitors. It also includes a critique of sources and case studies.

PART 2

Qualitative Marketing Research

7 Choosing Participants for Qualitative Research

Learning Objectives

1 Discuss the unique factors to consider when developing a participant profile
2 Explain how to construct a sample using the convenience, snowballing and purposive methods
3 Identify the steps involved in the purposive method of constructing a sample
4 Describe how to develop a participant profile using segmentation characteristics

THE SCOTS MIGHT LOVE SCOTCH BUT WHAT ABOUT OTHER SCOTTISH PRODUCTS?

Migration, which relocates groups of people from the country of their birth to a new home, is not new. It has been going on throughout history. What is new is that businesses are seeing these migrants as a marketing opportunity. However, the question remains as to whether or not these migrants prefer products from their home or their new countries. Research looked at residents of the UK who were born in Scotland or whose parents or grandparents were born in Scotland. Twelve exploratory in-depth interviews were conducted, along with a quantitative online survey of 131 participants. In addition, a survey of 2592 participants was held of which 435 participants were Scottish or of Scottish descent. The result? There was a clear relationship between country of origin (or association) and purchasing. Those who considered themselves Scottish were more likely to buy not only Scotch whiskey but also Scottish mineral water, food and clothing.

Question: What type of research would a company need to do to exploit the marketing potential of local immigrant groups?

Source: Nancarrow et al., 2007

7.1 Choosing Participants for Qualitative Research

The choice of subjects for qualitative research involves nonrandom sampling. When using nonrandom sampling everyone in the population does not have an equal chance to be chosen as part of the sample. However, nonrandom does not mean that a marketing researcher chooses the participants haphazardly or without thought. Even when conducting nonrandom sampling for focus groups, interviews and observational research, subjects will still need to be chosen carefully. There are three basic issues to be considered for selecting research participants which include demographic and psychographic characteristics, a knowledge of the research issue and the geographical location where potential participants live.

The description of which characteristics are important is called the 'participant profile'. While there are similarities in the process for choosing participants for each type of qualitative research methodology, there are also specific issues related to the selection process that differ. Table 7.1 below is a summary of the important issues to consider.

Table 7.1 Ranking important factors when choosing qualitative research subjects

Focus Groups	Interviews	Observation
1 Personal characteristics	1 Research issue knowledge	1 Location
2 Location	2 Personal characteristics	2 Personal characteristics
3 Research issue knowledge	3 Location	3 Research issue knowledge

7.1.1 Focus group research participant selection issues

Recruitment of individuals for participation in focus groups requires the selection of individuals with specific demographic and psychographic characteristics from within a population. Researchers may decide that the sample to include in the research study will be based on demographics such as age, gender, income or ethnicity. These characteristics may be the most important considerations when choosing a sample because the research involves examining the purchasing behavior of one of these specific consumer segments. In addition, a new product may be targeted at a specific psychographic group based on their lifestyle or interests. Therefore it is imperative that researchers include those participants who share these psychographic characteristics so that companies can learn more about their wants and needs.

The location where potential participants live is also a consideration when choosing the sample, as they must be willing to travel to the location where the focus group is being held. If participants do not live within a short traveling distance, they may not be willing to travel in order to take part. Least in importance is that participants have a particular knowledge about the specific research issues. Focus group participants may be selected by usage level, but they will not be expected to have any specific knowledge of the relevant industry or of its competitors.

7.1.2 Interview research participant selection issues

Researchers recruiting a sample for interviews will need to find fewer participants. However, because there are usually only a few interviews conducted it is important to choose each participant carefully. To do so researchers will develop a participant profile based on knowledge of the research issue with personal characteristics being a secondary consideration. This makes selection more difficult as potential interview subjects must be screened about their knowledge level. However, fewer participants are needed because of the time it takes to conduct the interviews. Personal characteristics must also be considered to ensure that the views expressed will provide insight on the target market segment of interest to the company involved.

Location is less important when considering the choice of participants. The knowledge the potential participants have is valuable but it is not reasonable to assume that potential research subjects will be willing to travel to meet with researchers. Therefore researchers will have to travel to interview these experts or the company concerned must be willing to pay for the research participants' travel expenses. The challenge in finding participants will be the time that it takes to choose the correct participants when arranging the interview.

7.1.3 Observation research participant selection issues

Observation also involves choosing participants. However, with observation the location is the most important choice criteria. Observational research will always take place where participants are involved in the behavior under study. Therefore it is this choice of location that is the most important decision when choosing a sample. If the wrong location is chosen, it will be impossible to observe the right participants.

Of course, the choice of location is also based on the personal characteristics of the desired research subjects who will be found there. Because not everyone at the location is of interest to the researchers, they will have to choose potential subjects based on their personal characteristics. For observational research, these characteristics must be discernable through observation. Even then researchers will need to make a judgment call. Therefore personal characteristics such as age would be described in general categories such as 'young', 'aged 18–22' or 'middle aged, 40–55'. When conducting observational research, researchers gain data without verbal communication. Therefore it is behavior, and not knowledge, that is studied.

7.1.4 Professional recruiters

It can take considerable time and effort to find qualified research subjects for qualitative research. Some researchers may also feel they do not have the expertise to find appropriate subjects. This is especially true if the research subjects are from a population that is ethnically or culturally different from that of the researchers. Professional research subject recruiting firms can provide assistance in these situations (see the box below). These companies continually recruit subjects who are promised payment for their participation. The subjects a research company may need could already be in an existing database compiled by a professional recruiter. Alternatively, they can recruit participants who will be needed for studying a unique segment.

7.2. Constructing a Sample for Qualitative Research

There are three basic methods for constructing a participant sample (see Table 7.2 below). Researchers can use convenience sampling where they ask any individuals who are willing to participate. Snowballing is a system where an appropriate potential participant is identified and is then asked to recruit others with similar characteristics. When using purposive sampling, researchers select potential participants that best meet the sample profile.

7.2.1 Convenience sampling

Convenience sampling is used when researchers choose any willing and available individuals as participants. This method can be implemented when it is known that a specific location tends to

Table 7.2 Methods of sample selection for qualitative research

Method	Description
Convenience	Find the correct location
	Choose those most likely to participate
Snowballing	Choose first participant based on profile
	Ask chosen participant to identify others
	Verify that the referrals meet the profile
	Invite referrals to participate
Purposive	Identify the characteristics
	Develop a list of potential participants
	Invite them to participate

attract the type of individual needed for that research study. The recruitment of participants can then take place in this location as it is where people who meet the profile tend to congregate. For example, if the research question involves a product used by college students, such as textbooks, the participant profile might describe those individuals who attend college. Locating such college students can be accomplished by visiting the college bookstore.

7.2.2 Snowballing

Another method of choosing participants is called 'snowball' sampling. With this method researchers choose the first participant to match the participant profile. This participant then refers others with similar characteristics. The theory for using this system is that the first participant is more likely to know someone like themselves than the researchers. This method is appropriate when the research calls for participants who may be from psychographic or ethnic groups that are very different to those of the researchers.

There are two reasons for using snowballing. Firstly, researchers may not have a knowledge of the relevant participants. Secondly, even if they did, potential participants may not respond to an invitation from the researchers to participate. This may be because they do not understand the process, or trust the researchers. Below is one example of how snowballing that can be used.

DRUG USERS KNOW OTHER DRUG USERS

One of the most difficult sampling issues is finding research participants who do not wish to be found. The UK's Home Office faced such a difficult task when the participant profile for a research study called for occasional drug users. Research executives recruited one group of subjects to be interviewed. However, all of the research subjects subsequently recruited were currently enrolled in drug rehab. This is really not surprising, as the executives in charge of finding participants would have felt comfortable approaching other executives at rehab centers for referrals.

Another approach, snowballing, was also used. A drug user was asked to recruit peers to participate in the study. This approach resulted in a much more diverse group of subjects, all of whom were drug users and none of whom had previously participated in a research study. This is not surprising either, as drug users know other drug users.

Source: Miles, 2006

When using the snowball process it is very important that the first participant is chosen carefully. The success of any research will depend on their accurate referral of similar participants. Once additional participants are referred, it should still be verified that they meet the stated requirements. When this has happened, participants are then sent information on the research study and an invitation to take part. Even when a nonprobability sampling method such as snowballing is used, the final group of participants should always be analyzed to see if they are significantly different from the profile (Piron, 2006).

7.2.3 Purposive sampling

The research question will define the characteristics of the participant profile. It is important that the participants chosen match this profile so that they have the necessary common experiences which will result in useful research data. If input is needed from more than one type of research subject, then more than one participant profile should be developed and two groups of potential subjects will need to be recruited.

The process of using purposive sampling first includes establishing the participant profile. Then a list of potential research subjects is identified that have the needed characteristics and knowledge. Finally, specific individuals from this list are asked to participate. Researchers may sometimes need to find participants for more than one type of methodology: it is not uncommon for large companies to conduct more than one type of qualitative research at a time. An example of the many types of research conducted by Proctor & Gamble is given below.

CONSUMER RESEARCH AT P&G IS CONSIDERED A SCIENCE

When Proctor & Gamble conduct qualitative consumer research to generate new ideas, some of the tools they use include:

Focus group discussions   Focus groups are used for exploring ideas and making initial evaluations. A small group of people is brought together and asked to talk about consumer preference issues.

In-home visits   Interviews are used to ask questions about how and why people use a product. Being in the home provides an opportunity to understand the actual conditions under which the task is performed and what the constraints are from the user's point of view.

In-context visits   Ethnographic research is used to study people performing a task or using a product. This type of research provides insight into the details of how people use a product, how they judge its benefits, and which improvements they require.

In-store interviews   Intercept interviews are used to ask shoppers questions to better understand how actual purchase decisions are made at the point of sale.

Proctor & Gamble also use quantitative research to generate facts on usage and to evaluate product prototypes. The tools they use are:

Habits and practices   These are large-scale studies that require respondents to keep written records of the details of product usage for an extended period of time.

Blind tests   Blind tests are product usage tests in which a new or upgraded product is given to participants who do not know the brand or the product. Participants are then asked to compare it with the current product or a key competitor's product.

Concept aided usage test / concept and use test   Participants are first presented with a concept and then given a product to learn to use to see if the product delivers as promised.

Quality monitoring   After people have purchased a product, they are asked if that product meets their expectations.

Source: Science in the Box, 2006

7.3 The Purposive Sampling Process

Qualitative research is only effective if the right participants are selected. Purposive sampling is the most effective method to ensure that this occurs. After all, researchers will have spent considerable time and effort on the design of a research methodology. However, the best methodology will fail if the wrong participants are chosen to participate.

Using purposive sampling to choose the participants to be included in a study is a task that must involve both the marketing researchers and the management personnel that have commissioned the research. The purposive sampling process first involves identifying key characteristics of the individuals who should participate. Once these characteristics are determined, management and researchers will determine the organizations or groups where individuals with these characteristics can be found. Specific individuals from these groups are then invited to participate in the research study.

7.3.1 Identifying characteristics

The first step in this process is to determine what common characteristics the participants should share. These will include their demographic characteristics such as age, gender, income, and education level. Psychographic characteristics such as lifestyle, attitudes, opinions and values may also be relevant. The geographic area within which participants should live is important for two reasons. First, it might determine if the participants may currently use or have need of a specific product. Second, the geographic area is also a matter of convenience, because if participants live at a distance they may not be willing to travel. The product knowledge or usage pattern of the participants is relevant if the research question distinguishes between non-users, occasional users, and heavy product users.

7.3.2 Identifying organizations or groups

After the characteristics that define the desired participants are selected, the next step in the process is to identify the groups with which these potential participants might associate. It may be that the researchers or management know people who fit the profile, but this would be the exception rather than the rule. Even if the researchers do know appropriate potential subjects, these are not the persons who should be selected. If the potential participants have an existing relationship with a researcher, they may not give objective answers.

If a participant profile calls for current product users, they may be found using internal company information, such as mailing lists or customer databases. For a small business, participants who are product users may be chosen from frequent customers who are currently known to the owner.

Usually a participant profile calls for people who are nonusers. These potential participants can be found by using organizational memberships. An effective means of finding participants is to choose an organization that has members who are similar to those who meet the profile of potential participants. Such an organization may be a business membership group, social or service club, civic organization, nonprofit group, church or sports team. If researchers have access to a membership list this can be used to invite participants. However, because of privacy concerns, such a list will probably not be available. For this reason it may be necessary to contact someone who holds a position of authority in an organization to ask for his or her cooperation.

For example, a sports equipment business that wishes to target college students could recruit focus group participants from sports teams on a campus. Initially, they will need to ask coaches for their permission.

Once the purpose of the research has been explained, these organizational officials may be willing to provide membership information. They are more likely to do so if they see that the purpose of the research is beneficial to their organization's members in some way. For example, if a company needs information on how to adapt products for older citizens to use, members of a senior group may be willing to participate. If the topic is seen as being beneficial to society, such as why do businesses fail, members of small business organizations may be interested in helping with the research. If an incentive is being offered, this should also be stated. However, all researchers should be aware that offering incentives can alter the type of people who agree to participate (see the box below).

IF THEY JUST COME FOR THE MONEY, ARE THEY REALLY ANY GOOD?

Market researchers know that it is becoming increasingly difficult to motivate consumers to participate in research studies, although getting people to agree to join a focus group is not yet as difficult as getting them to complete a survey form. However, even for focus group recruitment researchers often need to use financial incentives for participation. Does the fact that people are paid to participate affect the quality of participation?

That is the question that two researchers at the University of New York decided to research. Before the focus group, the researchers asked participants questions to determine if their primary motivation for attendance was the monetary incentive or if their motivation was an interest in the research topic and process. After the research, the focus group moderator was asked to 'grade' participants based on their level of insight and participation.

Overall, the moderators gave most of the participants high grades. However, when the grades were compared with the results of the survey administered to participants before research the pattern was clear. Of those participants who ranked the financial incentive as the primary motivation for participation, one-third received grades of C, D or F. Of those participants who ranked interest in the topic or research most important, only one-fifth received grades of C, D or F.

Source: Tuckel and Wood, 2001

Participants can also be found by advertising an invitation to participate. This method is used when potential participants may not be members of any official organization. For example, marketing researchers may need to conduct research concerning how to promote to young people who enjoy skateboarding. The researchers could advertise at a local skate shop that they are looking for research participants. In this case, the researchers may need to provide an incentive to encourage participation. This incentive, perhaps skateboard equipment, should be communicated in the advertisement.

Once a list of potential participants has been created, a few short screening questions should be prepared. These questions will verify if the potential research subjects meet the profile determined by the researchers. The questions can be administered orally and the answers recorded, or a potential participant can be asked to complete the questionnaire.

7.3.3 An invitation to participate

Once all the groups have been identified and the participants have been screened, those that meet the profile and are selected to participate will be sent a letter or email. The letter or email should provide both the name of the research firm and also the name of the company commissioning the research. A short description of both the research firm and the company should be provided to supply credibility. A webpage link or telephone number should also be included so that participants can contact a relevant person if they want more information.

In the letter the purpose of the research should be clearly described without using any research terminology. For example, the methodology and sampling process should not be described in technical terms. Instead, if the invitation is to participate in a focus group the letter should describe how a focus group functions. If the invitation is to participate in an interview, potential participants should be informed of which subjects will be discussed.

The details as to time and location should also be included in the letter. This will ensure that participants are able to commit to the scheduled date and location. The letter should also assure potential participants that the information obtained is confidential and that their participation will not be disclosed. The letter should provide potential participants with a number to call if they are interested in participation. However, it more than likely will take a personal phone call, in addition to the letter, to get a commitment to participate.

For some qualitative techniques, particularly those that require significant participant interaction, another step may be added to the process. If participants will be required to work extensively with projective techniques, researchers will want to know if they will be sufficiently motivated to give their full attention and creativity to the process. In this instance, researchers may want to hold a short pre-focus group where they can get to know the personalities of potential participants. Only those who the researchers feel will add to the dynamics of the focus group would be invited to participate (DeNicola, 2007).

Invitation letter components

- Name of company commissioning the research
- Names of research firm and researchers
- Purpose of research
- Research details
- Benefits of research to society or consumers
- Incentives for participation

7.4 Using Segmentation Characteristics to Develop a Profile

Consumers are at the heart of the marketing concept and the marketing mix of product, price, place and promotion is designed to attract a specific market segment. Therefore it is not

Table 7.3 Profile for research participants based on segmentation characteristics

Segmentation	Possible characteristics	Example of participant profile
Demographic	Age, income, education level, gender, ethnicity	Age 65–75, middle income
Psychographic	Attitudes, opinions, values, lifestyle	Active, adventurous
Geographic	Availability of product, convenience	Live in the UK
Usage	Non-user, user of competing product, occasional user, frequent user	Currently nonuser

surprising that participants for research studies are often chosen to match the characteristics of a company's current or potential target market segment of consumers. Of course the company will want to know more about what this segment of current or potential customers feels about issues such as their marketing mix for current products or about new product ideas. Table 7.3 provides a summary of how these characteristics can be used.

Organizations can, however, use qualitative research to gather information on those consumer segments to which they currently do not market. Information from these participants will be specifically needed for research on such subjects as proposed new products. For example, during a focus group session product ideas can be described and the potential consumers' responses recorded. This information can then be used as one factor in the decision-making process. In addition, interviews with participants from a potential target market segment can use questions on such issues as product quality, customer service and the additional services that could be offered to customers.

Because of the time, money and staffing that are needed to design and conduct a qualitative research study, the choice of participants in any research study is critical. This is why time must be spent developing the participant profile. One method to begin the process of developing the participant profile for a qualitative research study is to start with segmentation characteristics. The main bases for segmentation are demographic, psychographic, usage and geographic.

The research question will provide information as to who should be included in the research sample. However, the information provided in the research proposal might not be specific as to details. For example, the proposal might have stated that research was to be held with current customers, or with young single professionals who were not currently customers. When the proposal has been accepted and the study is being designed much more detailed information on the participant profile as to who will participate must be specified.

7.4.1 Choosing participants based on demographics

Probably the easiest place to start developing the participant profile would be to define the potential research study sample participants by demographics. These characteristics will include gender, age, education, income, ethnicity, and even physical characteristics such as height and weight. Because of the nature of the research question it might be easy to decide that only males or females are needed or desired. Products that are specifically designed for one gender may require a group that consists of men only. For example, a company might wish to expand their skin lotion product line with a product designed specifically for men. However, even if the product is for men, if potential purchasers will include women they may also need to be included in the participant profile.

The age of potential research participants also needs to be considered. Once again, this may be determined by the research question. If it specifically asks about the opinions and attitudes of younger or older consumers, then those participants must be chosen with their age in mind. Likewise groups should be composed of participants from the relevant income, education and ethnicity groups specified by research question. However, today there is less reliance on age than other characteristics when choosing participants, as it has been found that it does not readily correlate with other psychographic characteristics as once had been believed (Stroud, 2005).

If the research question does not specify what demographic characteristics are needed, then researchers must decide what criteria should be considered. Even if the benefits a product offers are not specifically designed to be targeted at males or females, gender might still be important. For example, an automobile company may not be aware of why sales for a specific product are below expectations. The company's management may believe that the issue has to do with the higher price of gas, making the automobile less attractive to consumers than more fuel efficient vehicles. Even when gender is not under consideration as a factor, it is important to have both males and females represented in a study. During research on the mileage issue, for instance, it may be discovered that male participants were unhappy with a recent redesign of the vehicle while females were unaffected.

If a research study does not specify that a certain gender, age, education, income or ethnicity is relevant, participants should be chosen to represent as many of these characteristics as possible. Researchers might learn (when analyzing the data) what demographic characteristics are actually relevant to the research question. Sometimes it can be nationality that is relevant. This is particularly true if a researcher is recruiting participants for expert interviews. In the box below is an example of how doctors in India gave Proctor & Gamble the idea for a new product.

THE ANSWER TO THE QUESTION MAY DEPEND ON THE NATIONALITY OF THE ANSWERER

What factors help a baby develop? When ACNielsen surveyed over 200 pediatricians in India, the six factors that were mentioned most often were breast feeding, balanced diet, uninterrupted sleep, physical contact, outings and massage. In fact 93 per cent of pediatricians felt that uninterrupted sleep helps babies to be healthier.

These data led Proctor & Gamble to develop a different type of Pampers diaper for the Indian consumer market. The product, 'New Pampers', has an absorbent gel material that prevents leaks. If babies are not woken by wet diapers, they will sleep more comfortably.

Why develop a special Pampers product just for India? Secondary research showed that India has the largest number of babies of any country in the world. In fact India has a huge market potential market of 45 million babies. Proctor & Gamble's 'New Pampers' can now give these babies what doctors recommend – a good night's sleep.

Source: Vyas, 2006

7.4.2 Psychographic characteristics

Choosing participants by demographic characteristics is quite easy to accomplish. After all, some of these characteristics can be determined simply by looking at a person. A researcher can determine other characteristics with a quick question about the potential participant's income or education level.

Psychographic characteristics, on the other hand, are not so easy to determine. However, they may be even more important in choosing research participants than demographics. Psychographic characteristics focus on a consumer's lifestyle, including their opinions, interests and attitudes. These are more often the characteristics that influence consumer purchases than demographic factors.

A consumer lifestyle, such as an interest in extreme sports, may still predominately attract a specific demographic group such as young males. Their interests would focus around sport, including viewing the sport on broadcast media and reading about it in specialist publications. For these young males their identity would be based on the values associated with the sport, including a glorification of risk taking and an anti-establishment attitude. Consumers today are less likely to identify themselves based on the traditional demographic categories of age and gender. Instead they are more likely to identify with groups based on lifestyle. Age in particular can no longer be looked upon as a predicator of consumer behavior (Stroud, 2005).

For example, other lifestyle groups such as snowboarders may have started out with a specific demographic profile say, young males. However, this demographic profile may now also include females, older consumers and families. A company would then have to define the population and participant profile based on psychographic interest instead of demographics. Once a lifestyle involves new demographic segments, other aspects of lifestyle such as opinions, values and attitudes might remain the same or they may change. Families involved in snowboarding may value the interest as a way to spend time together rather than as an extreme sport. They would not be likely to value risk and in fact may be quite concerned about safety issues.

Lifestyle can be defined as how people cope with the choices they need to make in their everyday life. This would include choices about their physical environment such as their dwelling, clothing and food. It also includes the values that develop as a result of family and social influences. Marketers know that it is lifestyle that often influences the choice of a product. Therefore, a participant profile for qualitative research is often chosen based on lifestyle choice. In fact, the trend now is to segment even more finely. As an example, grocery stores now segment on lifestyle and attitude by a single store when researching what products consumers want to purchase (Harris and Margraff, 2007).

Predetermined psychographic profiles

It isn't necessary for researchers to construct a psychographic profile. There are standardized profiles that are available for defining research samples. These standardized systems have been developed by commercial companies. Unfortunately, many researchers who are academically trained are unaware of the availability of products from the commercial research sector (Keegan, 2007). Two that can be considered when trying to determine who should participate in a qualitative study are VALS and PRIZM.

VALS (Values, Attitudes and Lifestyles) is a system of categorization by psychographic characteristics and is based on the idea that our actions are determined by our personality. These actions include consumer purchase behavior and brand choice. VALS is a short survey that divides people into one of eight categories (SRI, 2006). The categories are based on consumers' primary motivations and resources. VALS defines motivation as the guiding principle that defines a consumer's actions. Consumers' purchases are made to give expression to these guiding principles of who they are. VALS uses the term 'resources' not just to refer to whether or not a consumer has enough cash to make a purchase, it also refers to whether a consumer has the inner drive to make the purchase. These aspects are then combined with basic demographic data to create profiles.

VALS profile motivators

- Innovators – many resources, successful life
- Thinkers – ideals
- Achievers – achievement
- Experiencers – self-expression
- Believers – traditional, concrete beliefs
- Strivers – opinions of others
- Makers – self-created self-expression
- Survivors – few resources, narrow life

Market researchers could use this system by first working with the client company's management to identify which of the VALS' types of consumers would most likely be able to provide the information needed to answer the research question. Participants could then be chosen who would meet this profile.

The PRIZM system of consumer classification is based on research that has been gathered from many different sources, including psychological studies and census data (Claritas, 2006). The classification system combines consumer behavior information with family status and geographic information. The family status information includes household income, family size and age, while geographic information includes housing condition, housing prices and the percentage of home ownership. Using this psychological and demographic data, PRIZM has identified 14 different groups with 66 different segments. PRIZM then allows researchers to identify the predominant groups in a geographic area. Even the names of the groups give an indication of the characteristics of lives in an area, as can be seen in the box below.

THE PRIZM DIFFERENCE

Williamsport, Pennsylvania is a small city of 27,000 people located in rural North Central Pennsylvania. Virginia Beach, Virginia is a large city located on the Atlantic coast and Chesapeake Bay. While both communities contain a range of people in terms of demographic and psychographic characteristics, when looking at the community in terms of groups there are distinct differences. According to PRIZM, the following groups dominate in each city.

Williamsport, PA	*Virginia Beach, VA*
Bedrock America	Boomtown Singles
City Startups	Middleburg Managers
Family Thrifts	Up-and-Comers
Hometown Retired	Upward Bound
Park Bench Seniors	White Picket Fences

(Continued)

7.4.3 Geographic characteristics

Researchers may consider geographic location when developing a participant profile based on product availability. If the product to be researched is only available in specific geographic locations, then the research subjects must also come from these areas. For example, if researchers are conducting a study on consumer motivation when purchasing a locally brewed beer, the potential research participants will need to by recruited from the area where that beer is sold.

To motivate potential research subjects to participate in the research, they will need to perceive the location as being convenient. Therefore the distance a potential participant might be willing to travel would need to be considered when developing the profile. This distance will vary based on the demographic and psychographic characteristics of the research subjects. Working professionals will want to have the location of the focus group or interview close to their offices so that additional time is not wasted in a second commute. Suburban dwellers may not be willing to travel to the city. Certain populations, such as the elderly, may find transportation a problem as they may no longer drive. Researchers should remember that they must chose participants within a certain distance so that they are willing to participate.

7.4.4 Usage characteristics

Another aspect of usage to consider as part of a participant profile is product loyalty. Sometimes researchers may describe the participant profile as consumers who are new, lapsed or frequent product users. These characteristics cannot be determined without occasional screening questions about the type of product usage. Therefore the screening questionnaire must ask if a potential participant is familiar with the product, their level of usage and if they have used competing products.

WHAT DO CHILDREN REALLY WANT? SANTA KNOWS

Every year approximately half a million children send letters addressed to Santa at the North Pole, Alaska. (The North Pole is a real city in Alaska – and of course Santa is equally real, in case any children are reading this book.) Duracell Batteries sponsored an

(Continued)

analysis of the content of the letters sent to Santa at the North Pole to determine which gift items were most requested. This is the only known occasion when Santa has been assisted by secondary marketing research, as normally Santa relies on one-on-one intercept interviews with children at store locations. While secondary research does have the personal touch, personal interviewing limits the number of children involved in research as not all can travel to a store. Analyzing the letters allowed the gift choices of many more children to be discovered. The top ten gift choices for children were:

1   Clothing
2   Dolls and action figures
3   Gaming systems
4   Portable gaming devices
5   Video games
6   Sports equipment
7   Toy vehicles and planes
8   Portable music players
9   Remote control vehicles
10 Movies/DVDs

Even a quick analysis of these secondary data by Santa's elves will quickly let them know that technology is hot, with almost 60 per cent of children requesting this item! (Santa is still shaking his head about the child with the very long letter who requested 118 toys.)

Source: Proctor & Gamble, 2006

Summary

1   Qualitative studies use participants chosen as a nonrandom sample. Fewer participants are used and this means that extra care must be taken to choose the correct research subjects. If the wrong subjects are chosen the research findings will be useless. The most important criteria for focus groups are personal characteristics, while for interviews it is usage or product knowledge. One of the most important criteria for observation research is the location where the subjects can be found. Researchers must decide if they will need the help of professional recruiters.

2   Samples can be constructed using convenience sampling, where anyone who is willing and available is asked to participate. The snowballing method finds one qualified participant who then recruits others. Purposive sampling first develops a profile of the characteristics that a qualified research subject should possess.

3   The process of finding the participants for purposive sampling uses organizations and advertising. A list of qualified participants is developed using organizations to which they belong. It is possible that a person in a position of authority in an organization may

supply researchers with a list of members. However, due to privacy concerns it is more likely that the head of an organization will relay the invitation to interested members. Letters or emails of invitations are then sent. If the invitees agree to participate, additional information as to the time and place of the focus group is sent.

4 Segmentation characteristics can be used to develop the research participant profile that is needed in snowball and purposive sampling. The profile will describe the relevant demographics of participants, which might include age, gender, income or a combination of characteristics. Psychographic characteristics are also important including lifestyle, attitudes, opinions and value. Geographic characteristics are important if the product or issue under study is only relevant to a specific area. Usage characteristics will describe in the research subject a non-user, an occasional user, a frequent user or the user of a competing product.

Key Terms

convenience sample   research subject selection method that asks any available and willing individual

incentives   providing money or products to potential qualified research subjects to reward them for participation

participant profiles   description of who should be recruited to be included in the research

professional recruiters   companies that maintain databases of willing research participants or will find qualified research subjects for a project

purposive sample   sample that, while not a probability sample, does select participants based on specific characteristics

snowballing   participant recruiting method that uses one appropriate participant to recruit others with similar characteristics

Discussion Questions

1 Why are personal characteristics more important choice criteria for focus groups than interviews?
2 What type of problems would you encounter when recruiting research participants for a study on young people's opinions on TV reality shows?
3 How could the use of incentives to recruit participants bias the outcome of the above study?

4 Can you name a situation where you feel it would be more appropriate to use a professional recruiter to find research subjects?
5 How could snowballing be used to choose participants for a focus group on the entertainment choices of students involved in alternative lifestyles?
6 What would be the steps in using purposive sample selection for finding participants for a study of professors' attitudes toward student athletes?
7 What argument could be made for including participants who have an existing relationship with a researcher?
8 Which characteristics that might be used when choosing participants for a qualitative marketing research study on cosmetics do you feel are the most critical?
9 Why could it be argued that psychographic characteristics are even more important to consider than demographic characteristics?
10 If you were conducting research to determine why students were not enrolling at your university, what segmentation characteristics would you consider important when choosing participants?

Recommended Reading

Belk, Russell W. (ed.) (2007) *Handbook of Qualitative Research Methods in Marketing.* Cheltenham: Edward Elgar. An excellent resource on everything that is new in qualitative research methodology.

Daymon, Christine and Holloway, Immy (2002) *Qualitative Research Methods in Public Relations and Marketing Communications.* London: Routledge. A practical guide that thoroughly covers all aspects of qualitative research. While the book focuses on public relations and communications it also applies to any type of marketing research project.

Hackley, Chris (2003) *Doing Research Projects in Marketing, Management and Consumer Research.* London: Routledge. Focuses on how interpretive research fits into the qualitative research methodology. While the book covers philosophical perspectives it is also useful for new researchers.

Stevens, Robert., Wren, Bruce., Sherwood, Philip K. and Ruddick, Morris E. (2005) *The Marketing Research Guide.* New York: Business Books. This book is written from a management perspective and covers how marketing research can be used to solve marketing problems. It also includes chapters on industrial and international marketing research.

Stewart, David W., Shamdasani, Prem N. and Rook, Dennis W. (2007) *Focus Groups: Theory and Practice.* London: SAGE. While covering all aspects of planning and conducting focus groups, the book specifically looks at the issue of participant recruitment and selection.

8 Planning and Conducting Focus Groups

Learning Objectives

1 Introduce focus groups and their advantages and disadvantages
2 Describe the steps in developing the focus group methodology
3 Explain the personal characteristics and skills needed in a moderator
4 Relate how group conflict can be minimized
5 Explore alternative methods of conducting focus groups

EVERYTHING YOU NEED TO KNOW IS ON THE WORLD WIDE WEB: BUT CAN YOU UNDERSTAND IT?

Students might not have thought much about pensions. However, their professors certainly will have! Employers often tell their employees that everything they need to know about pension plans is available online. Researchers from the University of Edinburgh and Herriot Watt University decided to conduct research to see if these pension information websites were meeting the needs of those seeking help. They conducted a study of current and archived websites and also used focus groups and observational research to gather data. What they learned was that the information that pension providers put onto the website was not the information that consumers wanted and needed in order to make better decisions.

Questions: What research methodologies should be conducted before a company's webpage is created to ensure it meets the needs of consumers? Who should be involved as research subjects?

Source: Harrison et al., 2006

8.1 Rationale for Using Focus Group Methodology

A marketing research focus group is a methodology that uses participant interaction and moderator probing to uncover consumer wants, needs and desires. A focus group is sometimes misunderstood as being a mere discussion group where a moderator introduces a topic and then sits back and takes notes. However, it is the interaction between the moderator and group members and also between the members themselves that gets beyond participants' first responses to explore deeper ideas.

The focus group is designed to collect data and not just to air opinions. This interaction distinguishes focus groups from other types of group sessions, such as group interviews that do not encourage interaction between research participants (Carson, 2001). Used correctly, focus groups are an excellent method of generating new ideas for product benefits and promotions, exploring the causes for problems or failures, and gaining insights that can then be used to design quantitative research studies.

Focus groups are probably most frequently used as a means of generating new ideas. Product development is ultimately the responsibility of company employees. Although these employees may have marketing expertise, it is customers who will make the purchase decision. It only makes sense to ask customers for assistance in generating ideas for new or improved products. In addition, focus groups can be used to generate ideas on effective promotional campaigns including effective marketing messages and appropriate choices of media.

Focus groups are also used to learn the 'why' or cause of problems or failures. The problems explored in a focus group could be why a product is not succeeding in the marketplace. Of course it may seem to be a simple task to ask consumers why they don't like a product. For example, a simple question such as why consumers do not purchase a food product might receive the response that consumers do not like the taste. In the case of an automobile, consumers may respond by saying they do not like the design.

The problem is that simply telling the marketing department to improve the taste or style of a product does not provide any information on what consumers did not like and what they would like instead. In the case of a service product, consumers might say that staff were rude. However, without any information on why consumers felt staff were rude there is nothing for management to use in order to improve. Focus groups will explore the reasons for these problems in depth, thus providing ideas a company can use to solve the problem.

Appropriate questions for focus groups

- What do you think should be done?
- Why do you prefer … ?
- Why don't you prefer … ?
- How do you feel about … ?
- What would you like changed?

Focus groups are often conducted to generate a hypothesis that will be used in future quantitative research. For example, they can be used to gain insights that would help a researcher to write future survey questions. While the survey questions about why a product is liked or disliked are easy to write, the answers are not. This is because there are so many potential answers as preferences vary widely. Focus groups can be used to gather information on the answers that should be provided. For example, focus groups may have provided information that consumers are concerned about a specific product's color, size, and shape, and this information can then be included on the subsequent survey form.

8.1.1 Advantages of using focus groups

An advantage of using focus groups is the opportunity they provide for researchers to probe issues in depth by encouraging interaction between members. In addition, if a moderator is unsure of any point made by participants, they can be asked follow-up questions. Finally, a focus group can be combined with the use of projective techniques to elicit nonverbal responses.

Participant interaction

The major advantage to using a focus group is the interaction and synergy that increase spontaneity (Andreasen, 2002). In a one-on-one interview methodology a participant might place a researcher in a position of authority. As a result, this participant may not want to disagree or express negative opinions. However, in a focus group participants will not feel that they must agree with the opinions of other participants. As a result, they will be much more likely to disagree and express their own ideas. In addition, unlike an interview, participants do not need to speak until they feel that they have something they want to say. As a result, individuals will find a focus group a much less intimidating experience than an individual interview.

Use of follow-up questions to probe

One of the advantages of a focus group over a survey is the ability of the moderator to ask follow-up questions. When a participant responds to a question with a general comment that they do not 'like' a product, the moderator can keep asking for additional information. The final answer may be that the participant does not like the color, size, taste, packaging or cost. The moderator can then ask what they might prefer.

Combine with other techniques

While focus groups allow participants to interact with each other and the moderator, they also allow participants to interact with their physical surroundings. To help gain information, a moderator may allow the participants to handle or taste the physical product. This method could not be used when conducting a survey. In addition, the focus group methodology can be combined with projective techniques by using video clips or photos of the product in action.

8.1.2 Disadvantages of conducting focus groups

While focus groups are an excellent means of generating ideas, they are not useful for proving facts. In addition, results from focus groups are dependent on the correct choice of research participants and the use of a skilled moderator.

Doesn't supply proof

One of the disadvantages of focus group methodology is that it cannot be used to support a hypothesis. Only quantitative techniques using an appropriately chosen sample can do so. Management can use focus groups to gather data to make decisions on such topics as brand names, advertising copy or new product ideas. However, they should not base decisions solely on focus group evidence. Even though focus group participants will have been chosen to reflect a target market segment, the range of views in a focus group is still too small to generalize to the larger population (Hackley, 2003). If the wrong research subjects are chosen to participate, the wrong information will be obtained. Even where the participants are chosen carefully, if the moderator is unskilled, the results will be useless.

Results dependent on skill of moderator

A disadvantage to conducting focus group research is the effect that an unskilled moderator can have on the results obtained. An ideal focus group uses the interaction between members to spur new ideas and insights that may not be uncovered if the participants were interviewed individually. However, this interaction depends on the skill of the moderator to keep the discussion on the topic without leading the participants in the views they express. In addition, a skilled moderator will ensure that every participant is treated equally. The moderator must also, in a non-confrontational manner, ensure that the group members are respectful of each other's ideas and opinions.

Results dependent on choice of subjects

The success of a focus group in producing useable research data depends on the appropriate choice of research subjects. A well moderated focus group will produce useable research data. However, if the wrong research subjects are included the information provided will be worthless. Even worse, the management of the company commissioning research may not understand the importance of verifying how the participants were chosen. They will therefore base decisions on the information and then be surprised when their actions are not productive. They might blame the methodology when the true cause of such a failure was actually the choice of participants.

While there are disadvantages to the focus group methodology, they continue to be a popular choice among researchers. In the box below are some suggestions on how focus groups could be improved.

REINVENTING THE FOCUS GROUP

The first focus groups, held in the 1930s to gather information on consumer products, were conducted in the evening. This time of day worked well, as it allowed Mom to attend while Dad watched the kids. While a lot has changed in society since then, focus groups have basically remained the same. However, market researcher Naomi Henderson asks fellow colleagues in the field to consider the 'What If?' of the following questions.

What if a focus group didn't have to be two hours long?
What if the researchers used videotape to study subjects in their natural setting?
What if the researcher worked more closely with the client to ensure that the right participants were chosen?
What if the research clients actually sat in on the focus group rather than observe from behind a mirror?
What if researchers and clients met in person immediately after the conclusion of the research to discuss issues?
What if researchers met at the beginning of the year with clients so that research needs could be anticipated?

Addressing these 'What Ifs?' could help focus groups become more aligned with modern marketing theory.

Source: Henderson, 2006

8.1.3 Combining focus group and survey research

In the past, marketing research was often viewed as an either/or proposition. Either researchers believed in the primacy of quantitative research or they were believers in qualitative research.

While there is more attention being paid to qualitative research than in the past, academic researchers continue to focus on quantitative studies for their own research. A study of 1,195 articles in three marketing journals found that 25 per cent used qualitative methodologies, while 46 per cent used quantitative. What was of particular interest was that between 1993 and 2002 there was no increase in the usage of qualitative methodologies (Hanson and Grimmer, 2007).

Even if researchers prefer using quantitative research, they should consider combining methodologies. Once ideas (such as new brand names, promotional messages and product benefits) are generated by a focus group, the ideas can then be further researched using a quantitative technique such as a survey. This type of two-stage research project uses the advantages of both qualitative and quantitative research by first generating ideas and then confirming them. While more costly in terms of time and resources than a single study, such a two-stage study makes sense when expensive decisions must be made. This is because the cost to a company of a wrong decision can be very high.

8.2 Steps in Developing the Focus Group Methodology

The focus group methodology consists of the three stages of preparing, conducting and analyzing as shown in Table 8.1. Preparation for a focus group requires that researchers meet with management to discuss the research objectives. The researchers together with management will then develop the research participant profile, after which the participants will be invited and a moderator will be chosen. The researchers will then use both the research objectives and the participant profile to write a focus group script. Conducting the research involves preparation of the facilities, moderating the group, and gathering the material. After the research has been conducted, the researchers must transcribe the proceedings, code the results and prepare the report.

Table 8.1   Focus group process

Preparation	Meet with management to clarify issues
	Develop the participant profile
	Invite subjects to participate
	Choose a moderator
	Write the focus group script
Conducting	Prepare the facility
	Moderate the proceedings
	Gather and maintain the information
Analysis	Transcribe the information
	Code the information
	Write the report

8.2.1 Focus group preparation

During the preparation stage of the focus group methodology researchers meet with management and also those staff from departments that have a stake in solving the problem. Qualitative research is conducted when management is exploring new ideas or the cause of a problem. Therefore at this meeting it is important to have a broad, wide ranging discussion on the issues that management is concerned about. The vaguer the research issue, the more important it is for researchers to clarify what management wants and needs to know.

One of the problems researchers may face in the preparation stage is communicating to management that the focus group discussion must stay 'focused'. Unfortunately management may have the misconception that an hour long focus group with eight participants will result in eight hours of information. As a result of this belief, they will give researchers a long list of topics they want covered during the focus group. Of course in a focus group only one person can speak at a time, which limits the amount of information that can be gathered. In addition, it is important to remember that besides the time limitation the purpose of a focus group is to discuss an issue in depth. A focus group should not be conducted as a group survey, where researchers have a list of questions and then allow each member to respond only quickly. Researchers should come away from the meeting with management with two to three topic areas at most that the focus group will address.

Participant profile

After the research issues have been defined, the participants for the focus group must be chosen. Researchers and management will together develop a participant profile. For example, the research question may ask about the opinions of current customers. In this case, the participants will be chosen to represent the segmentation characteristics of the particular segment the question addresses. Groups that do not wish to participate may require a special means of invitation (see the box below). At other times the research question may ask about the opinions of a potential market segment and it will be chosen with these characteristics in mind.

HOW DO YOU GET YOUTH TO PARTICIPATE IN A FOCUS GROUP? MAKE SURE THEY ARE WITH THEIR FRIENDS!

Researchers from the University of Strathclyde and the University of Edinburgh conducted a study of British young people, aged 13–17, to determine how they used their mobile phones and their attitudes toward commercial messages sent to them on their phones. To determine the answer, the study involved 175 participants from three different schools on the east coast of Scotland. First the researchers asked each participant to complete a questionnaire on phone usage and their attitude towards marketing. The researchers then wanted to conduct focus groups. However, they already knew that young people would not be interested in the traditional focus group format of six to eight strangers sitting around a table. Instead, the researchers conducted mini-groups containing three people in each. These mini-groups consisted of young people who were already friends. This way they already had a bond and were willing to talk. The research findings? Their phone is 'a friend in their hand', so they hate it when a commercial appears.

Source: Grant and O'Donohoe, 2007

Choose a moderator

After the participants have been invited a moderator must be chosen. If a company or organization is large enough to support their own marketing research division, the moderator may be someone internal to that company. If not, a moderator must be hired to conduct the focus group. Moderators may be professionals who work in a full-service advertising agency, or they may be consultants with their own company.

The moderator should not be familiar with the participants. In fact, it is best if the moderator has no contact with the participants before the focus group session. Having a pre-existing relationship with a member of the group makes building a rapport with others in the group more difficult. A pre-existing relationship may cause a division in the group between those who know the moderator and those who do not.

Focus group script

The final step in the preparation stage would be to write the focus group script. The script will include the questions that will be asked during the focus group. These main research topic areas will be addressed with general questions that will then lead to additional follow-up questions. The script should be broken down into the three sections of a focus group; building a rapport, probing and closing. Besides the questions, the script will describe the techniques that will be used to gather information. The technique may be simply a question and discussion format. Alternatively, the focus group may use projective techniques. A focus group script may appear deceptively easy to produce. However, to have everyone agree on the final script can take as much effort and time as writing a survey form. In the box below is a sample focus group script.

SAMPLE FOCUS GROUP SCRIPT WITH PROJECTIVE TECHNIQUES

Research questions to be addressed in park use focus group:

1. Which parks are frequented by the participants and why?
2. What are their opinions of the facilities/activities?
3. What suggestions do participants have for improvements?

BUILDING A RAPPORT

Purpose: To relax and bond the group and to connect the group to the subject.
Method: Welcome and general discussion.
Question: Which park do you usually visit?
Additional questions: What other community parks are you familiar with?

Technique: To spur thought and conversation a map and photos of the city's parks will be on display.

PROBING

Purpose: To uncover information useful in answering research questions.
Method: General discussion followed by projective techniques.
Question: Why do you or why do you not visit your community park?

(Continued)

Technique: Speech bubble sentence completion, with picture of person in the park commenting to fellow park visitor, "The reason I visit (or would visit) the park is _____."

Additional questions: What is your favorite activity? Do you feel safe in the park? What type of facilities or activities should be in the park?

Technique: Ideas generated by participants will be listed on large pieces of paper. Each participant is given five pretend $100 bills and push pins. They will use these to vote for where to spend money. They can pin all their money on one idea or spread it around.

CLOSING

Purpose: To move the group towards the next step.
Method: Discussion to determine depth of commitment.
Question: If you had the power to insist the Mayor take one action to improve the parks, what would it be?

Technique: Pass around index cards. Ask participants to each list their idea for the Mayor.

8.2.2 Conducting a focus group

A marketing research firm or large corporation may have a specialized focus group facility. This facility would consist of a reception area where focus group participants would be greeted. A separate room where the focus group would take place would provide a table with comfortable seating. Also in the room would be projection equipment for showing any video clips the moderator might use. A table for displaying products, an easel with paper for writing and a side table with refreshments would all be in place. In addition, the room would contain a means for taping the proceedings. Attached to the focus group room would be a side room that would be used by researchers and management to view the proceedings using a one-way mirror.

While such a setting is very professional, it is also costly, and it is not necessary to have such a suite of rooms to conduct a successful focus group. In fact it may be argued that it is counter productive. This type of corporate setting is the natural environment of researchers and corporate employees. However, it is not the natural environment of most consumers and many might find it intimidating.

It is possible to have a focus group in any type of location where eight to ten people can be comfortably seated. If technical equipment is needed, it can easily be brought to the location. For example, if a corporation wants to study the needs of young people, it makes more sense to have the focus group in a bar or restaurant where young people congregate. Likewise, people from a specific ethnic group would be more likely to speak candidly if the focus group were held in a community center in their own neighborhood. A focus group with children requires special planning (see the box below).

It will take additional planning to run a successful focus group with children. Despite the added difficulty, companies that sell products geared to children, such as toys, must rely on focus groups if they are to have successful product development. However, companies that produce other products such as food, clothing, furniture and even tourism understand that children must also be included in their research plans because they have input into the decision-making process. To ensure that their ideas and opinions are included in product development and promotion, focus groups are necessary. However, when recruiting children for focus groups it is important not only to assess their demographic characteristics but also their verbal ability.

Of course any focus group involving children should ensure that they will be comfortable and protected. In addition, to run a successful focus group with children the following guidelines are suggested:

Group size: Keep it small, four to five is enough, don't mix by age and it's best to separate by gender.
Time: Keep it short, one hour at the most.
Setting: Adapt the physical environment by making it kid-friendly.
Skills: The process should be at the appropriate cognitive level, as age six is very different from age ten.
Play: Use games to bond and reward, as kids get bored very quickly.
Tasks: Give familiar tasks and get responses through nonverbal means, as marking a smiley face or frowning face is easier for children than giving a verbal response.

Source: Faulkenberry Summers, 1992

A focus group consists of three stages. The first stage is used to build a rapport. This can be accomplished by having the participants give first name introductions. The moderator can then introduce the subject by asking an easy, non-threatening question. Once a rapport has been established, the moderator will move on to more probing questions on the issue. During this portion of the focus group interaction will be encouraged and follow-up questions will be used. Finally, the moderator will provide a sense of closure by asking a final question or by requesting some last thoughts on the subject.

After the conclusion of the focus group, the moderator will thank the participants for their attendance. Once they have left it is the moderator's responsibility to maintain all information in an orderly fashion. Any large sheets of paper should be taken down and labeled. Projective material such as drawings should be collected and placed in a file. Finally, the recording of the proceedings should be labeled together with the date and the topic.

8.2.3 Focus group analysis

After a focus group has been conducted, the final step is to analyze the research findings. This is the responsibility of the moderator, as part of the skill they bring to the role is their ability to interpret

Table 8.2 Successful moderators

Personal characteristics	Interest in research process
	Empathy with participants
Skills and knowledge	Knowledge of research methods
	Skill in group dynamics
	Skill in analyzing data and writing reports

what has occurred. The focus group proceedings may have been videoed or taped. In addition, there may be written notes and also material from projective techniques. All the recorded and written information will be analyzed by the moderator for common themes and unique insights.

After the analysis is completed, a final report will be written. A research report for quantitative techniques will have statistics that are presented in graph or chart form to support its findings. A qualitative research report will rely on supporting its findings using quotes or projective materials. The final task of the moderator is to provide an oral report of the findings.

8.3 Desirable Moderator Characteristics and Skills

One of the key measures in having a successful focus group is to write a focus group script that addresses the research question. In addition, the subjects must meet the participant profile. Lastly, the right moderator must be selected. A skilled moderator will be able to run a successful focus group even if the subjects aren't as motivated to participate as would be desired and the questions are a bit too vague or too narrow. However, a poor moderator will result in an unsuccessful focus group – even with the most carefully chosen and motivated participants and the most well-written script. Choosing a successful moderator requires paying attention to both personal characteristics and skills as shown in Table 8.2 above.

8.3.1 Desirable personal characteristics

Successful moderators will find the research process interesting. It is not necessary, or even advisable, for them to be knowledgeable about the research topic. However, good researchers continue to find the process of obtaining needed information exciting no matter what topic is under discussion. A moderator will treat each focus group as being important and will be concerned that it provides the information needed by the company or organization. If they do not feel like this, they might not be willing to spend the time in developing a script and other techniques that will provide the needed information. Instead, they may conduct a focus group using the same procedures and techniques that they used last time.

A moderator also needs to be comfortable with and feel empathy for the participants. This is especially important if a moderator is a different age and from a different income level, religion or ethnicity. Empathy cannot be faked. If focus group participants come from a group whose opinions are usually ignored, they will quickly notice if a moderator does not treat them as equals. For this reason it is best to have a moderator with at least some similar demographic or psychographic characteristics as participants. If this is not possible, the moderator should have at least worked with similar types of participants in the past.

8.3.2 Required skills

A moderator should not only be familiar with focus groups, but should also have at least a basic understanding of all research methodologies. Management is often unclear as to what research method should be used to answer each type of research question. A knowledge of research methodologies will help a moderator to know when the information a company wants would be best discovered through the use of another method.

A moderator should also understand group dynamics. They will be unable to direct a group in a productive direction without a strong understanding of how groups function. Finally, a moderator should be skilled in the analysis and reporting of focus group data. Survey data can be analyzed by someone who had no input into the design or conducting of a survey. This is not true of a focus group, which is an interactive process between the moderator and the participants. The box below provides information that can be used to assess a moderator.

IS YOUR FOCUS GROUP MODERATOR UP TO THE JOB?

Much has been written about the abilities needed by a moderator. Not as much has been written about how to know if the focus group moderator is doing a good job. Here are some suggested questions. (The answer should be yes for all of these except for question five and question eight.) Does the moderator:

1. Flow from point to point without abrupt shifts?
2. Keep the discussion 'on purpose'?
3. Probe for clarity?
4. Ask questions that allow respondents to open up so they can give full answers?
5. Lead the respondents, put words in their mouths, or inappropriately summarize/paraphrase?
6. Establish and maintain a rapport?
7. Include everyone in the discussion?
8. Conduct serial interviewing?
9. 'Read' the room, stay with the respondents, and keep attention off of self and the guide?
10. Keep self/ego out of the discussion and avoid talking too much?
11. Attend to nonverbal communications?
12. Give clear ground rules/purpose statement/full disclosure about mirrors/microphones/observers/stipends?
13. Use a variety of research tools/techniques?
14. Provide linking and logic tracking for respondents and observers?
15. Listen to rather than inform participants?
16. Vary their voice tone during the process?
17. Change location/body position during the focus group process?
18. Give clear instructions/direction to respondents/set up and appropriately introduce stimuli?

Source: Henderson, 1992

8.4 Handling Group Conflict

The success of a focus group depends on the interaction between group members. There is no reason that a focus group should not be a pleasant experience with friendly interaction between participants. Of course, not all people have pleasant dispositions. As a result there may be times when focus group discussion becomes a bit 'heated'. One of the causes of having a focus group become confrontational is simply group dynamics. Before a group can work together successfully there are always some formation issues that must be worked though. An understanding of group dynamics can be helpful in learning to diffuse these conflicts.

8.4.1 Stages of group development

There are many different models of group dynamics. One that has gained popularity in the business world is called Tuckman's Stages (Tuckman, 1965). This model, which was originally created to explain the behavior of work teams, describes four stages of group dynamics: forming, storming, norming and performing. While a focus group differs from a work team in that there is a moderator facilitating the process, this model remains useful as these stages will still be in evidence during the focus group process.

Tuckman's Stages applied to focus groups

- Forming – strangers sit down together and must quickly make judgments about each other
- Storming – opinions are expressed which may result in conflict
- Norming – the moderator handles conflict by acknowledging the importance of all contributions
- Performing – the focus group can now concentrate on the topic rather than each other

'Forming' occurs when the participants, who are strangers, make judgments about each other. They need to know how other people in the group should be treated and how they will treat them. People will often make these judgments based on stereotypes rather than knowledge. 'Storming' is where strong opinions may result in strong reactions. Personalities may very well conflict, as the focus group participants are not chosen for their compatibility. During the 'norming' stage the moderator's role is to diffuse the conflict while acknowledging the contributions of all members. If the moderator can successfully diffuse the conflict, the focus group can then settle into a discussion. Even if at times there is disagreement, focus group members must have trust in the moderator's ability to handle any conflicts. At this stage the focus group can perform by having an interactive conversation on the topic. Even the most skilled moderator may have participants that never fully participate in discussion of the topic. However, after diffusing conflict during the storming stage enough so that the focus group can continue, the moderator will strive to have everyone participate during the 'performing' stage.

8.4.2 Focus groups using nominal grouping

Sometimes focus group proceedings can become heated because of the topic being discussed. There are some topics that evoke such strong responses that the usual interactive focus group will not work. It is the marketing of ideas that most often elicits these types of responses rather than the marketing of products. Consumers may have strong feelings about the color, taste, style or design of a consumer product. They may even strongly disagree with the opinions of fellow focus group members, but rarely would such disagreements be so vehement that it would disrupt a focus group.

Market researchers working on issues regarding ideas may find that some of these do elicit very strong responses. Research involving political campaigns, environmental issues, health care accessibility and other social issues may prompt very strong opinions and disagreements. For example, if a focus group was held where members felt so strongly either for or against the introduction of genetically altered food, they may either become argumentative or stop participating altogether. Sexual behavior is another sensitive topic. If a focus group needs to be conducted to get ideas on how to prevent teenage pregnancies, the participants may have strong ethical and moral beliefs. Even the food you eat can provoke strong feelings, as can be seen in the example below.

HOW WOULD YOU LIKE YOUR STEAK?
CLONED OR NOT CLONED?

A current issue before the US Food and Drug Administration (FDA) is whether to allow meat to be sold from cloned animals. A five-year study and almost 700 pages of testimony found that cloned animal products are safe to consume. However, the International Dairy Food Association decided to research consumers' views on the issue. The participants in the study were all women who were the primary food buyers in their families. The study found that consumers have very strong feelings about cloned food that will not be changed by any FDA report. The research found that 14 per cent of the women would stop using dairy products altogether if cloned food was introduced. A similar study by the Pew Initiative on Food and Biotechnology found that 46 per cent of consumers were 'very uncomfortable' with using cloning in food production.

Experts believe that farmers will use cloning to breed prized livestock, not to produce food. However, even with cloning one generation away from the steak on their plate, consumers still have strong negative opinions. So don't go looking for cloned food in your local grocery store anytime soon!

Source: Pollack and Martin, 2006

Under most circumstances a skilled moderator can prevent or diffuse conflict amongst focus group members. However, a technique to handle focus groups on especially sensitive topics is called nominal grouping. Using nominal group session techniques is a way to gain opinions and insights when the topic under discussion may prompt either overly disruptive arguments or silence on the part of participants. Nominal grouping involves first grouping participants by common characteristics and then having the participants silently list their ideas. These are presented in turn without discussion. Each idea is then discussed for its importance and relevance to the issue. However, they are not criticized based on merit. Each member ranks the ideas and then the rankings are discussed until a consensus is reached.

For example, a researcher for a community organization might want to gather information on why young people engage in sexual activity. This information will then be used to create a public service announcement. Participants in such a focus group would be young people who were currently sexually active. Each participant lists a reason why teens become sexually active. However, here the moderator does not allow participants to argue their ideas with each other. Instead of criticizing each other's ideas, they will discuss how these ideas should be ranked by importance.

Nominal technique for sensitive topics

- Have participants silently write their response to a question.
- The moderator gathers these responses and lists them on a board.
- The responses are discussed for relevance, not correctness.
- The participants rank these responses by importance.

8.5 Other Venues for Focus Groups

The traditional focus group is conducted with the participants and the moderator sitting around a table. However, focus groups can take place using other means than face-to-face personal communication, such as by videoconferencing and online.

8.5.1 Videoconferencing focus groups

Videoconferencing is a technology that can be used to conduct focus groups. Using videoconferencing research firms can reduce the expense of bringing the moderator and participants together in one location. Videoconferencing has the advantage of allowing the participants and moderators to see each other. They can therefore react to each other's body language and communicate more effectively. A sophisticated videoconferencing system allows all the members to see everyone's reactions to each other even when they are in many different locations. Another advantage of videoconferencing is that it allows products that are the subject of research to be shown and some projective techniques can also be used.

The disadvantage comes in that focus group participants must travel to a special facility where videoconferencing equipment is available. These types of facilities are generally only found in corporate offices and large universities. Not all participants would feel comfortable going to such locations. Even if they do go to the facility, not everyone would be familiar with communicating using this method. It might take a while for participants to feel comfortable enough to actively participate. In addition, the research firm sponsoring the research would need to pay for use of the facility.

8.5.2 Online focus groups

Online technology is being adapted for use with focus groups. This includes using existing Usenet user groups or internet chatrooms that attract people who have mutual interests. This shared interest or lifestyle might vary from a love of comic books to the enjoyment of gourmet foods. Therefore online focus groups are very useful when the research participant profile calls for subjects who are similar psychographically. A focus group can be conducted 'live', with a moderator posting questions while subjects respond immediately online.

137

Even more importantly than with a traditional focus group, when conducting a group online moderators should always identify themselves, the topic of the research and for whom the research is being conducted. It is unethical for a moderator to conduct research while posing as just another user.

Often members of an online community are eager to communicate their opinions. After all, people who chat online are a self-selected group that wants to communicate. Using this method can be helpful in gaining insights from groups that would not normally attend a traditional focus group. Groups that feel disenfranchised from society, such as the young, ethnic groups, or people who live alternative lifestyles, can be successfully reached with this method. In fact, how the online experience can be used in marketing can be explored (Sweeney and Perry, 2004).

Using such online sites limits the use of demographic criteria as there is no way to control for gender, age and economic level. Another consideration when using online focus groups is that this method will not reach a cross section of everyone interested in a topic. Instead, it will attract only those who are comfortable or interested in communicating online. This will mean that participants are more likely to be younger and better educated. Another disadvantage is that a moderator cannot see body language, although the online community is quite skilled at communicating feelings by using both words and symbols.

A moderator should have experience in conducting online focus groups because opinions can become extreme when expressed online. In addition, people may adopt a very different persona to the one they use in their everyday lives. Whether the opinions of alternative personas are more or less real is a question best left for psychologists and philosophers. However, moderators need to be aware that extreme opinions may not be acted upon in real life. There are now specialized tools for conducting online focus groups. In this case, participants come online specifically to participate in a focus group.

Summary

1   Focus groups are a qualitative research methodology that is used to generate ideas, explore the causes of problems and gain insights for use in the design of quantitative research. The major advantage in using focus groups is that interaction between group members can result in new ideas and insights. Another advantage of focus groups is that superficial answers can be further explored in depth by asking follow-up questions. Focus groups can easily be combined with projective techniques to allow participants to communicate ideas in ways other than verbal answers. However, focus group data cannot be used to prove a fact. In addition the quality of the data is dependent upon the appropriateness of the participants and the skill of the moderator.

2   Focus group methodology consists of three phases of preparing, conducting and analyzing. In the preparation stage the researcher meets with management to define the research issues, to develop a participant profile and chose a moderator. The researcher will then prepare a research script. The conducting phase will involve preparing the facility, moderating the proceedings and collecting the information after the group has concluded. The analysis stage will include transcribing and coding the information. The final report will then be written.

3 Much of the success of the focus group methodology depends on the skill of the moderator. The moderator should have an interest in the research process and an empathy with the participants. The skills needed include a knowledge of research methods, the ability to handle group dynamics and skill in analyzing and reporting data.
4 Conflict can arise during focus groups. A knowledge of group dynamics including the forming, storming, norming and performing stages can help a moderator to constructively direct the conversation. Nominal grouping can be used when particularly sensitive topics are discussed. With this technique, participants first privately list ideas that are then discussed for relevance rather than correctness.
5 Other means of conducting focus groups include videoconferencing and online. Each has its advantages that include cost savings and reaching particular groups. However, they all have the disadvantage of limiting the personal interaction between a moderator and focus group members that forms the basis of the focus group technique.

Key Terms

focus group qualitative research technique, led by a moderator, consisting of 6–10 people who exchange views

focus group script written overview of the topics to be covered during the focus group including opening, probing and closing questions

moderator leader in a focus group who poses the questions, encourages responses, and handles conflict to obtain useable research data

nominal focus group technique focus group technique for use with sensitive topics that reduces conflict by encouraging prioritizing rather than disagreement

participant profile description using segmentation characteristics of who should be chosen in a focus group

Discussion Questions

1 What are the advantages and disadvantages of using focus groups to explore the consumer preferences of young people?
2 How would you answer the claim that focus groups are not useful because too few participants are involved?
3 What issues could be explored using a focus group made up of students?

4   What argument would you present to management for the expense of conducting both a focus group and a survey on the food service available at a university?
5   Why should both management and researchers be involved in the development of a participant profile?
6   Why would moderators be able to obtain better data when they have empathy with the research subjects?
7   Which is more important to a focus group's success – a skilled moderator or the right participants? Support your argument.
8   How could Tuckman's Stages of Group Dynamics be used when conducting a focus group that consisted of sports fans from rival teams?
9   Why would nominal grouping be used to conduct a focus group that discusses better ways to promote HIV awareness on campuses?
10 What would be the advantages and disadvantages of using an online focus group to discuss older consumers' purchasing of travel tours?

Recommended Reading

Carson, David., Gilmore, Audrey., Perry, Chad and Gronhaug, Kjell (2001) *Qualitative Marketing Research*. London: SAGE. The authors of this book believe that statistical information must be balanced with intelligence gathered through qualitative methodologies. The book includes chapters on focus groups, observations, ethnography and grounded theory.

Michman, Ronald D. (2003) *Lifestyle Marketing: Reaching the New American Consumer*. Westport, CT: Praeger. This book stresses the importance of segmenting the consumer by lifestyle. It also has a chapter that discusses Asian, Jewish and Italian market segments.

Moisander, Johannna and Voltonen, Anu (2006) *Qualitative Marketing Research: A Cultural Approach*. London: SAGE. Examining qualitative methodologies from a cultural perspective or how products affect consumers' lives.

Puchta, Claudia and Potter, Jonathan (2004) *Focus Group Practice*. London: SAGE. A book that deals with the issue of the moderation of focus groups based on interaction theory.

Stewart, David., Shamdasani, Prem N. and Rook, Denis W. (2007) *Focus Groups: Theory and Practice*. London: SAGE. Thoroughly covers all aspects of focus groups from planning to implementation. It also presents information on the application of online and video focus groups.

9 In-depth, Intercept and Expert Interviews

Learning Objectives

1 Explain the advantages and disadvantages of using interview research
2 Examine the unique features of in-depth, expert and intercept interviews
3 Identify the different types of interview questions
4 Describe the different methods of screening potential interview participants
5 Explain the guidelines to be used for well-written interview questions

WHY AREN'T BRITISH ARTS AND HUMANITIES STUDENTS FINDING JOBS WHEN THE JOBS ARE THERE?

Studying a field in the arts and humanities and assuming you won't be able to find a job? You're not alone. A survey of 17,170 British students found that only 27 per cent of students studying in arts and humanities expected to find a job after graduation. In contrast, 58 per cent of engineering students and 57 per cent of business students expected to be gainfully employed on completion of their studies. Pity the poor arts and humanities students! Yet further research found that companies stated that 80 per cent of all positions would be open to applicants who studied any subject.

Question: If you worked in career placement, what additional research would you conduct to gather more information to help your arts and humanities graduates?

Source: Boone, 2007

9.1 The Rationale for Conducting Interview Research

Interviewing is a qualitative research technique using personal communication between researchers and research subjects. The purpose of conducting interviews includes gaining insights into consumer behavior, obtaining factual information and developing hypotheses for quantitative research. Besides in-depth one-to-one interviewing between researchers and research subjects to gain insights on consumer preferences, researchers may also conduct intercept and expert interviews. Intercept interviews only use three to four quick questions and are given by researchers at locations where specific subjects can be found. The purpose of expert interviews is to gather information on product, industry or consumer segments.

The purpose of research interviews is to explore ideas, gain knowledge or develop hypotheses that can then be tested using quantitative research. Research interviews use a partially structured approach to questioning. Some of the questions will be asked verbatim of each research subject. A researcher will determine other questions to ask as the interview progresses. The fact that some of the questions are the same for each research participant allows comparability. At the same time, a researcher can also add additional questions, which allows flexibility. The fact that interview methodology may be only partially structured does not mean that the interview process can be treated casually, as an interview is not simply a conversation. A researcher must spend time in carefully preparing research questions if an interview is to be successful.

9.1.1 Interview stages

In-depth interviews go through four stages. However, expert interviews only have three stages and intercept interviews two. All start with an opening phase where introductions are made and the purpose of the research is explained. In-depth interviews move on to a short questioning phase that includes easily answered, predetermined questions about a participant's consumer behavior or opinions. The probing phase asks follow-up questions based on the responses received during the questioning phase. During the closing stage, a researcher will thank a participant and answer any questions they may have about what will happen to the information he or she has provided.

Research interviewing stages

- *Opening*: communicates the purpose of the interview and establishes trust regarding confidentiality and ethics
- *Questioning*: uses predetermined questions
- *Probing*: uses follow-up questions based on earlier responses
- *Closing*: A researcher gives their thanks and answers the participant's questions

9.1.2 Advantages of using interviews

Interview methodology has the advantage of allowing research participants to express ideas in their own words. The length of an interview allows a participant time to develop their ideas fully. If a researcher is still unclear as to a participant's meaning, he or she can ask probing follow-up questions. Interviews are also used for gathering information that can be developed into an hypothesis that can be tested in turn by using quantitative research. Finally, the expert interview is useful for gathering factual knowledge.

Respond in own words

The purpose of an interview is to uncover consumer motivation by allowing participants to respond to a question in their own words. The advantage of this approach over survey research is that the answer is not based on the researcher's preconceived ideas. In survey research, even if the question is general in nature, a researcher will have predetermined possible responses. For this reason, it is difficult for new insights to emerge from survey research. For example, a survey question on why consumers do not buy a brand of breakfast cereal might provide possible answers concerning it's price, taste and availability. However, in an in-depth interview it might be found that these three factors had nothing to do with consumers not purchasing the product. Instead, consumers might mention that this cereal is for kids, and not for adults such as themselves. Interviews can lead to deeper insights that might be missed in other forms of research (Anderson, 2007).

Allow time to develop ideas
Interviews allow researchers to probe underlying reasons for consumer behavior, such as why a particular segment of the population is not purchasing a product. For example, the American National Football League has been trying to expand interest in the sport in Europe. While many Europeans enjoy watching sports teams compete, despite the NFL's best marketing efforts American football has had limited success expanding their fan base in Europe (Owen, 2007). If consumers who routinely purchase a competitor's product refuse to purchase a company's similar product, there may be a deep-rooted reason for such purchasing behavior. In-depth interviews with potential fans may be needed to uncover the reason why American football is having trouble attracting fans in Europe. These will allow researchers to spend enough time with research subjects to find out the cause of the purchasing behavior.

Develop hypotheses
Interviews can be used to develop hypotheses that can then be tested using quantitative survey research. For example, the owner of an amusement park might wish to conduct a survey on motivations for attendance. The information obtained will then be used to develop future promotional campaigns. Attendance at the park is strong and, therefore, management does not believe there are any serious problems that need to be explored with a focus group or in-depth interview methodology. On the other hand, they do not want to construct a survey form without some input from current customers. They might decide to use intercept interviews of guests leaving the park to quickly gather information. If the majority of respondents list 'quality time with my family' as the motivation for attendance, a survey can then be developed to confirm or deny this hypothesis.

Probe for underlying reasons
Interviews also allow researchers to probe beyond the initial answers given by participants. Sometimes this is necessary because the original answer is unclear. Often participants will use negative terms, such as 'boring', 'ugly' or 'useless', or positive terms such as 'great', 'best' or 'exciting'. The problem with this type of terminology is that it is too general to be of use to the company commissioning the research. In an interview, a researcher can ask for clarification on what a participant means by a word such as 'ugly'. Is it the packaging or the product design? Is it the product's color, size or shape that the consumer finds so unappealing? Once this negative information is obtained, a researcher can then obtain information on how the product can be improved by asking what color or shape the participant prefers.

Ask follow-up questions
Another advantage of conducting interviews is that researchers can probe unexpected insights. For example, if during a interview a participant mentions that they enjoy cereal as an evening snack a researcher can probe for more information on how often that participant consumes

cereal of an evening. The researcher may then decide to ask other participants about their consumption habits. From this first insight, that researcher might find that a number of participants consume the same product in the evening. Communicating these unexpected data to the company may provide them with a new promotion idea.

Gain factual knowledge

Expert interviews are used to gain factual knowledge on subjects that are of interest to researchers. This knowledge may be about benefits that consumers prefer in a product or information regarding a target market segment's behavior. For example, a company that produces medical equipment for hospitals may be developing a new design for wheelchairs for obese patients. To ensure that the chair will be developed with the right benefits they may arrange expert interviews with nursing supervisors. From these interviews, researchers might learn that an important criterion in chair design is the height of the seat as nurses have difficulty helping obese patients transfer from a bed to a chair.

9.1.3 Disadvantages of using interviews

A disadvantage of the interview methodology is that researchers must be highly skilled if an interview is to provide useful information. Because each participant is allowed to develop their own ideas every interview will be unique, making the information between interviews difficult to compare. A final disadvantage is that because of the time and expense of conducting interviews, only a small sample of participants can be used.

A skilled interviewer

One disadvantage of interviewing is that it will require a moderator who is skilled in interviewing techniques. An interviewer must have experience of working in the social sciences or have past marketing research experience in interviewing. Interviewees do not always cooperate with the interview process, and may in fact try to disrupt the flow of an interview and take control. A skilled interviewer needs to know how to handle these situations and regain control by returning to the topic under discussion (Sands and Krumer-Nevo, 2006).

A skilled interviewer will understand that an interview is a type of controlled conversation and not a monologue where only the participant speaks. An interviewer must not only listen for unclear or insightful answers but also must keep the interview focused on the research question without leading the participant. Unlike focus groups where group interaction can prompt responses, interviews rely on an interviewer's skill to ensure that the participant provides the needed information. This can be difficult with shy, quiet or resistant participants.

In addition, researchers must encourage participation while letting participants do almost all of the talking. A researcher must elicit from a participant information of which they may only partially aware or which they (wrongly) deem unimportant. Because of the difficulty in conducting interviews, skilled interviewers are expensive to hire. However, without a skilled interviewer interviews will waste time and money and may lead a company to accept faulty information upon which to make decisions.

Data not comparable

Because researchers use probing questions without knowing exactly what answers may surface, each interview will be unique. Therefore it is difficult to compare data although, through analysis, common themes may be found. For this reason interview methodology is often used as a prelude to further quantitative research. Because data are difficult to compare, management should be careful when basing important decisions on data obtained through interviews alone.

Small sample size

A series of in-depth interviews will involve many fewer participants than a survey. Because there are few participants, interview research cannot be used to prove or disprove an hypothesis. While interviewing can provide valuable insights, the quality of such insights will depend on the quality of the research subjects. Therefore extra care must be taken to ensure that the interview subjects meet the participant profile.

9.2 Types of Interviews

The choice of marketing research interviewing methodologies includes in-depth interviews. With this technique a researcher spends most of the interview exploring consumer motivation and behavior. Expert interviews are used to gather information from people who are not necessarily direct consumers of a specific product, but have knowledge of either that product and industry or the needs and wants of the market segment that is being targeted. Intercept interviews are short person-on-the-street interviews that only ask a few predetermined questions. This information can be used to develop hypotheses that can then be proved or disproved by using quantitative research.

Types of interviews

- *In-depth*: one-to-one on a single topic for an extended period
- *Expert*: with a person other than the research subject to obtain facts
- *Intercept or person-on-the-street*: short interviews with many participants

9.2.1 In-depth interviews

In-depth interviews are conducted between an interviewer and a single participant. The interview is partially structured with some of the questions being predetermined. These questions are written by researchers and based on the research question. A researcher will ask other questions based on information provided by the participants during the interviews. In-depth interviews usually last a little under an hour and go through four phases: opening, questioning, probing and closing. During the 'opening' phase an interviewer will explain to a participant the purpose of the research. Once this is concluded the research will move into the 'questioning' phase. The questions will start by being very general in nature and then will move on to more specific information.

For example, if an interviewer is discussing breakfast cereal the opening question will be if the participant eats cereal. Asking this type of question will establish the purpose of the research while at the same giving the participant an easy question to answer. The interviewer will then ask predetermined questions about brand preference and move on to more probing questions regarding why the participant chose this particular brand. The interviewer will then ask

Table 9.1 In-depth interview structure

Opening phase	(The researcher explains the purpose of the research concerns breakfast cereal preferences.)
	Do you eat breakfast cereal? (predetermined)
Questioning phase	What brand do you eat? (predetermined)
Probing phase	Why do you prefer this brand? (predetermined)
	What do you mean by 'not so sweet'? (unstructured)
Closing phase	Thanks for participation.
	Do you have any questions?

additional probing questions to ensure that the information the participant has provided has been correctly understood. Finally, a researcher will close the interview by thanking the participant and asking if they have any questions. An example of the process is shown in Table 9.1.

Sometimes research questions will touch on sensitive issues. Some industries, such as health care, assisted living for the elderly or organizations that work with the disabled, often need to conduct research that asks participants questions about difficult times in their lives. Interviewers for these types of research projects need to have special training so that the research does not leave any emotional scars. A research study conducted in Britain found, that if it were conducted with sensitivity, research participants may find the interview process therapeutic rather than harmful (Lowes and Gill, 2006).

9.2.2 Expert interviews

Expert interviews are usually conducted early on in the research process as a means of clarifying a research problem. They can also be used to gather data during research, but only in combination with other research methods. An expert interview is conducted to gather factual information about a problem from someone with a specific product, consumer or industry knowledge. Because this expert is usually a busy professional, the time for an interview is kept as short as possible. The expert interview consists of only two phases – opening and questioning. Because the purpose of the interview is to gain factual information, and not the underlying causes of behavior, probing is not used. This also allows for the interview to be conducted in a shorter time.

In the breakfast cereal example above, during the early stages of the research process researchers might wish to conduct expert interviews with grocery store managers. The managers can provide information on what cereals have sold well in the past and the current sales trends. In addition, researchers may wish to conduct expert interviews with nutritionists regarding current consumer eating habits.

During the research process, expert interviews might also be conducted among people involved in the distribution process and the development of promotion. If the research uncovers that package size is an issue, the researchers should discuss with distribution experts what reaction would be received if the company involved produced unique packaging that would require a modification to shelf space. If an issue involves a new promotion idea, such as marketing cereal for evening consumption, researchers may wish to interview advertising agency managers to see if they have handled such a unique product repositioning promotion for other clients. An example of the process is shown in Table 9.2.

Table 9.2 Expert interview structure

Opening phase	(The researcher explains the purpose of the research with a nutritionist regarding breakfast food consumption.)
Questioning phase	How important is nutritional information in food choice? (predetermined)
	Is portion control an issue with breakfast food consumption? (predetermined)
	Are there other issues that you think are important? (predetermined)
Closing phase	Thanks for participation

9.2.3 Intercept interviews

Person-on-the-street interviews also ask open-ended questions. In this case though the interview is kept very short. An intercept interview should only take a few minutes and is therefore limited to three or four questions. The participants are chosen and interviewed at the location where they can be found. This technique is often used when the subjects needed for the research are unwilling to agree to an in-depth interview. Because the interviews take a short period of time, many more can be conducted. However, the short time period for person-on-the-street interviews means that there isn't time for probing questions. Therefore interviewers used for this type of interview does not need the same level of technical skill. Instead, it is more important that the potential participants view the interviewer as someone who is friendly and approachable. Below is an example of how intercept interviews are used in researching fashions trends.

HOW DO YOU KNOW WHAT THE NEXT FASHION TREND WILL BE?

According to marketing researchers in the fashion industry, the first step in deciding next year's fashions is secondary research on social trends. In-house reports, government statistics and data from academic sources are studied for information on social changes that might affect what people want from fashion.

Secondly, researchers study the media to find any recent cultural changes. These media would include both cutting-edge and mainstream TV shows, magazines and movies.

Thirdly, researchers hit the streets to interview the 'fashion-forward' who are the first to be knowledgeable about the newest trends.

Finally, the researchers use observational research to see what trend-makers are wearing and also visit those retailers who are known for starting these trends.

Even with all these research efforts only 50–70 per cent of all of new fashions that make it into a retail store are successful.

Source: Retail Week, 2004

For breakfast cereal preferences, intercept interviews might take place wherever a target market segment congregates. If working adults are the target market segment, the interviews might take place outside an office building. If families are the target, the interviews might take place at a shopping center or grocery store. An example of the process is shown in Table 9.3.

Interviews

147

Table 9.3 Intercept interview structure

Opening phase	Explain purpose of research
Questioning phase	Do you eat breakfast cereal? (predetermined)
	What brand do you eat? (predetermined)
	Why do you prefer this brand? (predetermined)

9.3 Writing Questions

Types of interview questions include descriptive, causal, consequence and non-directional (Ember and Ember, 2001). Descriptive questions ask for facts concerning behavior. Such questions are usually both easy to ask and easy to answer. Causal questions ask research subjects to think about why a certain behavior takes place. These questions ask for underlying motivations and take more time and thought to answer. Even more difficult are consequence questions. These types of question ask research subjects to construct a hypothetical example in their mind and to then respond on how they would act. Non-directional questions ask research participants to determine if there is a relationship between two facts.

9.3.1 Descriptive questions

Many of the early questions used during an interview will be descriptive. These types of questions ask participants to describe their consumer behavior. Because these are factual they are both easy for researchers to ask and easy for participants to answer. An example of a descriptive question would be 'How often to do you go shoe shopping?' If an interview only consisted of these types of questions, an interview, which is both expensive and time consuming, would not be necessary. Such descriptive data could be easily obtained by using a survey form.

Descriptive questions: ask for facts

- How often do you shop for shoes?
- When do you shop for shoes?
- How much money do you spend on shoes?

9.3.2 Causal questions

Causal questions address how one variable acts upon another. For example, if the research question is 'What motivates women to shop frequently for shoes?', the first descriptive questions would address the facts of shoe shopping. The participants will first be asked how often they go shopping, when they go shopping, and how much they spend.

The causal questions will then address the motivation for shopping. In this case the research subject has already been identified as a frequent shoe shopper. The causal question can be asked as an open-ended question, such as 'Why do you frequently shop for shoes?' or the question may be phrased using a suggested cause, such as 'Do you shop for shoes when you are depressed?' The interviewer could then move on to other suggested causes, such as stress, relationship problems or an active social life.

Casual questions: ask for reasons that a behavior exists

- Why do you shop for shoes?
- Do you shop for shoes when you are depressed?
- Do you shop for shoes as the result of difficulties at work?

9.3.3 Consequence questions

A consequence question will address behavior by a shopper that results from the frequent shopping behavior. Once again, an open-ended question could be asked regarding how subjects feel after they have finished shopping. Or alternatively, the question can provide a suggested answer by asking 'Do you feel relaxed after you have finished shopping?' These questions would provide information on the intangible benefits provided by shopping that cause the behavior.

Consequence questions: what happens as the result of a behavior?

- How do you feel after shopping for shoes?
- Do you feel relaxed after shopping?

9.3.4 Non-directional questions

A non-directional relationship question asks whether two variables are related. The question is asked without implying either a positive or negative aspect to such a relationship. An interviewer may want to know if frequent shoe-shoppers read many fashion magazines or have many family responsibilities. There is no clear direction to these questions because the researcher will still not know if reading magazines causes people to buy shoes, as people who read about shoes may not necessarily feel a need to buy them. In addition, some people who read magazines may feel the need to purchase what they see. Here all that will be known is that a relationship does exist. Further research will be needed to prove this relationship.

Nondirectional relationship question: are two variables related?

- Do you frequently read fashion magazines?
- Do you have many family responsibilities?

9.4 Screening Participants

Because interviews are a qualitative process, it can sometimes be forgotten that as much care should be taken when selecting participants who fit the profile as when designing a sample for a quantitative survey. It is true that it is generally more difficult to have a potential participant agree to an interview than a survey because of the time involved. Therefore, researchers may be tempted to focus more on who is willing to be interviewed rather than who fits the profile. Unfortunately, if the research subjects for interviews are not carefully selected, both time and money will be wasted. A willing, but inappropriate, participant will result in not obtaining the needed information and the interview will be wasted.

Interviews

A company's management along with researchers will have to meet to determine a participant profile. First of all they must decide if they want to interview current customers, potential customers or both. They must then decide on the demographic and psychographic profile of the subjects. The profile should be very specific and the researchers involved should explain to management if extra time will be needed to recruit appropriate research subjects. The example below in Table 9.4 gives some profiles that might be developed for the study of breakfast cereal consumption.

Table 9.4 Sample participant profile

Usage status	*Demographic*	*Psychographic*
Frequent cereal eaters who are currently not users of the brand being researched.	Young males; family status is single; living independently; employed.	Lifestyle is active and sports oriented; not interested in cooking; casual housekeepers.

9.4.1 In-depth interviews

It is important when conducting in-depth interviews that the profile must be very specific. It might focus on only one of the segmentation characteristics, or two, or all three can be used in combination to describe appropriate research subjects. To find potential participants who meet this profile a short questionnaire must be developed. The screening questionnaire can be administered in person, over the phone, or online. Only participants who have the needed characteristics that match the participant profile will be invited to participate in the research. A researcher should not provide information to potential participants on what specific characteristics are necessary to be chosen. If they do so, some potential participants might be tempted to answer so they will be chosen, even if they are not appropriate subjects. An example of a screening questionnaire is provided in Table 9.5.

9.4.2 Intercept interviews

For on-the-street interviews a participant profile will be provided for interviewers. By using the profile, an interviewer will need to ask a single screening question.

Sample participant profile for intercept interviews

- Young males
- Physically fit
- Not with young children
- Dressed in a style that suggests the person has money for clothes (most likely employed)
- Dressed informally (not too fussy about appearance)

When a potential subject is identified, a researcher will then ask a single screening question, such as 'Do you eat cereal?' This method is not as scientific as the screening questionnaire used for an in-depth interview. The reason a full screening does not take place is that potential participants

Table 9.5   Screening questions

Usage Status	Demographic	Psychographic
How often do you eat cereal? Do you eat 'Healthy Berries'?	What is your gender? What is your age? What is your family status? With whom do you live? Are you employed at least 30 hours a week on a job with a wage?	How often do you engage in sports or other physical activities? How often do you cook a meal from scratch (using ingredients and following a recipe)?

will normally not be willing to provide such information to a complete stranger on the street. However, because more interviews are conducted, there can be less emphasis placed on each participant exactly meeting the participant profile. The example below shows how research was used to discover the reading preferences of young people.

DO YOU KNOW WHAT MEDIA YOUNG PEOPLE ARE USING? BELIEVE IT OR NOT, THEY'RE READING MAGAZINES

Everyone knows that 18 to 24 year old consumers exist, but marketers don't know how to reach them with traditional broadcast advertising. Research proved as true the common belief that this age group are not users of traditional media. Research found that only 8 per cent were heavy users of radio, probably because they are listening to their iPods. Only 6 per cent were readers of quality newspapers. Television was watched heavily by 17 per cent on weekdays and 15 per cent on Saturdays. A hint of what media were being used was that 24 per cent were readers of magazines. What might surprise marketers, who believe that this group of young people is unreachable, is the fact that 55 per cent of magazine readers are heavy users of commercial magazines tied to specific products and brands. According to researchers, the reason for this heavy use of commercial publications is that young people are highly brand conscious. They want to read a publication that reinforces an image of themselves as consumers.

Source: Smith, 2006

9.4.3 Expert interviews

Participants for expert interviews are usually chosen on the basis of referrals, but researchers may be tempted to rely only on people they know in order to save time. Instead, researchers should ask the management of a company commissioning research for the names of people who would have knowledge of the subject being researched. These experts might work in the industry under study, such as the cereal industry. They may also be experts on a specific consumer target market segment, such as young men, or be expert on a specific product type, such as breakfast foods.

9.5 Constructing Questions

One of the major responsibilities of an interviewer will be writing the questions for in-depth, expert and intercept interviews. Of course the questions should be of the correct type and provide the information needed to answer a research question and its objectives. However, there are some general rules researchers should follow so that all such questions will be well written and clearly communicated. After a researcher has written the interview questions they will need to be tested before they are used in research. The box below provides more information on writing good questions.

WHY ASKING QUESTIONS IS NOT AS SIMPLE AS IT SEEMS

Asking questions is something anyone can do. First thing in the morning we ask 'How did you sleep last night?' At work we ask 'When would you like this report finished?' And when we get home we ask 'What's for dinner?' It would seem that asking questions would be easy, and yet asking the right question in the right way is very difficult. Author William Foddy describes the reasons why this is so.

1   Factual questions sometimes elicit invalid answers.
2   The relationship between what respondents say they do and what they actually do is not always very strong.
3   Respondents' attitudes, beliefs, opinions, habits and interests often seem to be extraordinarily unstable.
4   Small changes in wording sometimes produce major changes in the distribution of responses.
5   Respondents commonly misinterpret questions.
6   Answers to earlier questions can affect the respondents' answers to later questions.
7   Changing the order in which response options are presented sometimes affects respondents' answers.
8   Respondents' answers are sometimes affected by the question format.
9   Respondents often answer questions even when it appears they know very little about a topic.
10 The cultural context in which a question is presented often has an impact on the way respondents interpret and answer questions.

No wonder asking questions isn't as simple as it first seems!

Source: Foddy, 1995

9.5.1 General rules on writing questions

Of course the rule here is that researchers should write the questions that address a research issue. In addition to the questions being grammatically well written, there are some guidelines that will help researchers to write good interview questions. First, researchers should only ask questions that the participants have the knowledge to answer, should write questions so that they address only one issue at a time, and should a use language and style that will be understood by all participants.

Questions that can be answered

Researchers should always remember one of the most important guidelines when writing questions, which is to never ask a question that a research participant does not have the knowledge to answer. This guideline may seem self-evident. However, researchers in their quest for information may write questions without considering if the research subjects have the required knowledge to answer these.

Participants can only know what they have learned or what they have experienced. However, they may still try to answer other questions simply to be helpful. Therefore, if a researcher asks questions about experiences they have not had or products that they have not used, participants can only answer hypothetically. For example, a researcher may ask participants if they would use a new product if it were available. However, the company client should carefully consider whether to base future action on the answers they receive. This is because it is difficult for people to be accurate when they try to predict the future. It would be much better to ask about the specific qualities participants desire in a product, as they can than refer back to previous real experiences. Researchers can then analyze this information and make recommendations about products that should be introduced in the future.

One question at a time

Another important guideline for researchers to remember when writing questions is to only ask one question at a time. Any more than this will prove confusing for participants to answer. It may also confuse the researcher concerned who will not know if the answer was to the first or second question. A question such as 'How did you chose your last vacation destination and did you enjoy the trip?' is too complicated for an easy response. It can also make analysis of the data more difficult if a participant had had a difficult time choosing their destination (unhappy response) but enjoyed the trip (happy response).

Write in the words and style of participants

Market researchers, because they have similar educational backgrounds, most often communicate with each other using the same educational level of English and a similar vocabulary. Written language is also often more formal than spoken language. Therefore the questions researchers write must be 'translated' into the everyday language of participants so they do not sound stilted when asked. This translation will not only include terminology but also grammar, the length of a sentence or question, and sentence structure. Therefore, it is important for researchers to be familiar with how participants use language. This would include any jargon that is used by younger people or by persons from minority ethnic groups. The use of their own language when writing questions will not only help in communication, it will help in establishing legitimacy and trust.

9.5.2 Testing questions

It is not possible to run sample interviews to test questions because it takes too much time. However, it is still important to test the questions that will be used in an interview for the use of jargon, clarity, and appropriateness. One way to do so is to first have a potential participant listen to a researcher read through the questions. The researcher should then ask if there are any words that were not understood. Second, the researcher should ask the listener to rephrase the question in their own words. Third, they should ask the listener if they would be willing to answer the question.

This test allows researchers to replace any words that are not understood. If terminology needs to be included, researchers can provide an explanation within the question itself. Asking the listener to repeat the question is another test to see if a question communicates the topic clearly. It may also provide researchers with alternative wordings that they may want to incorporate. Finally, asking a test participant if they would be willing and able to answer a question provides information on whether a topic is too sensitive to be easily answered.

9.5.3 Location of interviews

The type of interview research being conducted will dictate its location. In-depth interviews should be held at a location that is free from distractions so that both the researcher and the participant can concentrate on the issue. Locations where an interview can be conducted include at a researcher's office, in a participant's home, or by telephone. Expert interviews are held at locations that will be convenient for participants so as to minimize the inconvenience. These interviews could be conducted at a participant's place of employment, over dinner or lunch, on the phone or online. Some interview methodologies have even combined interviews with an analysis of the content of emails (Clegg et al., 2006). Intercept interviews are held where the participants can be found. This might be at a location, such as a store or business. In addition, an intercept interview might be conducted in a public place where potential participants may congregate.

In-depth interviews

There are two choices of locations where in-depth interviews can be conducted – either at a researcher's office or in a participant's home. In addition, in-depth interviews can be conducted over the telephone. Choice of location is more than just a matter of convenience, and can affect the outcome of an interview. Therefore a participant should be allowed to have an input into choice of location for the interview, because when they feel comfortable they will feel more free to communicate (Herzog, 2005).

Intercept interviews

An intercept interview can be conducted at the store or business where the consumer behavior under study takes place. They can also take place in public places where likely participants tend to congregate. When conducting intercept interviews, interviewers should station themselves somewhere out of the main flow of people traffic when the questions are asked so as not to antagonize the management of a business.

Expert interviews

An expert interview will often take place in a participant's place of employment. If this is not possible such interviews can also be conducted over the telephone. In addition, online interviewing is appropriate for conducting expert interviews. The possible location choices are summarized in Table 9.6.

Table 9.6 Interview type and location

Type	Location	Advantages	Disadvantages
In-depth	Researcher's office	Time saving for researcher	Possible intimidation
	Participant's home	Comfort, recall	Reluctance of participants, travel time
Intercept	Store/business	Interest level	Only current customers
	Public place	Lots of participants	Security, privacy
Expert	Place of employment	Sign of respect, convenient for participant	Lack of privacy, lack of candor
	Phone	Cost/time savings, privacy for participants	No nonverbal cues, interruptions
	Online	Time and money savings, privacy, transcript	No nonverbal cues

Summary

1 Interview research can be conducted to explore ideas, to obtain factual knowledge and to gather information that can be used in developing hypotheses that will be tested using quantitative research. The advantages of using an interview research methodology include discovering the underlying reasons for consumer behavior, allowing participants to respond in their own words, and the fact that researchers can follow up unclear answers with further probing questions. The disadvantages include fewer participants being involved, the need for a skilled interviewer, and the fact that each interview is unique which makes comparisons of data difficult.

2 Interviews can be in-depth where topics are explored for an extended period. Intercept interviews are short but are conducted with many participants. Expert interviews are used to gather facts. All types of interviews use predetermined questions. However, only in-depth interviews use unstructured questions to probe more deeply into issues.

3 Interview questions can be descriptive, asking participants to describe behavior. Causal interview questions try to determine the effect of one variable by asking about the 'Why' of certain behavior. These questions will take more time and thought to answer. Consequence questions try to determine what happens as the result of behavior. Non-directional questions ask about the relationship between two variables.

4 When screening potential participants for in-depth interviews a profile should be very specific as to usage, demographic and psychographic characteristics. A screening questionnaire will be developed for this purpose. For intercept interviews a sample profile will be developed that will rely on visible demographic characteristics. The only important consideration for expert interviews is that participants have the required knowledge about a specific industry, consumer segment or product type.

5 Interview questions should only ask what participants can answer and should only allow for one question at a time. In addition, questions should be put in words and phrases that will be familiar to participants. Finally, any questions should be tested. The type of interview will partially determine the location where it should be held.

Interviews

155

Key Terms

causal questions   ask participants about why a behavior takes place

consequence questions   ask what results from a consumer pursuing a particular behavior

descriptive questions   ask participants to describe consumer behavior

expert interviews   an interview with someone who possesses specific knowledge of a consumer segment, industry or product type

in-depth interviews   lengthy interviews about consumer preferences and purchases

intercept interviews   short person-on-the-street interviews of only two or three questions

non-directional questions   asked to determine if two variables are related

unstructured questions   these are not planned in advance but are determined by the answer to a previous question

---

Discussion Questions

1   Why would you argue that a research study of students' attitudes toward drinking should use interviews rather than focus groups?
2   What different types of questions would be asked during the questioning and probing stages of the above interviews?
3   Why should expert interviews be part of a study on why students drop out of college?
4   What three questions could be asked of students during an intercept interview regarding their music purchases?
5   What is the difference between causal and consequence interview questions?
6   Why would it be important to consider psychographic characteristics when determining a participant profile for intercept interviews on dance club attendance?
7   Why should interview questions be tested?
8   How could expert interviews be conducted online?

Recommended Reading

Denzin, Norman K. and Lincoln, Yvonna S. (2005) *The Sage Handbook of Qualitative Research.* London: SAGE. While there are many interesting chapters on various aspects of qualitative research, the book also specifically addresses interviewing.

Gubrium, Jaber F. and Holstein, James A. (2002) *Handbook of Interview Research: Context and Method*. London: SAGE. The book covers many aspects of interviewing from gender issues to cross-cultural interviewing. It also includes chapters on survey interviewing and interviewing as part of the grounded theory process.

Postoaca, Andrei (2006) *The Anonymous Elect: Market Research through Online Access Panels*. New York: Springer-Verlag. Explores the dynamic between interviewer and interviewee when the communication is online. While a marketing book, the author also brings in sociology, psychology and linguistics.

Rubin, Herbert and Rubin, Irene (2005) *Qualitative Interviewing: The Art of Hearing Data*. London: SAGE. Business students are not taught how to listen, so this book addresses the issue of listening and using probing to uncover information.

Seidman, Irving (2006) *Interviewing as Qualitative Research: A Guide for Researchers in Education and the Social Sciences*. New York: Teachers College Press. While it addresses the subject of interviewing more broadly than just for marketing, this book contains excellent information on interview structure and participant selection.

10 Projective, Observational, Ethnography and Grounded Theory Techniques

Learning Objectives

1 Explain the types and uses of projective research techniques
2 Describe the uses of observational research
3 Discuss the advantages of using ethnography as part of marketing research
4 Explore the use of grounded theory when researching consumer interaction

RESEARCHING THE WORLD OF AUSTRALIAN HIP HOP

Hip Hop culture may have been born in the Bronx in New York City, but it is now global. However, not all Hip Hop cultures are the same and Australian Hip Hop has unique characteristics. How do we know? Marketing research, including observation and ethnography, was used to explore the world of Australian hip hop culture. These techniques were necessary to get close to a group of individuals who weren't interested in helping market researchers learn more about their culture. Using these qualitative techniques the researchers learnt that Australian Hip Hoppers viewed themselves as different from the American-style Hip Hop culture. While not wanting to be involved in 'commercial' research, interestingly, the Hip Hoppers expressed their unique Australian identity through the consumption of particular products.

Questions: What local cultures or groups would be resistant to traditional marketing research techniques? Why do you believe this is so?

Source: Arthur, 2006

10.1 Projective Techniques

Projective techniques are used to encourage communication using nonverbal methods of response. They include completion tasks and other techniques such as component sorts and thematic appreciation tests. These techniques elicit information through writing, drawing and a variety of ways other than answering verbally. These techniques, borrowed from psychology, are gaining increased use in marketing. The aim of such projective techniques is to gain insights from participants of which they may not be totally aware.

10.1.1 Advantages of using projective techniques

Projective techniques are usually combined with other research methods. An advantage of combining the use of projective techniques with other methods, such as focus groups or interviews, is that they provide an additional means of gathering information. Projective techniques have the advantage of obtaining information of which participants may not be fully aware. They also allow shy or quiet participants to take part without speaking. In addition, they can be used to make other research techniques more interesting and participative.

One reason for using projective techniques is to gain information on topics that a participant may be unwilling to discuss. This unwillingness may be due to embarrassment regarding the subject. It also may result simply from shyness. For example, if the research question asks for opinions on adult-themed entertainment, participants may be reluctant to express either too negative or too positive an opinion. Having these opinions expressed anonymously by having them written allows participants to express views they might not state out loud (Ramsey et al., 2006).

The use of projective techniques makes research sessions more interactive and interesting. In today's technology-driven world, where people have immediate information and entertainment at the press of a button, sitting still while a topic is under discussion can be difficult. Unless the research participants are very interested in the topic, they may find an hour-long focus group a bit boring. Projective techniques can be used not just to gather data that cannot be obtained in any other way, but also to keep the research session more interesting. If participants are bored they will not provide the necessary information, while an interactive environment will result in richer data.

10.1.2 Disadvantages of using projective techniques

Projective techniques do not work well with research subjects who are unable to express themselves nonverbally. The idea of drawing a picture or completing a cartoon may be beyond their ability. Others may feel that they will be judged on their creative talents and will therefore not feel comfortable taking the risk. Another disadvantage to projective techniques is that they are not useful as a stand-alone research technique. They must be used to compare and contrast with other verbal information provided by participants.

10.1.3 Types of projective techniques

There are many different projective techniques that researchers can use individually or in combination with other research methods. These are creative tools that are especially appealing to researchers working in nonprofit organizations and creative industries. The most common projective techniques are completion tasks, such as word associations, sentence and story completion, and cartoons. More advanced projective techniques include thematic appreciation and component sorts. Creative researchers may even develop their own techniques.

Many projective techniques involve the completion of a task that a researcher has begun. Such techniques allow participants to describe an experience in their own words but without speaking. These tasks include sentence or story completion. If a researcher feels that participants will not find the tasks too challenging, they can also include advertisement completion and product design. Even more creative would be for a researcher to ask participants to prepare the copy for an ad about a specific product that would motivate them to make that purchase. If the product under research is an experience, the participants might be asked to construct what they consider to be an ideal event or performance.

Other projective techniques include the thematic appreciation test, which uses photos to elicit responses, and component sorts where words and ideas are placed on cards which participants are then asked to associate with products and segments. All of these tasks allow participants to provide information about products without using themselves as subjects, which in turn allows them to reveal information in a non-threatening manner.

Types of completion tasks

- Word association
- Sentence completion
- Story completion
- Cartoon completion
- Ad and event creation
- Thematic appreciation tests
- Component sorts

Word association

Word association is simply asking for a participant's first response to a name, photo or event. The idea is to get emotional, rather than intellectual, responses. Word association can be used with individuals or in focus groups or interviews. One example of its use would be if a business was planning a redesign of their store. A researcher, rather than just describe the store, may show a photo to a focus group and ask the participants to write the first three words that come to mind. Using this technique a researcher could also show participants a product or photo of a place.

The participants must then record their answers on small cards which are gathered up by the researcher. Alternatively, participants may be asked to record their answers on large sheets of paper so that they can be immediately shared with others. Words that might be listed when participants are asked about a new store design are 'exciting', 'confusing', 'boring', 'crowded', 'lovely', 'feminine', or 'manly'.

EXAMPLE OF A WORD ASSOCIATION TASK

Three words that come to mind when I see the new store design are:

_____ _____ _____

Sentence completion

An example of a sentence completion task would be to have the participants complete a sentence on their motivation for choosing a new product. If the research is being conducted regarding a service, participants might be asked to complete a sentence about a happy or unhappy customer that uses this service.

EXAMPLE OF A SENTENCE COMPLETION TASK

The Corner Billiards Parlor is _____

The people who visit the Corner Billiards Parlor are _____

The Corner Billiards Parlor should _____

Sentence completion allows for comparison between participant responses. Some responses to the sentences might express the fact that the Corner Billiards Parlor is a fun place where people can socialize. Other participants might answer that the Corner Billiards Parlor is a place where people drink too much and make trouble. These negative views might not be expressed using other methods. Researchers can than compare the demographic profiles of those participants who expressed negative views.

Story completion

Story completion is a bit more challenging for participants. They will be asked to finish a story that a researcher has prepared. For example, story completion could be used when researching how young people view a university. The participants in this research would be current students who might have difficulty when questioned about why they decided to attend that university. A more creative and interesting technique would present them with the following story. To see if opinions about the university would vary because of gender, the name Tom could be substituted. If researchers wanted to see if the story would change by ethnicity or religion, the names Anu, Pierre, Jacob, or Mohammed could be substituted.

EXAMPLE OF A STORY COMPLETION TASK

Amy has just returned home for the Christmas holidays after her first semester away at Small Town University. That evening she decides to have pizza with two friends who decided to attend Big City University. After they have talked about their own experiences, they ask Amy what she would say to someone who was thinking of attending Small Town University. Amy's response was _____

Cartoon completion

Cartoons can also be used as a means for participants to communicate ideas nonverbally. Cartoons can be used to enable participants to, almost literally, put their words into someone else's mouth. This can save a participant from the potential embarrassment of stating opinions in front of strangers who may disagree. Another advantage of this technique is that it can make responding to a question more fun.

The cartoon usually consists of two characters with speech bubbles over their heads similar to those in comic books. One character's speech bubble will ask a question, the other character will have an empty speech bubble in which the participant will put a response. One character might be saying 'Hi Alan, I was thinking of visiting the new billiard parlor. Want to go?' The survey participants will than put their own answers into the other speech bubble. This allows them to communicate their own ideas through someone else. It also assists participants in responding by helping them to picture the circumstances.

When using cartoon completion, the characters shown in the cartoon can be varied by age, gender or ethnicity. This can be used to see if the responses vary based on the consumer characteristics shown in the cartoon. In addition, the same characters can be used but the product being shown can be varied. This allows researchers to compare and contrast responses based on demographic or psychographic characteristics.

Thematic appreciation test

Thematic appreciation tests are used to give information to participants by using nonverbal means. Even a very skilled researcher may have difficulty describing people, places, or products with which participants are unfamiliar. Using thematic appreciation tests, a researcher will show participants a picture or photo and then ask for a written response. For example, a researcher may show a picture of a specific psychographic group and then ask which products the participants believe the group would buy. Participants might also be shown a picture of a place, such as a tourist attraction, and asked if this would be a place they would visit. Alternatively, they may be shown a picture of a product and asked how it could be improved.

Besides saving researchers the difficulty of trying to describe people, places or products, another advantage this technique provides is consistency. When a researcher describes people, places, or products verbally, there is always the possibility that participants will have actually created different mental images based on this description. If this is true then their responses will not be comparable.

Component sorts

With this technique, participants are provided with cards that show or state the different features of a product. They then sort these cards into categories provided by a researcher. Another technique allows the participants to create their own categories.

For example, participants may be given different descriptions of consumer market segments along with a list of a company's products. The participants would then be asked to sort the cards by the type of consumer that might choose each product. For example, a soft drink company may create categories such as 'young urban youth interested in music', 'suburban youth interested in sports', 'retired people interested in travel', and 'middle-aged consumers involved with family life'. The participants are then given cards with the company's different products by brand name and description. The participants then sort out which of these brands each group uses.

The purpose here is not to learn about actual consumption patterns, as each participant will only have a knowledge of their personal consumption and those with whom they closely associate. Rather, the purpose in this case is to learn about brand image amongst the participants. Using this technique companies can learn that a certain brand has a family image while another has a youthful image. They can then use this information to either reinforce or reposition a brand image.

10.1.4 The process of conducting projective research

Using projective techniques requires preparation just as any other form of research does. First of all an idea must be created that will help to answer a research question. Projective techniques should not be used simply to engage the attention of participants. Instead, each technique should obtain the information that will help to answer a research question. Once an idea has been created materials must be prepared. These might include cartoons, drawings, half-completed ads, cards, or any other suitable material. A little creativity and a computer will allow a researcher to create interesting and useful materials.

When projective techniques are used, a researcher must explain the reasons for using the technique without leading participants as to what to create. This can be difficult, as participants may look to a researcher to provide the 'right' answer. While people understand how to answer questions verbally, answering them nonverbally may be a new experience. If a researcher finds a group unwilling to cooperate, they must be ready with a different technique for obtaining the required information.

Once the research is completed, a researcher must gather and label all the information. The names of participants aren't important, but their characteristics and the date of the research should be noted as this will help in the analysis of the data. The data will be examined for the range of responses provided, with the researcher noting common themes and unusual insights. The completed projective material can be very useful when preparing a final report. Drawings can be reproduced and used in the body of the report or else included in the appendix, while quotes provided through sentence completion may be used verbatim. These examples of projective techniques provide a unique insight into the research subject's thinking.

The projective technique research process

- Create ideas
- Prepare materials
- Have alternatives available
- Record and maintain information
- Analyze data
- Insert examples of completed materials into report

10.2 Observational Research

Another research method that can be used by organizations is observation. Observational research is based on analyzing what people do rather than what they say. The research is conducted without communicating with people, but rather by noting their behavior. Observational research is being conducted in new ways as technology is now making it possible to 'observe' using the internet, scanner-tracking, video and neuroimaging (Lee and Broderick, 2007).

10.2.1 Advantages of observational research

Observational research allows researchers to study behavior without involving research subjects. Using this technique can confirm what people actually do rather than what they say they do. Observational research can also expand perspectives without spending money on more expensive research. In addition, the research subjects do not need to answer questions about behavior that they might find difficult to recall.

Observational research should be considered when a research question calls for confirming the actions of consumers. For example, a retail organization might want to know if customers have difficulty following the signage to the fitting room facilities in its stores. Rather than ask, they can station someone near the signs to see if customers appear confused.

Another rationale for using observational research is if there is a research question that would be too difficult or expensive to address with another research technique. A downtown association might wish to know if their store's Christmas window displays effectively engage the attention of shoppers. While an interesting research question, it might be too expensive for them to conduct a survey to ask people if they visited downtown and, if they did so, how effective the window display was in catching their attention. It would be much cheaper to conduct an observational study in order to see who stopped by to look in the window and how long they stayed.

An important advantage of conducting observational research is that it will determine what people actually do versus what they say they do. Research subjects may give inaccurate information when surveyed about their behavior because they might recall incorrectly what they did either because of inattention or because of a poor memory. They may also wish to give an answer they perceive as correct or appropriate. If visitors to a museum are asked how they spent their visit, they might respond that they spent the majority of their time contemplating the art. Observational research may find that they actually spent the majority of their time in the gift shop and café.

Another occasion for conducting an observational research study is when the research subjects may not remember their actions. For example, a museum can observe the behavior of specific groups of visitors, such as families, to help their organization determine which exhibits attract the most attention. This method will often give more accurate information than surveying, as most families on their way out will have tired children to get home and might not remember their visit in detail as a result.

10.2.2 Disadvantages of observational research

The disadvantages of observational research include an inability to accurately profile who is being observed. When conducting observational research it is not possible to ask potential participants questions about demographic characteristics such as their age, education level or income. Therefore, the sample selection depends on the ability of a researcher to estimate these characteristics. This researcher is also dependent on who happens to be at the location at the time and date when the research is conducted. For example, they might have planned to observe consumer behavior at the shopping mall. However, if the weather outside is beautiful many young people might be outdoors playing sports. Thus the sample observed might be older than anticipated and the research effort may not be as effective as originally planned.

10.2.3 Types of observations

There are three distinct types of observational research. When using the complete observer approach, research subjects will not be aware they are under observation. Using another type of observational research, researchers will participate in the behavior at the same time as they are observing. A third approach is for researchers to completely immerse themselves in a behavior.

Complete observer

When using the complete observer approach, a researcher will have no interaction with participants. Using this method the marketing researcher should attempt to be invisible to the participants. This can be accomplished through actually being hidden from view. In this case, the researcher may be watching from a location outside the sightline of customers. If this is not possible, the marketing researcher will try to be almost invisible by not being noticed by the research subjects. The researcher can stand behind a counter where they will be thought to be just another clerk. This type of observation is conducted when the presence of the researcher may change the behavior of those being observed (for example, if a marketing researcher wants to observe children at play, as the presence of an unfamiliar researcher would affect how the children interact).

The complete observer approach does not require a researcher to record the data. The behavior being researched can be videoed and then analyzed. For example, security camera tapes from a store could be examined not for evidence of shoplifting, but to watch how customers interacted with the displays. Below is an interesting example of the type of information that is collected on a routine basis.

CARDS CAN TELL A LOT ABOUT A BRITISH SHOPPER

Everyone knows that when a loyalty card is used to purchase products at a grocery or drug store, that store is recording purchase information. Few people will have thought about what can be learned from an analysis of the recorded data.

Researchers used the purchases of an anonymous female British shopper at a chain drug store to compile a composite of her demographics and lifestyle. They called her 'Brenda' and using information from her purchases alone they described her as a 'large woman whose desire to lose weight is thwarted by her appetite. She has long hair, bad skin and is shortsighted. Her parents are still alive; she lives for holidays; and has a long-term boyfriend'. How did they know so much about someone they had never met? Here are some of her purchases:

- Large size tights
- Healthy foods, but in large quantities
- A set of scales
- Hair accessories for long hair
- Contact lens products
- Regular purchases of tanning products
- Christmas cards for parents and boyfriend

Stores collect this information to better target consumers with the right products and promotions. The data compiled are used in product line and promotion decisions. Researchers do not analyze such data on an individual basis. So don't worry about your secret purchases becoming public!

Source: Farrar, 2004

Techniques

165

Participating observer

Another type of observation has researchers participating in the behavior that is being observed. This type of observation is used when it is impossible to conceal an observer. In some social settings the use of a silent person observing a behavior would draw others' notice. For example, the manufacturer of sports equipment installed in public parks may want to know how the equipment is being used. Using a video camera in public would be an invasion of privacy and would certainly raise concerns among people using the park. Even a silent observer taking notes might result in calls to the local police.

In this type of situation, an observer might visit the park and bring a book or magazine to read while sitting comfortably on a bench. While they will seem to be just enjoying the park, they will at the same time be observing the behavior of park users. Of course the problem is that this participation can interfere with observation. This problem can be handled by having some hidden means of recording data, such as concealing the observation form in the book or magazine. Another way of handling this issue is for the researcher to observe for only a short time and then record the notes elsewhere. Of course, if a researcher is noticed and asked about their note taking, they should explain what they are doing and the purpose of the research. It might be wise for the research firm concerned to supply them with an official letter explaining the purpose of the research and who can be contacted for more information.

Complete participant

A third way of conducting observation is for the researcher to be a complete participant. With this method, a researcher engages in the same consumer behavior as the research subjects. If an airline wants to learn more about the experience of being a passenger on a shuttle flight, a researcher can travel on that flight as just another commuting passenger. They will not only be able to observe behavior, they will also be able to overhear comments. Because researchers can blend into the action, they don't have to worry that their presence is distorting the behavior of the research subjects around them.

10.2.4 Designing the observational research process

Observational research involves more than just watching people. If research findings are to be useful it is important that the research methodology is carefully designed and that trained observational researchers are used. Once a research question has been written, the first step in the process is to determine exactly what behavior should be observed. This question is just as important as asking what questions should be included on a survey form or writing a script for a focus group. If the wrong behavior is observed, the findings will be useless.

For example, a company that designs clothing might want to know more about the relationship between the clothing they produce and teen consumers. The research questions they might want answered could include why teens chose that company's clothes, what items they chose and how they decided exactly what to buy. Each question will require a different behavior to be observed. If the company wants to know why teens chose their brand of clothing, observational research will not be appropriate, as observation can reveal what people do, but not why they do it. If the research question is what items teens chose, an observer can watch young people at the checkouts at a store where that product line is sold. (While a store might have total sales figures in a computer database, this information will not be broken down by age.) In fact, the salespeople themselves can be trained to gather this information. If the company wants to know how young people chose the company line, they can be observed while they shop.

How a behavior will be observed also needs to be specified. The research descriptions should describe the sample to be observed using demographic terms. The description should also use psychographic terms if attitudes, values and lifestyles can be determined by observing behavior. For example, if a company produces skateboards, they may decide upon observational research to discover what types of tricks skateboarders do. The research directions might provide a demographic description of young males, aged 16 to 20, who live the skateboard lifestyle. It will be up to researchers to use visual clues to both estimate age and to determine lifestyle, which could be based on the way skateboarders are dressed.

Observer training

Observation is difficult. It requires patience, attention to detail and the ability to be unobtrusive. When selecting observers it is important to consider whether they have the patience to sit or stand quietly while watching others. If someone does not have the necessary patience, no amount of training will correct this. However, training can help observers to pay attention to detail and learn to be unobtrusive.

A well designed observation form will help to keep an observer watching what needs to be observed rather than any other more interesting behavior they may notice. An observation form that uses the systematic recording of specific types of behavior during specific time periods will help a researcher stay focused on the important details that are needed to answer a research question (see the box below).

SAMPLE OBSERVATION FORM

Store: _____ Shopper number: _____

Date: _____ Start time: _____

Demographic description of shopper: _____

Observations:

Period	Location	Purchase behavior
Start	_____	_____
15 min	_____	_____
30 min	_____	_____
45 min	_____	_____

Take a 15-minute break and repeat

Additional Notes: *In the area below make any additional notes regarding constraints/ problems or unexpected activities you observe.*

Shopping Project Observation Form Directions
Once at the store, note your location on the form. If people are already shopping, choose three 'subjects' to observe. If possible please try to choose a variety of individuals, groups, couples or families. Record the start of the observation for each subject. Describe the individual subjects and note their behavior every 15 minutes.

Before the observations occur, a researcher should carefully chose a location for the observer to be stationed. This should be a site where the observer can see the relevant behavior without being unduly noticed. This could be sitting on a chair in a seating area of a department store set aside for customers. It could be leaning against the bar at a nightclub or pushing a grocery cart in a warehouse store. The location should be as comfortable as possible without being too noticeable.

The researcher should first try out various observation time periods and locations to ensure that they will allow the observer to be successful. They should also accompany the observer for the first observation period to ensure that the instructions have been understood.

Observational research process

1 Select the type of behavior to be observed
2 Select the sample to be observed
3 Select a location based on where the sample and behavior can be found
4 Select the time for an observation
5 Write out an observation form
6 Train the observers
7 Analyze any notes and forms
8 Write up the report

10.3 Ethnography Research

Ethnography is a research technique originally used by anthropologists and sociologists to gather information on how groups of people interact on a daily basis. Rather than ask questions or simply observe behavior, a researcher becomes one of the members of that specific group for a period of time. This allows researchers to more clearly understand the values and attitudes that underlie a group's behavior.

Ethnographic marketing research studies consumption behavior and can take place in a research subject's home or at their place of employment, although gaining access to conduct research in these settings may be difficult (Canniford, 2006). While a researcher is involved with a group, they will be keeping track of behaviors by preparing notes and, if possible, gathering photographic or video evidence.

For example, a company that designs office furniture might wish to market a new type of office desk. Rather than use a survey or focus group to ask what features employees might like, the researcher concerned could conduct ethnographic research to learn how employees use office furniture. To conduct the study, this researcher would remain in the worksite taking notes, talking to key individuals and gathering visual data. The research might reveal that office workers do not have a convenient place to set their cups of coffee and lack a desk area where they can work jointly.

Ethnography is used to study the behavior of groups that would not, or could not, participate in traditional research studies. These groups might be based on lifestyle or demographic factors such as religion or ethnicity. Another rationale for using ethnography is to gather details of behavior that are so engrained into the fabric of everyday life that they are difficult for people to describe. For example, if researchers want to know how families do their laundry so that a better container for laundry detergent can be designed, they can stay with a family on laundry day. The company can then use this information to make strategic decisions and also to build a stronger relationship with consumers (Agafonoff, 2006).

10.3.1 Advantages and disadvantages of conducting ethnographic research

The advantage of conducting ethnographic research is that researchers not only observe a behavior, they also share the experience with research subjects. Ethnography therefore provides insights that cannot be gained from merely observing or discussing behavior. In addition, ethnography research is a valuable tool to use when researching consumers in other cultures where stating your opinions directly to a stranger is not considered appropriate behavior. In countries such as Indonesia and Thailand, ethnography has been helpful in overcoming cultural barriers to providing information (Fielding, 2006b).

One disadvantage of conducting ethnographic research is that it takes time to develop the necessary trust to gain access to a group or family in order to conduct the research. In order to allow for a behavior to unfold naturally, the research time will need to be longer than for other types of research. In addition, this process must use researchers skilled in this technique so that useful marketing information can to be obtained.

10.3.2 The process of conducting ethnographic research

The first step in designing an ethnographic study is to determine the group and the behavior that are to be researched. The most important decision will be to decide upon the location where this research will take place. The location might be in a store, at home, in the workplace, or at a place where the research subjects socialize. In addition, researchers must establish trust with the members of the group that is to be observed. Because the researchers may be entering the private space of the research subjects, taking the time to establish trust is imperative. To establish trust both the purpose of the research and the research process should be carefully and fully explained.

Using ethnographic research, a researcher both watches and listens while the subjects go about the behavior under study. If the observation reveals that there are key individuals in a group that are determining the behavior, informal interviews may take place to clarify issues. Besides watching and listening, a visual record of photos or videotapes may also be taken. All of the data are then analyzed for common behavioral patterns and why these patterns exist.

Ethnographic research process

1   Decide on the research subjects and behavior to be studied
2   Gain their permission and build up trust
3   Observe the behavior of individuals and the group
4   Informally interview key individuals
5   If needed, photograph or video the behavior
6   Analyze the written and visual data

10.3.3 Participant involvement in ethnographic research

A unique aspect of ethnographic research is participant involvement (Durante and Feehan, 2006). This can be accomplished by having the participants complete logs or diaries, or using photography. Research subjects can be asked to keep a log of their behavior that can then be analyzed. For example, a fast food restaurant chain may wish to know more about the lunchtime habits of office workers. The restaurant's management may believe that business is falling because more people are taking shorter lunch periods while working at their desks. One method to gain insights is to ask workers to participate in a study where they log in how long they take for lunch each day. Diaries will ask for more detailed recorded information. For example, teenage girls may be asked to keep a diary of their clothing purchases that also records how they feel about the items bought.

An advantage of combining logs or diaries with ethnographic research is that it can track a research subject's behavior over time. The disadvantage is that it is difficult to have people maintain their interest in recording the data in a timely fashion. If they do not, they are likely to go back and fill in entries for previous days with estimated information. However, this method can easily be adapted to online use which makes the entire process much easier. A research subject can either log onto a website where they will record the information each day, or they can email the researcher with the information. If they forget, the researcher can email them a reminder.

Another method to have research subjects become involved as researchers is to provide them with either digital or video cameras. They can then record objects or interactions that they feel are important. For example, children might be asked to photograph their favorite toys at home. This material is then provided to the researchers for analysis.

Researchers still continue to find new ways to integrate technology into the practice of ethnography (Chen et al., 2006). Examples of how ethnographic research is used are discussed below.

ETHNOGRAPHIC RESEARCH SUCCESS STORIES

Ethnographic marketing research has gained in popularity because of a growing dissatisfaction with the data that are provided by focus groups. Here are a few examples of success stories.

Frontier Airlines had discovered via focus groups that people liked the animals that were painted on the tailfins of their planes. However, it took ethnographic research to discover that parents and children enjoyed seeing which animal would be on their plane. The airline now has a marketing campaign where the public can vote for their favorite animal.

Whirlpool discovered that people did not want to wait until a dishwasher was full before running a cycle. As a result, Whirlpool designed a smaller machine.

Whole Foods groceries discovered that their customers shopped at their stores at a more leisurely pace than at traditional supermarkets. Shoppers also spent most time in the fresh food section where they made their menu decisions based on produce availability.

Eastman Kodak researched how 18 to 24 year olds used disposable cameras by studying their behavior in dorm rooms. What they discovered is that students shared cameras and enjoyed taking gag photos of their friends. This behavior became the basis of a promotional campaign.

Duracell studied people replacing their hearing aid batteries. They found that many users had a problem removing the old battery. As a result of this research, Duracell improved their batteries by simply attaching an extra long tab that could be pulled when it was time to be removed.

All of these behaviors would have been difficult to understand using more traditional research methods.

Source: Wasserman, 2003

10.4 Grounded Theory

Most research starts with a theory of why people behave the way that they do. A research methodology is then designed to test whether this theory is correct. Grounded theory starts with the opposite approach. Rather than the researchers first establishing a theory and then observing the behavior to determine if they are correct, the researchers observe the behavior to determine a theory.

Conducting grounded theory is useful when the consumer behavior to be studied involves social interaction. For example, a clothing manufacturer might want to know more about who makes the purchase decision when female 'tweens' go shopping for clothing with their mothers. Unless the researchers happen to be mothers with daughters aged nine through twelve, they will probably have very little knowledge of the purchase process. Grounded theory would be the recommendation here, rather than hypothesizing with very little knowledge.

Grounded theory does not start with an extensive secondary research process about what is already known. Instead, the goal is to start field research as soon as possible. Rather than theorize, marketing researchers use the methodology to find patterns or ideas that will help explain this behavior. Rather than holding a traditional focus group or interviews, behavior is researched in its natural setting (Daengbuppha et al., 2006).

When conducting grounded theory, research data are collected and analyzed simultaneously. Grounded theory, like ethnography, involves research that takes place in the 'field' or where a specific consumer behavior is taking place. What is unique about grounded theory is that the analysis does not wait until after the research has been conducted. Instead, the analysis of the data takes place on an ongoing basis. As a result of this analysis, the next subject observation or interview question will be adjusted. Thus, theory is built from the ground up rather than imposed from above.

10.4.1 Advantages and disadvantages of conducting grounded theory

An advantage of conducting grounded theory research is that researchers do not need any preliminary knowledge to begin research. In addition, researchers observe a behavior as it occurs in its natural setting rather than in the unnatural setting of a research focus group or interview. Such a formal research setting may skew the results on sensitive or decisive topics. In addition, as some groups of consumers become more resistant to being involved in traditional research methods, grounded theory can offer a means to research consumer behavior.

A disadvantage of conducting ethnographic research is that researchers skilled in building theory must be used. In addition, management commissioning the research may have difficulty understanding the rationale behind grounded theory.

10.4.2 The process of conducting grounded theory

The first step in the grounded theory research process is to determine the research group behavior to be studied. After this decision has been made, the next step is close observation of the group while they are engaged in the behavior. After observing the behavior, the research subjects are immediately asked questions to clarify the behavior being observed. The information obtained is then used to choose the next research subject or group and what behavior will be observed. The process is repeated until a theory can be determined that causes the behavior.

Using the previous example of mothers and daughters shopping, if the first observation notes conflict during the purchase process, this is what will be addressed in the questioning. The daughter may state that the sales assistant recommends the clothing and that the mother is being unreasonable in her objections. On the basis of the analysis of these data, the next research observation will include interaction with the sales assistant. The observation, interview, and analysis process continue. However, the subject and interview questions will be adjusted each time based on the analysis. At the end of the process, the researcher should have developed a theory of how the purchase decision was made.

Grounded theory research process

1 Observe the group behavior to be studied
2 Ask interview questions based on observation
3 Analyze the data
4 Choose a second subject to observe, based on analysis of the first data set
5 Observe the research subject
6 Ask interview questions based on the observation
7 Analyze the data
8 Continue the process until a theory is developed

Summary

1 Projective techniques are methods that allow research subjects to respond to questions in ways other than giving verbal answers. These creative techniques allow for interactive participation in the research process, making the experience more enjoyable for subjects and providing researchers with unique insights. Techniques include completion tasks, thematic appreciation tests and component sorts. Projective techniques can stand alone or be used as part of the focus group or interview process.
2 Observational research is based on analyzing what people do rather than what they say they do. This method allows for subjects to be the focus of research without directly involving them in the research process. This method is useful when research subjects may not remember past behavior as it is simply a routine part of their daily life. Observation can be conducted without the knowledge of subjects or researchers can participate in the behavior while conducting research. The observational research process requires a skilled observer who will follow a process of watching and noting subjects' behavior.
3 Ethnography is a research technique borrowed from other social sciences. It is used to research group behavior that may be difficult for participants to describe. Therefore it is conducted in the environment of the consumer. Ethnography observes reality rather than relying on a description of reality. To conduct this type of research requires the permission and trust of research subjects and a researcher skilled in the process. First of all the behavior is observed and then any key individuals are informally interviewed.

4   Traditional research starts with secondary research to develop a theory and then observes or questions to test its reality. Grounded theory starts in the field in order to construct a theory of behavior. This method is particularly helpful when the consumer behavior under study involves social interaction. Grounded theory is also distinguished by the fact that the research process evolves as research is conducted. Any data collected are analyzed in the field and the subjects chosen and questions asked will be adjusted based on the information that has been received. This method also requires a skilled researcher.

Key Terms

component sorts   research subjects are provided with cards that show or state features of a product and are then asked to sort them by category

ethnography   researchers become involved, through observation and interviews, in the daily lives of research subjects in order that they can learn more about consumer behavior

grounded theory   researchers observe consumer behavior in order to develop a theory

observational research   researchers watch what research subjects do, rather than rely on what they say

projective techniques   methodology that allows research subjects to provide information in nonverbal ways

thematic appreciation tests   researcher shows a photo of a product, place or person and asks for a response

Discussion Questions

1   Why are projective techniques sometimes used in focus groups? Why would some researchers argue they should not be used?
2   What type of projective technique would you recommend if you wanted to find out students' attitude toward this class? Why would you recommend this technique?
3   What type of observation would you recommend for a study of how students use the library at your university?
4   Why is ethnographic research growing in popularity?
5   What are the issues that result in it taking longer to gain permission to conduct ethnographic research?

Techniques

6   How can logs and cameras be used to allow the research subjects to participate in the research?
7   For what type of studies would you recommend the use of grounded theory?
8   Describe the grounded theory research process and why it needs to be adapted in the field.

Recommended Reading

Abrams, Bill (2000) *The Observational Research Handbook: Understanding How Consumers Live With Your Product.* Lincolnwood, IL: American Marketing Association. A basic primer that introduces the reader to observational techniques and the various steps in this process.

Goulding, Christina (2002) *Grounded Theory: A Practical Guide for Management, Business and Market Researchers.* London: SAGE. The book first explains how grounded theory fits in with other qualitative techniques. It then covers the data collection and analysis process and also includes a case study.

Mariampolski, Hy (2005) *Ethnography for Marketers: A Guide to Consumer Immersion.* London: SAGE. While the book covers the theory of ethnography, it also explains how to plan and implement an ethnographic research project.

Pink, Sarah (2006) *Doing Visual Ethnography.* London: SAGE. While covering the subject of ethnographic research in general, the book focuses on the use of video, hypermedia and photography.

Seale, Clive, Gobo, Giampietro, Gubrium, Jaber F. and Silverman, David (eds) (2006) *Qualitative Research Practice.* London: SAGE. An extensive collection of articles on all aspects of qualitative research designed for both beginning and advanced researchers.

PART 3

Quantitative Marketing Research

11 Determining Probability Samples

Learning Objectives

1 Understand types of sampling and sources of sampling error
2 Learn to determine the correct target population and develop the sample frame
3 Examine probability sampling including simple, stratified, systematic and cluster
4 Describe the steps involved in determining the size of the sample

---

WHAT YOUNG EUROPEANS NOW WEAR ON THEIR FEET WAS FIRST WORN IN TOKYO

No, young Europeans are not wearing used shoes. But the styles they are wearing might have been first tested on young Japanese. Young residents of Tokyo are known for pushing the envelope on what is fashionable. After all, where do you think the Goth-Loli style came from? (Just in case you aren't in the know – it's a popular style in Tokyo that combines the Sid Vicious look with Little Bo Beep sentimentality.) Marketing researchers looking for new ideas for the designer Gola went to Tokyo to conduct observational research. After watching these fashion savvied consumers, the researchers developed the idea for shin-high boxing boots for women. They were first a hit in Japan and then exported to Europe where they also sold well. Who would have known the opinions of Tokyo teenyboppers would predict what young Londoners would wear?

Questions: If you were going to conduct research on the latest in music trends where would you go? What about entertainment? Education?

Source: Rowley and Tashiro, 2007

11.1 Sampling Issues

One of the questions researchers face when developing a research plan is who will be chosen to be research participants. The word 'population' is commonly used to define everyone of interest who could be possibly included in a research study. Researchers may define a population by geographic area. In addition, they may also define a population using such demographic data as age, gender, income, or ethnicity. Because marketing promotion is often targeted based on psychographic segmentation, researchers may also define a population based on interests, values or lifestyles. Product usage can also be a means for defining a population, such as nonusers, occasional users and frequent users. Of course these variables can also be used in combination. The resulting population may be very large, such as daily users of toothpaste who live in Germany, or very small, such as people over the age of 70 in the UK who are attending university as full-time students.

One of the ways that a sample frame is often first defined is by the geographic area where people live or work. Once an area is defined individual participants can be contacted using telephone numbers. However, this is becoming even more difficult due to a mobile population, homes without a landline phone and people working from home or living temporarily near a worksite (Wynter, 2006).

11.1.1 Using a census

When conducting quantitative research, researchers are attempting to support a fact or hypothesis. This fact might be how many consumers would buy a product, what type of new promotion would work best, the effect of pricing on purchase behavior, or the best store in which to distribute a product. Of course if a 100 per cent accurate answer is needed, researchers must ask every person who is included in a population.

Asking everyone in a population is called a census. Conducting a census is possible if the number of people from whom information is needed is small and all of the members can be reached. For example, a professor might wonder if students in his class study each evening. A census could be used for surveying all the members of this class about their plans for the evening. However, if even one student is absent due to illness the census would be incomplete. Even if everyone is present, if one student refuses to answer this question, again, the census would be incomplete.

Obviously, there are problems with trying to conduct a census. Some people will not be present and some may refuse to participate. A census might be conducted despite these difficulties in reaching everyone but any errors in the answers obtained from this research would be very expensive. For example, a medical equipment supplier might be developing a piece of equipment that would be used by only a very few doctors treating a rare condition. If the cost of developing such equipment for the marketplace is very expensive, the company may wish to ensure that the design of the equipment is exactly right so that it will be purchased. When only a small number of people are in the population, such as a few doctors, conducting a census is possible.

11.1.2 Using a sample

However, most research will involve the sampling of a population rather than a census. For example, researchers might be developing a new toothpaste flavor that they plan to introduce in France. Asking everyone in the population will simply take too much time and money. In addition, the company commissioning the research does not need to know with 100 per cent accuracy that the new flavor will be acceptable. Less accuracy will still provide the information as to whether the flavor will be acceptable to a significant percentage of adults in France. Thus asking a sample of the population will still provide an accurate enough estimate of consumer preference and this will allow the company to proceed with product development plans.

In this type of research situation, researchers will save money and time by surveying a sample of the total population. This money will be saved because not as many surveys need to be conducted. Time is an issue here, not just because increased time spent in conducting research means increased staff expenses. It is also important in this case because while the toothpaste company is conducting a census of everyone, a rival company may introduce the same new flavor.

11.1.3 Sampling errors

The data obtained from asking a sample of a population can never provide as accurate an answer as a census of everyone. A professor who wants to learn how many students study at night could ask all of his students. However, if the same professor only asks ten out of the 30 students enrolled in his class, there is the possibility that the answers provided are not representative of everyone. This is called sampling error. This error might result if the professor asked those ten students who always attend class. They would respond positively that they study nightly. The professor would then believe that all his students worked hard. On the other hand, he could also include too many of those students who didn't attend class regularly, get the response that they didn't study and, as a result, will believe that all his students are lazy. No sample can perfectly represent a total population.

11.1.4 Nonsampling errors

Other types of errors that result from using a sample are called nonsampling errors. These errors do not result from the fact that a sample was used instead of a census. Instead those designing and conducting the research cause these errors. Because they are caused by human error, nonsampling errors can be controlled. Types of nonsampling errors include specification errors, design errors, and selection errors.

Specification errors
Specification errors result when the wrong population is specified in a research design. A university admissions office may wish to study students' views on what type of art classes should be offered. For convenience, the admissions office might choose to survey students on the campus where the admission office is located. However, if most of the students who attend classes on the campus are business students, the survey results will be flawed. Business students may have little interest in art classes. They may not even know what type of art classes could potentially be offered. Their opinions will have no comparability to what students interested in art might want. Therefore the wrong choice of population will result in data that are not useable.

Design errors
Design errors occur because of human failure and include data recording, data entry, data analysis and nonresponse error. When the same researcher conducts many surveys, it is possible that some responses may be recorded incorrectly. With self-administered surveys, respondents may also make mistakes in recording data. To minimize data recording errors, it is important that survey takers be properly trained and also motivated to do their job correctly. Survey forms should also be designed so that respondents will be able to easily find the response they wish to indicate. The answer space should be designed so that once an answer is indicated, it will not be

confused with other possible responses. For example, if the question requires a yes or no answer whether a respondent is to make a tick, cross out, circle or underline should be clearly stated. In addition, the blanks for completion of open-ended questions should be far enough apart to ensure there is no confusion when an answer is indicated.

Even if participants and respondents are very careful when administering surveys, there are still occasions for error. Once surveys are collected all the information must be input into a computer software program. Even if the number of surveys is so low that computer software is not used, the responses must still be counted and tabulated. Because this work requires a low level of skill, clerical assistants often perform the data entry task. And because of the repetitious nature of this task, errors can result when the responses are input incorrectly. This is a difficult type of error to eliminate, but careful hiring can help reduce errors. Because of the possibility of data entry error the data should be doubled checked once they are entered.

Data recording errors and solutions

- A researcher makes a wrong entry: training and motivation
- A respondent makes a wrong entry: clear design and instructions
- Data entry personnel make a wrong entry: careful hiring

Selection errors

Selection errors occur when the correct population has been chosen, but the sample taken from the population is not representative of the entire population. For example, a university may decide to ask students who are enrolled in art classes what additional classes they should offer. A selection error occurs when the students who are asked are still not representative of the whole student population. For example, a young male student employed to conduct the survey might view the task as a good opportunity to chat up lots of young women. As a result, a much larger population of women then men will be included in the sample. If women want different types of classes than men, this could result in the survey returning inaccurate information due to selection error.

11.2 Determining the Target Population and the Sample Frame

One of the most critical steps in the quantitative research process is determining the target population to be researched. It is not unusual early in the research process for both marketing researchers and management to speak in generalities. They may discuss the need to research the attitudes of current customers. They may also discuss wanting to research potential customers who are older, retired couples. At first these might appear to be reasonable research requests. However, marketing researchers will understand that both of these definitions of a population are too vague. A target population always needs to be clearly defined so that the correct individuals are included in the sample frame from which the final participants will be chosen. This is especially true of the population and sampling frame for online surveys. Because geography does not need to be considered, when defining a population it is easy to do this too broadly resulting in a higher non-response rate (Dibb and Michaelidou, 2006). Below is an example of how Turkish Airlines decided to use elite status as the sampling frame for their survey study.

An example of this process would be the management of a football team researching how a rise
in ticket prices would affect attendance at games. The first decision that must be made here in
defining the population is whether to research the effect on fans who currently attend games or
potential fans. If the decision is to research fans who are currently buying tickets, the next step in
defining the population is to discuss whether the population includes everyone in this category
or a smaller group. Management, with the assistance of market researchers, will need to define
what they mean by 'current', 'fans' and 'buy tickets'. This process is summarized in Figure 11.1.

Defining current ticket buyers at first seems self-explanatory. However, it is important to define
the time period meant by 'current'. Does this refer to just the most recent game, or to the past
month, the current season or the last one or two years? The answer to the question will depend
on whether attendance is consistent or varies over time. If management is aware that the same
group of fans attends each game, then a short time frame is acceptable. However, if attendance
varies a longer time period will be needed.

The next question that needs to be addressed is if a 'fan' includes those people who attend
occasionally or those who attend frequently. Management may decide it is more important to
learn the attitudes of those people who attend frequently. Finally, does it make a difference if
those who attend frequently buy season passes or purchase tickets for each game individually?
A final definition of the population could be those people who attended at least 75 per cent of
the games during the last season and bought season tickets.

11.2.1 Sampling frame

Once a population has been defined marketing researchers will be able to decide whether they
can do a census of the population or whether they will need to choose a sample. If the population is small and the research question demands 100 per cent accuracy, a census could be conducted. However, in most situations researchers will decide to use a sample of a population to

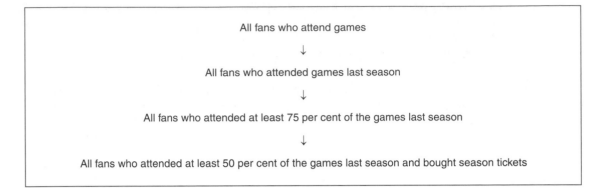

All fans who attend games

↓

All fans who attended games last season

↓

All fans who attended at least 75 per cent of the games last season

↓

All fans who attended at least 50 per cent of the games last season and bought season tickets

Figure 11.1   Narrowing the population

participate in the survey. In order for a sample of participants to be chosen, researchers must first have potential access to everyone in that population. For the football team mentioned previously this list of potential participants in the population, or sample frame, might be developed using data from the football team's ticket office database.

Using this database, researchers will be able to construct a list of ticket buyers and the frequency of ticket purchases for the past season. With this list researchers can then look for fans who have purchased season tickets for 75 per cent or more of the previous year's games. This method is still not foolproof. There may be ticket buyers who paid cash, or who refused to provide their names when they bought tickets. However, the frame should include a high percentage of people, if not everyone, who makes up a population.

When developing sample frames of customers, there are other sources of information besides ticket office data that could be used to construct sampling frames. Sampling frames can be developed from magazine subscription lists or lists of people who have signed up to receive company information via email. When constructing a sample frame for non-customers voting registration lists and telephone directories can be used.

11.2.2 Probability versus nonprobability sampling

Probability sampling uses techniques that result in an ability to calculate exactly the probability of a single person in a sampling frame being chosen to participate. This probability is based on the number of total people in that sample divided by the number of total people in the population. If the population is a known number this is quite easy to calculate. A survey that includes 250 people, out of a population of 1,000, means that every individual in the population has a 25 per cent probability of being included. The methods of conducting probability sampling include simple, stratified, systematic, and cluster.

Of course for most research studies the total number of people who are in a population at any given moment is unknown. For example, even at a university it is impossible to know exactly how many students are attending classes based on the last registration list. Since that list was compiled, students may have withdrawn or new students may have transferred in. There may also be students who have stopped attending classes but have not yet notified the university. Probability sampling can still be conducted with the probability calculated based on a reasonable estimate of the entire population. The process is summarized below in Figure 11.2.

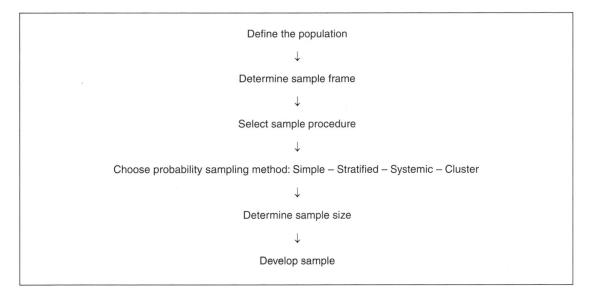

Figure 11.2   Sample definition process

11.3 Probability Sampling

The methods of probability sampling from which researchers can choose include simple, stratified, systemic and cluster. These vary in the randomness of the resulting sample. They also vary in their complexity and the time and effort it will take to construct a sample. Sometimes researchers may decide to use the services of a commercial provider (see the box below).

CAN A SYNDICATE HELP YOU?

The Target Group Index (TGI), started in the UK in 1969, is an example of a company that collects data that are then resold to other companies. Why would a company's management use a commercial data provider? The TGI can provide a broader range of consumer information than one company can collect on its own. The TGI collects information from over 50 countries on consumer product preferences, media consumption and attitudes and beliefs. All of these data can then be compared using demographic characteristics such as age, income, gender, employment and family status.

How many brands and products does the TGI cover? The service can provide information on the preferences and consumption of 500 types of products and over 4000 brands. For example, the information on media covers the press, all type of broadcast television, radio, cinema, outdoor media and the internet. The service can even provide information on how consumers view such issues as money, health, and the environment. So if you need to know what dog food young, single dog owners who care about the environment and attend the cinema buy – you can!

Source: TGI Surveys, 2007

Determining Probability Samples

11.3.1 Simple random sampling

The most easily understood method is simple random sampling. In this method each sampling unit has an equal chance of being chosen to participate in the research study. The probability can be calculated by dividing the number of people in that sample by the total number of people in the population. For example, a university's administration may wish to conduct a study of all of its students. They decide to survey 300 students out of a total population of 15,000. Thus the probability of being chosen is 2 per cent, or 300 divided by 15,000.

Probability sampling

$$\text{Probability} \;=\; \frac{\text{Sample Size}}{\text{Total number in population}}$$

Whilst it is easy to calculate the probability of being chosen, what is difficult is choosing the 300 participants so that this is done randomly. The university's administration could go to the entrance to the main building and ask the first 300 people to come in the door to participate. However, this would not be random because participation would be determined by who happens to have a class right after that time period. Even just going down the list of student names choosing every fiftieth name will not result in a truly random list because someone has to choose a starting point, so this first name is not random.

The problem is easy to understand if a low-tech solution to the problem is described. One way to achieve a random sample of student names is to write each student's name on a piece of paper and put all of these in a hat. Someone who is not looking then draws out the names. Each name will have the same 2 per cent chance of being drawn. After a name has been drawn a blank piece of paper is put back into the hat to represent that name, so that each time there is still one chance in 15,000 of being drawn.

Of course this would be somewhat cumbersome. Therefore most researchers will use a random number generator or table. A random number table consists of rows and columns of numbers that have no order or sequence. The first step in using the table is to give each unit, or name, in the population a number. Students could be numbered from 1 to 15,000. Then the researcher uses the list to choose the number of the first participant. The researcher will use the next 299 numbers in the random list to determine who is included in the sample. Other methods to ensure that a sample is truly random are using automatic dialing, a software program or a calculator that generates random numbers.

11.3.2 Systematic sampling

Even though it is a much simpler method to use, systematic sampling will result in a sample that is almost random. In systematic sampling, after the population has been determined, all units in the population are listed and counted. A skip interval is then calculated by dividing the total population by the sample size and this interval is used to choose who will be included in the sample. Using the example described above, the skip interval is 50, or 15,000 divided by 300. A random start point is chosen and then the skip interval is used to count off every fiftieth name on the list which is then included in the sample.

Calculating the skip interval

$$\text{Skip Interval} = \frac{\text{Population Size}}{\text{Sample Size}}$$

At first glance this may seem to be as random as simple sampling, but this is not so. The starting letter of family names is not random but often determined by ethnic and national origin. For example, if a university has a large number of students of Korean ethnicity, Korean student names would not be scattered randomly throughout a list of student names. A very common Korean name is Kim and students named Kim would not have an equal chance of being chosen because their names would be grouped together on the list. Using student numbers would also be a problem as these are implemented as students enter a university, resulting in a bias by time period.

One solution to this problem is to randomize the list before using the skip interval. If the list is computerized it can be sorted by a more random factor then name or student number. Another method is restarting the skip interval and counting once or twice when choosing the sample. Each time this happens a new random start would be chosen.

11.3.3 Stratified sampling

Stratified sampling is used when researchers believe that answers will vary depending on the demographic, psychographic, geographic or usage characteristics of each person in a population. There are two main reasons for choosing a stratified sample. First of all the population may be skewed in such a way that it is difficult to obtain a random sample using either a random or systematic method. In this case, stratified sampling is used to increase the randomness of the sample. Second, the research study may call for comparing results between specific groups within a population. The main reason for using stratified sampling is to ensure that any differences are diminished by the sampling procedure. Another reason is when the research study is designed to learn more about differences between groups.

Most populations can be divided into smaller groups based on shared characteristics. These characteristics can be based on demographic factors such as gender, age, income and education level. They can also be grouped by psychographic characteristics such as interests and lifestyles. Geographic grouping may be an important option to consider if the answer to a research question might vary depending on where participants live. Finally, product usage status (such as nonusers, occasional users and frequent users) might be of interest to researchers.

The example of using stratified sampling when conducting a survey of university students can be used to clarify this method. Perhaps a university's administration is interested in learning the views of students from all ethnic backgrounds. The administration therefore wants to ensure that their sample includes at least some students from all the ethnic groups represented on the student body. Using a simple random or systematic sampling procedure might include students from all the ethnic groups or might not, because each student at the university has a random chance of being chosen.

Using a stratified sample allows marketing researchers to examine each of the strata separately. Initially, researchers must decide how many participants will be chosen from the population as a whole. After that researchers must decide on how to distribute the number of total participants among the different strata.

Using proportionate sampling, each stratum will be given same proportion of sample participants as the strata's proportion of the entire population. For example, the strata may have been developed using ethnic groups of students for a university in the USA that would include Americans of European descent, Asian-Americans, African-Americans, and those from an Hispanic ethnic background. The university also possesses census data that give the proportion of each group in the total population. This information is used to calculate how many participants will be chosen for each group if the total population is 15,000 and the sample is 300.

Mean of population

Mean	% of population	# in sample
Caucasian	40%	120
African-American	25%	75
Hispanic	25%	75
Asian-American	10%	30
Total sample	100%	300

To implement proportionate sampling, a separate list of units or names must be developed for each group and then the names must be chosen using systematic sampling. However, the university in this case may chose to use disproportionate sampling if they decide that they need much more information about groups other than the majority group of Caucasian students. They may therefore decide to decrease the number of people in the Caucasian sample and increase the numbers in the other samples.

11.3.4 Cluster sampling

Cluster sampling also divides populations into groups. However, cluster sampling differs by reason of why a population is divided and the number of resulting groups. In stratified sampling groups are based on a few demographic, psychographic, geographic or usage characteristics (see the box below). The purpose here is to ensure that at least a few individuals from each group will be included. In cluster sampling a population is divided into many groups. Rather than being different, the aim of the resulting groups is that each will include individuals who represent the total population. The purpose of cluster sampling is to economically and efficiently obtain a sample from a large population that provides an accurate representation of an entire population. Such a method could also be combined with other sampling methods to form subgroups. This method can also be used to measure joint group preference in comparison to individual consumer choice (Arora, 2006).

DON'T FORGET TO CONSIDER PRODUCT USAGE STATUS WHEN CONSTRUCTING A SAMPLE

Many sample profiles will describe a population in terms of demographic and geographic characteristics. However, within these similar groups there may be big differences in how people use products. Companies may find it is worth their while to consider product usage when designing a sample. For example, frequent product users can give added insight

---

Cluster sampling is often used when it is impossible to determine the exact number of individuals in a population. One example would be if a university's administration wanted to conduct a telephone survey of potential students living in the city. While the university could determine the exact number of current students, they would never know how many potential students existed. Another problem is that a telephone survey of the entire geographic area from which the university draws students would be too expensive. Therefore they may decide to cluster sample.

One common means of clustering the population is to randomly divide a geographic area. If the same university believes that potential students are evenly dispersed throughout the city, they can subdivide it into several geographic areas. The first step would be to choose how the city was to be subdivided, such as by postal code. Assuming that there was an even chance that potential students were living in any of the postal codes, the next step would be to randomly choose which of the postal code areas would be included in the cluster sample.

An additional step can be added here to the cluster sampling technique. Once the postal codes that are to be included in the study have been chosen, another probability technique could be used to sample individuals within each of the chosen areas. For example, the university may know that potential students are scattered evenly throughout the metropolitan area. However, they may also know that not all of the residents are likely to be potential students. They may wish to include in the sample in each cluster only those people within the population who are members of a certain age range.

11.4 Determining a Sample Size

Once a sampling procedure has been chosen, researchers must then decide upon the number of subjects that should be included in the research to ensure that the results are representative of the entire population. It is important for the management of the company commissioning the research to recognize that more is not always better when determining the number of research subjects to be included in the study. Research costs money and the more research subjects that are involved, the more the study will cost. Management must understand that if a research population is carefully chosen, a small sample from this population can be reasonably representative of the whole.

There are a few concepts that must be considered when sample size is determined. First, the more variation there is in a population as a whole, the larger a sample will need to be. For example, when planning the design of a new student center a university will need to know the recreational preferences of its students whether they are sports, arts-related or video gaming. The university may have a fairly homogeneous student population of the same nationality and age. Therefore, it can be assumed that their interests might be similar and it will take a smaller sample to determine their preferences. However, another university might have the same number of students but that this covers both traditional college age students as well as older adults who come from different countries. In this case, it can be assumed that a larger sample will be needed as it would be expected that the interests of the students will vary widely.

A second factor that must be considered in this example is the precision in the range between the survey answer results and the reality of the population as a whole. A survey question might ask how much of a fee each student would be willing to pay to use the new center. From these responses an average fee can be calculated. The university must then decide on how large a range or interval they are willing to tolerate between the average tabulated from the survey responses and the true answer that would be known only if everyone in the population was asked this same question.

A third factor that must be considered when determining sample size is the need for confidence that the research findings reflect the reality of the total population. Total accuracy requires a census of all participants. Since this is not possible, the university must decide what level of confidence they need that the survey data accurately reflect the whole. The larger a sample is, the higher will be the confidence that this is so.

Factors to consider when determining sample size

- Variation within the population
  o More variation means a larger sample
- Precision needed between range of given answer and true answer
  o A smaller range means a larger sample
- Confidence that research findings represent the population as a whole
  o Higher confidence means a larger sample

11.4.1 Calculating the size of a sample

To calculate the necessary size of a sample, it is not necessary to know the size of the population. What are needed for the formula are the variation in the population, the acceptable range of the estimated answer from the true answer, and the confidence level that the calculated answer is correct. Even a small sample size can save a company a great deal of money, as is shown in the example below.

SHOPPERS MIGHT LOVE CLEARANCE RACKS BUT RETAILERS DON'T

A new research method is being introduced into the fashion wear industry that attempts to help retailers with their purchasing. A consumer database of 500 to 600 shoppers has been developed that retailers can use to choose a sample for online research on product preference. This information can then be used by retailers to determine what products stores should stock.

The basic formula for calculating the sample when estimating an average or mean is quite simple.

Calculating the sample size

$$n = (z^2/H^2) *^{(est} \sigma^2)$$

In this formula, n represents the number needed in the sample. The symbol z represents the confidence level that is needed that the answer is accurate for the population as a whole. The usual z-scores that are used are 1.65 for 90 per cent confidence, 1.96 for 95 per cent and 2.58 for 99 per cent confidence. H is the half precision or one half of the range that the average from the survey results can be from the answer that is true for the population as a whole. The symbol σ represents the variation in the whole population. Using these three numbers the required sample size can be calculated.

For example, a university might be very interested in determining what annual fee to charge students for admittance to the new student center. Of these three numbers, the z-score is a given and does not need to be calculated by researchers. They only need to know that the university would be happy for the answer to be 95 per cent confident that it represents the whole population. In addition, the range would be supplied by the university. They might state that they want the answer to be within a 25 pound, dollar or Euro plus or minus range. This only leaves the variation in the population for researchers to calculate.

11.4.2 Normal distribution and variation

To understand the variability of data it is not necessary to have an advanced knowledge of a subject. However, when discussing variability the terms 'parameter' and 'statistic' need to be understood. If a market researcher could conduct a census on how much students spent on entertainment last weekend, a true mean or average could be calculated. This number is called the parameter. Of course, conducting a census is too expensive and time consuming so the researcher would survey a sample of students. From these data is calculated a number, or statistic, which is used as an estimate of the entire population.

Perhaps the researcher wants to further make sure that this statistic is an accurate estimate, so the survey is conducted a second time with a new sample. The same sampling procedure is chosen so the same number of subjects are asked the research question. However, the sample will now consist of different individuals. The researcher will again need to calculate the statistic. If the researcher were able to survey every possible sample in the population, this would result in a series of means. If all the resulting means were examined, it would be found that some answers will occur more frequently than others.

This similarity results from the fact that members of a population will have characteristics in common, which in turn will mean that many will behave in similar ways. However, there will also be some whose behavior will vary. When these similarities and differences are shown visually they result in a graph where the most commonly resulting mean is in the middle with diminishing returns on either side for numbers that are higher and lower. This is the classic 'normal' or bell distribution curve.

Fortunately most data will fit a normal distribution curve and, therefore, the variability within a population can be estimated. Normal variability is considered to be plus or minus three standard deviations away from the true value. Therefore, a researcher can take an estimated range of variability and calculate the variation. For example, the university's administration may estimate that the range in acceptable fees would be from £50 for those students with limited incomes up to a high of £500 for the wealthiest students. This gives a range of £450. Since the standard deviation is plus or minus three on each side, the number 450 is now divided by six to get the variability of the population, which would be £75.

Using the example above, the sample size for the study of how much students are willing to pay annually for the use of a new student center can be calculated.

$$35 = ((1.96)^2 / (25)^2) * (75)^2$$

For the estimate to be 95 per cent, with a range of 25 each way and standard variability, only 35 students would be needed to participate in the survey. However, a total of range of 50 when the variation is only 450 is quite large. Perhaps the university in question would like the answer to be more accurate. They may decide to change the range from 50 to 15. The sample size now changes to 96 students. If the university narrows the acceptable range to only five, the sample size necessary changes to 864! Likewise changing the confidence level will affect the sample size, as will a change in the variability.

11.4.3 Calculating sample size when estimating a population proportion

The university's administration may also be interested in calculating a proportion, such as the proportion or percentage of students who are involved in sports. In this case the z-score of confidence level will be chosen and the range estimated. The confidence level might still be 95 per cent and the acceptable range could be within plus or minus 3 per cent of the true answer. However, the difficulty arises when the researcher needs a number to represent variability in the population as a whole, which for a proportion is represented by the symbol π. In this case, theoretically, the variation can run from zero to 100 per cent of the total population. However, the university will know that is too wide an estimate of variability – after all, they can estimate that at least 20 per cent of students are interested in sports and 20 per cent are not interested in sports. Therefore, the variability should be set at 40 per cent or half of 80 per cent. The resulting sample size needed is 1,024.

$$n = (z^2/H^2) * \pi (1-\pi)$$
$$1024 = ((1.96)^2 / (.03)^2) * (.4*(1 - .04))$$

Therefore, to estimate the proportion of a population takes a much larger sample. Why does the proportion take such a larger sample size? The answer lies in the range as compared to the variation. In the calculation involving a mean the range was 50, which is 11 per cent of the total variation of 450 (50/450 = .11). However, with the proportion example the range of 6 per cent (plus or minus 3 per cent) compared with a possible variation of 100 per cent in the population as a whole. Because more precision is needed to estimate within 6 per cent than with 11 per cent, a larger sample is needed.

Summary

1   Including everyone in the population in a research study is called a census. A census includes everyone in the population, but is expensive and impractical for research purposes. Sampling is used when only certain people in the population are chosen to be part of a research study. When sampling is conducted it is inevitable that there will be errors. Errors result when the chosen sample is not absolutely representative of the whole population. Mistakes can also result due to human error when recording or entering information.
2   The first step in developing a sample is to determine the targeted population. It is important to narrow the definition of a population so that only those participants who can answer the research question are included. A list of names from this population is called a 'sampling frame'. The next step in the process is to select a sampling method, which can be based on non-probability or probability.
3   Probability sampling includes simple, stratified, systematic and cluster. The methods vary in the randomness of the resulting sample. The probability of someone being chosen during sampling can be calculated by dividing the sample size by the total number of people in the population. Simple random sampling provides the most random sample. Systematic sampling is easier and results in almost as random a sample. Stratified sampling divides a population into smaller groups based on shared characteristics and with a certain number of subjects chosen from each group. In cluster sampling the population is divided into many groups that are similar, rather than dissimilar as in stratified. Cluster sampling is an economical means of sampling a large population.
4   Factors to consider when determining a sample size include the acceptable range of error of the estimated answer from the true answer, the level of confidence needed that the answer is within that range and the variation within the population. The sample size can be calculated using these three numbers. The sample size for estimating a proportion will be higher than the sample size for estimating a mean.

Key Terms

census   including everyone in a population as participants in the research study

cluster   cost effective way of sampling a large population that is homogeneous

nonprobability sampling methods include convenience, judgment and quota, where each potential subject does not have the same probability of being included

nonsampling errors human errors that occur in the research process

population a group of individuals who share characteristics defined by a researcher

probability sampling methods include simple, stratified, systematic and cluster, where every potential subject has the same probability of being included in the sample

sampling errors errors that occur when a sample is chosen incorrectly

simple random sample sampling system where each unit in a population has an equal probability of being chosen

skip interval number used when counting off to choose participants from a list of the population

stratified sampling a population is divided by characteristics and each group is sampled separately, after which the mean and percentages are calculated for the entire population based on weighted averages

systematic sample sampling system where each sample unit is chosen using a random start and a skip interval

Discussion Questions

1   If you were to conduct a survey of students' favorite sports, would you use a census or sampling?
2   What would be the advantages of using a sample versus conducting a census for a sports study?
3   Can you give an example of a population at your school or college that would be best surveyed using a census?
4   Why is it necessary to understand the standard error of the population when conducting a survey of how much time students spend doing homework?
5   How could a sample frame be determined for members of a church congregation?
6   Which nonprobability sampling method would you recommend should be used for a survey on what classes should be offered in your degree program? Why?
7   Which probability sampling method would you recommend to determine the number of students who plan on going on to obtain an additional degree?
8   How would you determine the sample size for the above study?

Recommended Reading

Chakrapani, Chuck (2000) *Marketing Research: State-of-the-Art Perspectives.* Chicago, IL: American Marketing Association. This book includes articles on many aspects of marketing research including a chapter on sampling technologies.

Fink, Arlene (2003) *How to Sample in Surveys.* London: SAGE. A short book that first explains the various sampling methods and then provides a quick explanation of statistical sampling.

Good, James W. Hardin (2006) *Common Errors in Statistics and How to Avoid Them.* Hoboken, NJ: Wiley. This covers the mathematics of statistical sampling and analysis using many examples and everyday language. A good book for those who believe they can't understand statistics.

Riddick, Carol Cutler and Russell, Ruth V. (1999) *Evaluative Research in Recreation, Park and Sport Settings.* Champagne, IL: Sagamore Publishing. This book is a reminder that marketing research is used in a variety of organizational settings. Includes a chapter on sampling and sample size.

Van Belle, Gerald (2002) *Statistical Rules of Thumb.* New York: Wiley. An excellent reference on everything statistical, the book is organized by topic including sampling.

12 Questionnaire Design

Learning Objectives

1   Understand the purpose of survey research
2   Describe the process of planning the survey research methodology
3   Learn the rules for writing effective survey questions and answers
4   Appreciate the importance of layout in designing questionnaires
5   Examine how survey forms must be adapted when placed online

DO YOU WANT BIG BROTHER IN YOUR HOME?

A Sussex family let marketing researchers put cameras into their home as if they were part of *Big Brother*. The family – Mum, Dad and the two children – had cameras installed in their living room and kitchen for three months. It wasn't to save memories but rather they were paid £500 per month to let researchers from Brainjuicer, an online research company, watch them going about their daily business. If the family didn't perform what the researchers wanted to see, the researchers called in their request. What they learned was how the family performed daily tasks, from brushing their teeth to washing the dishes.

Why? The purpose was to see how people interact and behave without the distracting presence of researchers. The family stated that after a few days they forgot the cameras were even there!

Questions: Is the traditional survey dead? Can it be combined with other, newer, forms of marketing research?

Source: Grande, 2007c

12.1 Survey Research Methodology

Surveys are a quantitative research methodology that consists of a set of questions with predetermined answer choices from which participants must chose. In addition, some survey questions may be open-ended, where participants are able to respond in their own words. Surveys can be administered by a researcher, either in person or over the phone. Surveys can also be self-administered whereby they are sent via the postal service or put online. Whatever the form of survey administration, the survey design methodology and the questionnaire development process remain basically the same.

12.1.1 Uses of survey research

Surveys are most effective when obtaining information if marketing researchers already know something about the research problem at hand. This information will be needed as researchers must anticipate participants' responses when they write possible answers to questions. This knowledge can be the result of secondary research on the external environment or internal research on company information. However it is obtained, there needs to be some initial knowledge of the research problem so that there is enough information to write the correct survey questions and answers.

Surveys can be used to gather information on any aspect of the marketing mix including the customer, product, promotion, price and place as shown in Table 12.1. A survey can be used to learn if a company's current customers are satisfied with its products, or it may be used to determine the likelihood of a new target market segment being interested in purchasing. The effectiveness of a promotional campaign to motivate purchasing can be ascertained by asking if a consumer has purchased a product as the result of seeing or hearing an advertisement or sales incentive offer. For example, technology has increased the number of ways that marketing messages are being delivered and a researcher might be interested in how consumers are now receiving marketing messages. Of course, this researcher must first be aware of all the new methods of communicating such messages, otherwise these won't be added to the possible answers to a question (Fielding, 2006a). Survey questions can also be written to ask about the effect of price changes on purchase likelihood. In addition, where consumers could most conveniently purchase a product could be discovered through a survey question.

Table 12.1 Purpose of survey research

Marketing Mix Element	Possible Research Issues
Customer	Satisfaction of current segment toward product
	Find new customer segment to target with product
Product	Preferred benefits of current product
	Benefits desired from new product
Promotion	Awareness of promotional campaign components
	Effectiveness of promotional campaign to motivate purchase
Price	Appropriate pricing level
	Effect of price increase on purchase behavior
Place	Location where product should be sold
	Ease of purchase process

12.1.2 Questionnaire development needs

When designing a questionnaire for a survey a researcher must keep in mind the needs of a number of groups that may have an interest in what questions will be on the survey form. Each group will view the completed questionnaire from their own unique perspective. First, the management of the company that has commissioned the research will be concerned that the survey questions will provide the information needed to answer the research question. In addition, they will also want questions on demographic and geographic characteristics that will allow for comparisons and contrasts between groups of consumers.

The research participants will want the questions to be ones they can answer and that these are worded in a way that is easily understood. Participants will also want the form designed so that it is simple to record their responses. Those administering the survey (if it is not self-administered) will want the questions to be written clearly so that participants do not need to ask for clarification. The data entry clerk, who has to enter the information into a computer database, will want a survey form where the participants' answers are easy to understand, which will result in quicker data entry. In addition, the data entry clerk will require that the questionnaire should be visually designed, so that any errors are minimized while reading the entries.

Survey issues

- Management – that it asks the right questions
- Participants – that it includes questions that can be easily answered
- Surveyor administrator – that the questions are clearly written
- Data entry clerk – that the form makes it simple to enter data

12.2 The Questionnaire Design Process

After management has determined the research question, the questionnaire design process will begin with a meeting between the researchers and management. At this meeting, researchers and management will discuss the topic areas that need to be covered in the survey to provide the data needed to answer all aspects of the research question. The researchers will then write a draft survey form. This draft will be reviewed by management for the appropriateness of the questions. Another issue that needs to be addressed is how the process needs to be adapted if the survey study is to be conducted in a different country (Vallaster and Hasenöhrl, 2006).

This process will be repeated until everyone is satisfied with both the questions and the answers. The answers will then be coded and the questionnaire will be laid out in its final form. The last step will be to test the survey with potential participants.

Questionnaire design process

1 Meet with management to determine question topic areas
2 Write draft survey
3 Review draft with management

4   Write coding into answers and lay out questionnaire
5   Test survey

12.2.1 Question topic areas

Before the design process can begin, management must have determined the research question. It may be that researchers will simply be given the research question and told to write a survey form. However, it would be preferable for management and the marketing researchers to work together during the process. Marketing researchers should meet with the management of the company commissioning the research to discuss those topic areas for which questions will need to be written to answer the research question. In addition, any questions needed to qualify participants for the study and any demographic questions need to be discussed.

For example, a survey designed to answer the question of what factors motivate young people when purchasing a car might include question topic areas on preferred price, design and power. Several sample questions such as 'How important is price when making a purchase decision?' will be written for each question topic area to help management visualize the final questionnaire. At this meeting the management of the company may suggest questions to the researchers. However, they will only be viewing the question from a consideration of their own needs. Sometimes management will propose questions that are too broad and these would only result in general data that cannot be turned into useful information. It will be the researchers' responsibility to explain that the question is too broad or too complex to be answered.

12.2.2 Writing the draft and management review

Once the topic outline and sample questions have been approved a draft survey needs to be created. Researchers will then review the form with the management of the company to determine the appropriateness of the questions and any additional questions that should be asked. This process might to be repeated any number of times. While it is management's responsibility to decide on the topic areas, each time the form is reviewed it is the marketing researchers' responsibility to explain why certain questions should be included and why some should not be asked. The exact wording of the questions also needs to be reviewed. This process must be repeated until everyone is comfortable with the survey questions. Trying to save time at this step in the process may result in wrong or badly worded questions being asked and unusable data. In addition, the answers to the questions must also be written down. It is interesting to note that the popularity of online survey software is changing the relationship between researchers and management to one of even stronger partnership (see the box below).

THE MARKET RESEARCHER AS ADVISOR

Technology has allowed many processes to become 'self-service'. People now consider it standard to pump their own gas, withdraw their money from an ATM, and even check out their own groceries at the store. New tools are also having a profound impact on the relationship between the marketer and the marketing researcher. Online survey tools are making it easier for companies to construct their own online surveys.

(Continued)

No longer does a company always need the expertise of a marketing researcher when they need research conducted. In addition, they need no longer wait during every stage of the research process for input and results from the 'professionals', as survey tools will automatically analyze statistical results.

What does this self-service ability mean for companies? First, it means less waiting time for results and, second, less chance of miscommunication. What does this mean for marketing researchers? Just as in many other fields where the routine tasks of a profession have been automated, they will now be able to focus their attention on more complex marketing research tasks and issues along with providing advice to managers.

Source: Siesfeld, 2005

Other issues that will need to be discussed at this stage in the process will include translation issues that must be addressed even for single country surveys. In addition, the organization and design of the physical layout of the form need to be discussed. Finally, any special topics need to be clarified, such as adapting the questionnaire for online use or for use by the disabled.

12.2.3 Coding the question answers

Surveys are a quantitative research methodology. This means that statistics such as averages and percentages will need to be calculated during the analysis stage. To do so, answers in words will need to be converted into numbers. These numbers are referred to as 'coding' and should be designed as part of the survey form and not added later. This will save time and effort when the data are entered into a computer software program. For example, if a question calls for a research subject to decide if they agree or disagree with an answer, the form can be written so that a number is circled that corresponds to an answer. It is the number and not the word that is entered into the software program, as numbers can be manipulated statistically to find if there is a relationship between the data.

Coding example

	Agree	Neither agree nor disagree	Disagree
The product is well designed	1	2	3
The product's color is attractive	1	2	3

12.2.4 Pretesting the survey form

All survey forms should be pretested. When testing the survey form, both the content of questions and their wording should be examined. Each question should be one that the participant can and is willing to answer. In addition, the wording should be checked to see if a participant understands the question in the way that the researchers intended. Besides the questions, the answers should also be examined. The available responses for a question should contain the answers that most participants would provide. If the written answer does not do so, 'other' will be ticked too often, or participants will choose a response even though it does not accurately reflect their opinions.

In addition to the content and wording, the form of each question should be examined. If an open-ended question leaves participants confused, it could be rewritten as a close-ended question so that potential answers can be provided. The words used in the scale that is used to answer a question, such as 'strongly agree' to 'strongly disagree', should have the same meaning for all participants. Lastly, the instructions should be tested to ensure that they are written in an easily understood format.

Participant testing

The survey questionnaire should be tested with participants who are similar to the research subject sample. If the sample consists of a variety of subgroups, at least some of the test participants should be from each group. During the first step in the testing process, a researcher should be present while a participant completes the questionnaire. This way the researcher can make a note of any direction, question or answer that causes difficulty. If there are major problems with the survey form, the researcher should address these through changes and the testing should begin again. If there only a few minor changes that result from testing the questionnaire, the testing can proceed to the next step.

Methodology testing

The questionnaire should now be tested using the planned methodology, whether administered in person, over the phone, by mail, or online. The sample for the test can be small, with as few as five to ten individuals. The reason for testing the methodology besides the questions and answers is to determine the length of time that it takes for the survey to be completed. The amount of time it will take to complete will have an effect on the completion rate (Hansen, 2007).

Data entry testing

Once the survey delivery methodology testing is completed, a final test should be conducted of the data entry system. The completed and coded questionnaires should be entered into the software that will be used for the analysis. This should uncover any coding problems. It is much better to find these coding issues at this point so they can be corrected before the final version of the questionnaire is printed.

Testing of questionnaire form

- Personally administer to discover problems
- Administer with delivery methodology
- Test data entry

12.3 Writing the Questions and Answers

Most survey questions are close-ended, with possible answers provided from which a participant must chose. These answers are determined on the basis of previous qualitative research, such as focus groups or interviews. For example, the answers that focus group participants provide most frequently to a similar question will determine the responses used on the survey form. In addition, data discovered through observation and interviews will also be used to construct the answers to close-ended questions.

Open-ended questions allow survey participants to provide their own answers that they will write on the form or type online. Since the purpose of surveys, which are a quantitative research methodology, is to support a fact or hypothesis, open-ended questions must be kept to a minimum. This is because the answers to open-ended questions may vary so much that there aren't enough similar responses to allow for statistical calculations.

12.3.1 General guidelines for question writing

There are general guidelines that researchers should remember when writing any survey question. First, the questions should not be hypothetical as some people will have difficulty imagining such situations. For example, questions that ask for imaged responses such as 'How would you feel if you found out that you had bought defective merchandise?' are difficult to answer on a survey form. Such questions are best left to focus groups or interviews where researchers have the time to draw out responses. Survey questions should only deal with what participants already know or have experienced.

Problem Question: How should manufacturers change cars so that they get better gas mileage?

Rewritten Question: How important is high gas mileage to you when you purchase a car?

Use simple terms
Researchers are often very familiar with the terminology used by the industry commissioning the research. If not initially, they will have certainly become familiar with the industry terminology while conducting secondary research. It is important for researchers to remember that participants in a survey might not have this knowledge. Researchers should always write the question using words that are commonly understood.

Problem Question: What means of transport did you use to visit this establishment?

Rewritten Question: How did you get to the store today?

Reading level
Besides the issue of terminology, respondents may not read at the same academic level as researchers. Reading level involves the number of words in a sentence, the sentence's grammatical structure, and the length of the words used. It is very important to have questions written at the correct level. If researchers are unsure they should always write at a lower level, which will make a sentence easier and quicker to read for everyone.

Problem Question: In terms of motivational desires, what would you consider of primary importance?

Rewritten Question: What was the most important reason why you bought our product?

Ask one question at a time
It is important to keep a survey form short so that participants are motivated to complete it. However, the researchers should not be tempted to shorten the number of questions by combining more than one at a time. Asking two questions simultaneously will only confuse participants. If a participant is unsure of the question being asked, the answer will be meaningless.

Problem Question: How did you travel to the store today and did you encounter any difficulty?

Rewritten Question: How did you travel to the store today? How convenient was this method of transportation?

Avoid the passive voice

Questions that ask when 'a person' or 'someone' has done something will leave respondents confused. They will find it easiest to respond to questions that ask about their own activities. For example, a question that asks 'Do you purchase products that you have seen on infomercials?' is easy to understand. In addition, a question that asks if your family members buy products that they have seen on infomercials can be answered. A question such as 'Do people buy products that they have seen on infomercials?' cannot be answered as participants will not have such knowledge.

Problem Question: How enjoyable is a visit to the theatre?

Rewritten Question: Did you enjoy your visit to the theatre this evening?

Writing questions in more than one language

It is important that any common sayings are comparable when asked in more than one language. This translation may be necessary even when a questionnaire is being used in only one country (see the box below). Even simple words such as 'miserable', 'disgusted', or 'thrilled' will be difficult to translate.

HOW MANY LANGUAGES ARE THERE IN THE UK?

The British speak English right? The officials in charge of the 2001 population census in the UK needed to know what other languages were spoken in which to print the forms. To find the answer local authorities in England and Wales were contacted. From the information provided it was discovered that the forms would need to be translated into the following languages:

Albanian	Arabic	Bengali
Chinese	Croatian	Farsi
French	German	Greek
Gujerati	Hindi	Italian
Japanese	Polish	Portuguese
Punjabi	Russian	Serbian
Somali	Spanish	Swahili
Turkish	Urdu	Vietnamese

Obviously the issue of translating a survey, even if it is given in only one country, cannot be ignored.

Source: CILT, 2007

12.3.2 Writing the answers

There are two components to a survey answer – the wording of the answer and the means of response. The same rules that apply to writing the questions apply to writing the answers, but even more so. Because each answer consists of so few words, it is vitally important that these are the right words. There are several ways that participants can be instructed to answer a question. An answer to the question of 'What motivated you to enroll in this marketing course?' could be written using fill-in-the-blank, dichotomous, forced choice, multiple choice, checklist, rating and ranking responses.

Fill-in-the-blank

Open-ended questions, where respondents are only provided with a blank line, are used when researchers do not wish to lead participants. An example of an open-ended question in a survey would be 'Why did you enroll in this marketing course?' The advantage of this type of question is that it allows any type of response, including those which researchers might not have thought of. One surprising response might be 'A person I'm attracted to signed up'. After all, potential romance might not have been among the responses considered by researchers. The disadvantage of this type of fill-in-the-blank response is that every questionnaire will have to be read and the answer will need to be coded.

Fill-in-the-Blank

Question: Why did you enroll in this course?

Answer: _____

Dichotomous choice

A dichotomous choice answer allows respondents to choose one of two responses that are usually opposite. Examples would be answers that allow respondents to tick 'yes' or 'no'. A dichotomous choice answer directly addresses a research issue and forces participants to make a choice. Perhaps researchers are interested in discovering whether love of learning motivates students to enroll in a marketing course. However, this response may not be one that occurs to a student. This would leave researchers with the conclusion that love of learning plays no role in motivations for enrolling in the class. A dichotomous choice question would ask 'Is love of learning one of the reasons why you enrolled in this course?' The student will tick either 'yes' or 'no'. This type of answer forces students to reveal whether love of learning had any role in motivating their decision.

Dichotomous choice

Question: Is love of learning one of the reasons why you enrolled in this course?

Answer: ___ Yes ___ No

Forced choice

A forced choice question asks respondents to choose between two responses. However, the responses do not need to be opposites. In fact they can have no direct relationship with each other. Researchers would use this type of question when they want to determine which of the two responses is more important. It might be that researchers notice that mid-afternoon classes have the most enrollments. Is this because of a popular professor or the time of day? In this case the forced choice answers would be written as 'Like to take mid-afternoon classes' and 'Heard the professor was friendly'. Therefore a student cannot choose both. If most of the students tick the first answer, mid-afternoon might be the time to schedule professors who have lower enrollments because students do not perceive them as friendly!

Forced choice

Question: Which of these reasons more strongly motivated you to enroll in this course?

Answer: ___ Like to take mid-afternoon class ___ Heard the professor was friendly

Multiple choice

When researchers have a number of variables that might affect choice, they may wish to write a multiple choice question. The answers would then list the motivations that were uncovered during earlier exploratory research. Researchers must decide how many reasons to list. If too many are provided, participants may find it difficult to weigh them mentally and come to a conclusion about which are most important. Usually four or five possible answers are listed. Of course, the listed reasons might not include any of the reasons why an individual student might have enrolled in that class. This situation can be handled by adding 'none of the above' as a response, or by allowing a fill-in-the-blank line for respondents to write in their own responses.

Multiple choice

Question: What was the main reason you enrolled in this course?

Answer: ___ The right amount of outside classwork is given
___ The professor is friendly
___ It will help me get a job
___ It was scheduled at a convenient time
___ None of the above
___ Other: _____

Checklist choice

The problem with a multiple choice answer is that more than one of the answers may be true. A student might have been strongly motivated by two or even three of the reasons. A checklist solves this problem by allowing participants to choose as many variables as apply. Because participants do not have to weigh one possible answer against another, a checklist can include many more possible answers.

Checklist

Question: Which of the following were reasons why you enrolled in this course?

Answer: ___ The right amount of outside classwork is given
The professor is friendly
___ It will help me get a job

_____ It was scheduled at a convenient time
_____ I love learning about marketing
_____ My friend enrolled on the course
_____ I heard the professor gave good grades/marks
_____ My parents told me to take this course

Ranking choice

A variation on the checklist is the ranking question. This type of question and answer assumes that the listed responses will include a number of variables that will apply. It allows participants to indicate not only which of the reasons apply, but also the relative importance of each reason. Theoretically, researchers could ask participants to rank all of the answers that apply. However, this may prove to be too difficult for participants, so usually a question will ask participants to rank their top three to five answers.

The importance of asking a ranking question instead of just providing a checklist will become apparent when data analysis is considered. In data analysis, when calculating the frequency of responses, they will not just be counted but will also be weighted by choice. For example, the number one choice for students might vary widely while the second choice is almost always 'it will help me get a job'. When the variables are weighted, the choice that was second ranked may be the most common.

Ranking choice

Question: Of the reasons listed below, chose the top three that affected your decision to enroll on this course. (Use 1 to indicate 'most important', 2 to indicate 'second most important,' 3 to indicate 'third most important'.)

Answer: _____ The right amount of outside classwork is given
_____ The professor is friendly
_____ It will help me get a job
_____ It was scheduled at a convenient time
_____ I love learning about marketing
_____ My friend enrolled on the course
_____ I heard the professor gave good grades/marks
_____ My parents told me to take this course

Rating question

A survey multiple choice question and answer format allows researchers to learn which answer is most important. A survey checklist question allows researchers to learn which of many answers are important. A rating question will allow respondents to choose more than one answer and also to rank the importance of each. The answer can consist of three, five or seven possible rankings. One of the rankings will be that the answer had no effect on choice. This is always the middle of the rating. A researcher can then write the rating to allow a respondent to indicate whether the answer had either a positive or negative effect on choice, such as 'agree' or 'disagree'.

In addition, the ratings can allow participants to show how strongly the answer positively or negatively affected their choice. Even complex questions such as 'How happy are you?' can be answered in this way (see the box below). A researcher may obtain this information by adding more possible answers, such as 'strongly agree' and 'strongly disagree'. Along with the response of 'no effect', the answer now has five possibilities. A researcher can continue to expand the answer to add the responses of 'very strongly agree' and 'very strongly disagree'. Of course, it is still difficult to predict how each participant will evaluate the choice of rating (Schwarz et al., 1998).

Rating

Question: Rate how each of the following reasons influenced your decision to enroll in this course?

Answer:

	Agree	No effect	Disagree
The professor is friendly	___	___	___
It will help me get a job	___	___	___
It was scheduled at a convenient time	___	___	___
I love learning about marketing	___	___	___

HOW HAPPY ARE KOREANS?

How would you go about researching how happy people are? A research group in Korea started with focus groups, where they collected 152 statements about what made life happy. After analysis the responses were placed in 18 groups based on common themes. These statements were then tested on 517 Koreans to see if they resonated. Statements with low reliability at predicting what Koreans believed made for a happy life were dropped and some additional statements were added.

The result of this testing was a Happy Life Inventory of 156 items. A 6-point scale was developed to answer the questions. This questionnaire was then shown to 1503 adults to assess their happiness. Did it work? When the results were compared with the Psychological Well-being scale a correlation was found.

Source: Kim et al., 2007

12.4 Questionnaire Layout

For self-administered surveys, the way that the questions and answers are visually presented is critical. A poorly laid out questionnaire may confuse participants and result in unanswered questions. It may also confuse the data entry clerk and lead to input errors and faulty results. When laying out a form, researchers must remember the visual impact that results from the use of margins, spacing and font size. Proper use of these elements will result in a survey form that is easy for both the participants and data entry clerks to read.

Researchers will also want to keep a survey form to as few pages as possible, as fewer pages will keep reproduction costs down. In addition, a survey with many pages will discourage potential subjects from participating. However, these concerns should not lead researchers to print the survey in a font that is too small and therefore difficult to read. The use of white space, such as larger margins and extra lines between the questions, will result in a longer survey form but will also make the survey more attractive.

Routing is an issue that needs to be considered when a questionnaire layout is designed. For example, there might be a follow-up question designed only for those who drive an automobile to go shopping. A question that asks where participants park their car when they travel to the store will not be relevant for those participants who do not drive. Therefore these participants should be directed to skip the question and go on to the next question. The instructions for routing must be very clearly and simply stated on the survey form as most people will assume they will need to answer every question.

12.4.1 Question sequence

The questions should not be listed on the form in a random manner. The first questions should be for the purpose of qualifying a participant. The types of qualification questions asked would depend on the research question and the purpose of the survey. They may ask a participant about the frequency of purchase of a specific consumer product or whether they rent or own their own home. The questions may also ask about age or family status.

Even if basic demographic data are not part of the qualifications or research question they should still be included. These demographic questions should come first as they are the easiest to answer. For example, while the research question might not have asked about a gender difference in purchase habits or attitudes, when the data are analyzed it may be found that there is a gender difference in consumption. The same may hold true for age, education level and even geographic location.

The next questions should be general in nature, with more in-depth questions to follow. For example, a question that asks what brand of toothpaste a participant uses is easy to answer. A more specific question, as to why the participant chooses to purchase a specific brand of toothpaste, will take more thought. If difficult questions are listed on a survey form too early on, they may discourage participants from continuing and completing the form. For this reason also, any sensitive questions should be saved for last.

Question sequence

- Qualifying questions
- Demographic questions
- Easy to answer questions
- In-depth questions
- Sensitive questions

12.5 Electronic Survey Forms

The development of an online survey should be no different from that of a traditional survey. There are software packages now available that make the creation of a survey much easier. However, this does not make the decision of what topics to address and how to write the questions and potential answers any easier. The invention of word processing programs made writing much easier – but it did not automatically make everyone good writers (see the box below)!

HOW ONLINE SURVEYS ARE CHANGING MARKETING RESEARCH

Are companies using online research? According to the Research Industry Trends 2006 report, more than half of those companies using survey research now use the internet as their first method of choice. The newsletter *Inside Research* has stated that spending for online marketing research has increased from $253 million in 2000 to $1.3 billion in 2006. What has this growth meant to the industry? The effects have been profound.

Large corporations understand that online surveys are cheaper. Marketing research was once bought as an expensive specialty service from consultants. Now marketing research is being run through purchasing departments as just another commodity.

As a result of this change, large marketing research firms must now keep their costs low to get contracts. Smaller research firms, which cannot compete on price, now have to specialize in the services they offer. These small firms are targeting specific industries or consumer segments and specializing in developing a database of potential subjects for these areas.

These new online survey tools not only help design surveys, they also analyze data and come complete with downloadable spreadsheets and graphs. Large companies using these software survey tools are asking their product and service managers to conduct their own survey analysis of customer behavior and satisfaction. Any serious problems revealed by the data can automatically be reported to management.

Small businesses can now afford to conduct research using these software tools. The cost of running an online survey can be as low as $20 to $50 a month. If the business grows, they can then move up to more sophisticated marketing research products.

Companies' expectations about the quality of who is included in online panels have increased. While it is quite easy to establish a large database of willing participants using incentives, it is still difficult to find quality participants who meet specialized participant profiles. However, many companies do not make this distinction, putting pressure on marketing research firms to improve their recruitment ability.

Source: Gelb, 2006

There are a number of reasons for the increasing popularity of putting survey forms online. One is the difficulty in motivating individuals to participate in traditional survey research. An online form can be completed at a time that is convenient for a participant, unlike a phone or personal survey. Also, the completed form is automatically returned – unlike a mail survey.

In addition, there are design advantages to using an electronic form. With an electronic form there is less concern to keep a questionnaire to as few pages as possible. Participants only see one or two questions at a time and, therefore, will not be intimidated by the overall length. In addition, the form can be laid out so that it is easy to read, with a larger font size and more white space.

Coding of responses is not needed because the results from an electronic form are calculated automatically without data entry. In addition, the routing of questions can be handled automatically. The next question that needs to be answered will appear on the screen based on the answer to the previous question. On an electronic survey form, when a participant responds to a question on how they travel to the store with the answer 'by car' the next question will automatically ask about the difficulty of parking. If the response to the question is not 'by car', the next survey question will not ask about parking.

Another advantage to laying out an electronic survey form is the ability to use drop down boxes for answers to questions. In written surveys, researchers face the temptation of limiting the number of responses provided to any one question so that the survey form does not become too lengthy. Using drop down boxes – where participants use their cursors to pull up a menu of answers and then makes their choice – solves this problem.

12.5.1 Using technology to design new types of responses

Besides convenience, using an online format allows creativity in designing a questionnaire. This is particularly true in writing the answer format. For example, when product or brand preferences need to be indicated, they can be shown with pictures or logos along with their names. Participants may more easily recognize a package or logo than the name of a brand. Beside each picture would be a 'radio' button that a participant would click to indicate his or her choice.

Survey questions often ask participants to rank their choices of products or desired benefits. In a paper survey, such choices are ranked in the same order. There may be a bias here towards the early responses as research subjects may find a likely answer and stop before they read the complete list. With an online survey the order can be randomly generated so as to eliminate this bias. Below are some additional rules for online survey form development.

RULES FOR DESIGNING THE ONLINE SURVEY FORM

RAND is a nonprofit organization that sponsors research and analysis. RAND decided to take a look at best practice in the new area of online surveying. They developed the following criteria for a successful online form.

1 List only a few questions per screen
2 Eliminate unnecessary questions
3 Use graphics sparingly
4 Be aware of how respondents may interpret questions in light of accompanying graphics
5 Use matrix questions sparingly
6 Reduce response errors by restricting response choices
7 Force answers only on rare occasions
8 Make error/warning messages as specific as possible
9 Always password protect Web surveys
10 Ensure that respondents' privacy and their perception of privacy are protected
11 Provide some indication of survey progress
12 Allow respondents to interrupt and then re-enter the survey
13 Carefully handle respondents who fail a screening test
14 Give respondents something in return
15 Take advantage of the media's presentation capabilities

Source: Schonlau et al., 2002

Summary

1 Surveys can be used to research any aspect of the marketing mix. The development of a survey should be a joint undertaking between management and marketing researchers. Both participants and data entry clerks should also be considered when designing a questionnaire.

2 The survey development process starts with the research question and proceeds through meetings between the marketing researchers and management where question topic areas will be discussed. Drafts of the survey form are created and reviewed until everyone is satisfied that the questionnaire will provide the needed information. The questionnaire is then tested on potential participants and should be first tested verbally to check for understanding and possible confusion. After this it will be tested with a few survey participants using the planned delivery method.

3 Survey questions can be either closed or open-ended. The general rules for writing effective questions include using simple terms, writing at the correct reading level, asking only one question at a time and writing in the active voice. It should be remembered that questions may need to be translated into other languages. There are a number of different ways to structure the answers. These include fill-in-the-blank for open-ended questions. Close-ended questions can be answered using dichotomous, forced choice, multiple choice, checklist, rating or ranking responses.

4   The questionnaire's layout should ensure the form is easy to use and to read. It should look attractive so that people will be motivated to read the questions. The routing of the participant through the questionnaire should be clearly explained. The questionnaire should start with qualifying questions and then move on to demographic questions, easy to answer questions, in-depth, and finally sensitive questions.

5 If a form is to be administered online, the same development process must take place. One advantage of an online survey form is that the form can be designed so that only one question can be seen at a time and routing can be automatic. Another advantage is that answers can be constructed using graphics and drop down boxes. In addition, radio buttons can be used for answers and photos or products and logos can be shown instead of words.

Key Terms

coding answers   using numbers on the questionnaire form to represent answers so that the data entry clerk can enter numbers rather than words

dichotomous answers   when a participant is allowed to choose one or more answers

forced choice   an answer type that forces participants to choose between two opposite answers

ranking choice   an answer type that allows participants to provide more than one answer, ranking each in importance

rating choice   an answer type that asks participants to rate the importance of all responses

routing   the order in which participants should answer questions

---

Discussion Questions

1   What are three research questions regarding student activities that would be appropriate for survey research?
2   Why would it be useful to meet with university officials before such a survey is undertaken? What should be discussed at these meetings?
3   Which of the general rules for writing survey questions would be most important to remember when writing a survey form for students?
4   Why is it sometimes better to use a rating question rather than a ranking question?
5   Which type of question answers would work best for your student survey? Why?
6   How would you respond to the argument that survey questions should be written so that management get the results they want?
7   Why is testing of a survey form important?
8   Why does an online survey form need to go through the same development process?
9   How should a survey form be changed if it is administered online?

Recommended Reading

Campbell, Bruce (2000) *Listening to your Donors: The Nonprofit's Practical Guide to Designing and Conducting Surveys that Improve Communication with Donors, Refine Marketing Methods, Make Fundraising Appeals More Effective, Increase Your Income*. San Francisco, CA: Jossey-Bass . The ability to write survey questions is also needed by those working in nonprofit organizations. This book presents information on how to write questions and design surveys for nonprofits.

Corder, Lloyd (2006) *The Snap Shot Survey: Quick, Affordable Marketing Research for Every Organization*. Chicago, IL: Kaplan. A book aimed at the practitioner with many examples of different types of surveys written for a variety of purposes.

Czaja, Ronald (2004) *Designing Surveys*. Thousand Oaks, CA: Pine Forge. While comprehensive in nature, this book has specialized chapters on writing questions, organizing questions on a survey form and testing questions.

Fink, Arlene (2006) *How to Conduct Surveys*. London: SAGE. This book gives special attention to writing questions, creating measurement scales and the appearance of survey forms.

Fowler, Floyd (2002) *Survey Research Methods*. London: SAGE. While written about the social sciences, this book has useful chapters on designing questions to measure accurately and the evaluation of written questions.

Gratton, Chris and Jones, Ian (2004) *Research Methods for Sport Studies*. London: Routledge. A book that covers questionnaire development and question writing from the perspective of someone in the sports industry.

Presser, Stanley (2004) *Methods for Testing and Evaluating Survey Questionnaires*. New York: Wiley. This book is an overview of issues related to questionnaire design and testing. It is based on the papers presented at a joint conference of many organizations interested in the issue.

13 Conducting Surveys

Learning Objectives

1 Explain the advantages and disadvantages of conducting surveys
2 Describe the methods of conducting researcher-administered surveys
3 Describe the methods of conducting self-administered surveys
4 Explain the importance and components of cover letters and emails to survey participants
5 Explain the survey process including the training of survey takers

'FRUITY AND FUN': SURVEYS CAN BE USED FOR SOCIAL AND CONSUMER MARKETING

Public health officials in Indonesia were concerned about the spread of AIDS amongst young people. As a result, they asked researchers to help with the development of a campaign to build awareness of safe sex. The researchers' first task was to learn more about the sexual behavior of Indonesian youth. However, the challenge that researchers faced was that there were still many people in that country who held traditional, conservative views regarding sexuality. Therefore a large-scale survey of sexual behavior might be viewed as offensive. The first step to be taken was a review of youth media where it was learned that the content heavily focused on sexual relationships. A personal survey asking about behavior and attitudes toward safe sex was then conducted with young people at locations such as shopping malls. To increase response rates, the survey takers were of the same gender as the participants and the survey took place in a private location. The result? A public health message campaign aimed at young people, along with the launch of 'Fiesta', a range of flavored, colored condoms.

Questions: What controversial social issues would be difficult to research? How would you go about surveying people on these issues?

Source: Purdy, 2006

13.1 Methods of Conducting Researcher-Administered Surveys

After deciding upon a research question, researchers must chose the research methodology that will be used. The most common quantitative technique for collecting primary data is the survey. Survey research involves asking all the participants the same predetermined questions. If researchers decide to conduct a survey, they must then determine the appropriate population to be surveyed, the size of the sample and the sampling method. After these decisions have been made, researchers can write a survey questionnaire.

Researchers must also decide upon a survey method. Methods for conducting surveys can be divided into researcher-administered surveys and self-administered surveys. When researcher-administered surveys are used, participants are assisted in completing the survey either by a researcher or an assistant. With this method participants are helped with any questions they find difficult to answer and are encouraged, if necessary, to complete the survey. With self-administered surveys participants are provided with a survey form, which they then complete on their own.

13.1.1 Researcher-administered surveys

When conducting researcher-administered surveys researchers or their assistants ask the questions and complete the questionnaire forms. The primary methods of conducting researcher-administered surveys are personal face-to-face surveys and phone surveys.

There are three important advantages to conducting researcher-administered surveys. First, if a research participant does not understand the meaning of a question, the researcher can help to clarify the misunderstanding. This will ensure that the question is understood correctly and will, therefore, result in more accurate research data. For example, a college student taking a survey might wonder if a question on yearly income refers to their own or their family's income.

A second advantage of this surveying method is that a researcher can encourage a participant to answer all the questions and complete the questionnaire. Research participants may initially agree to take a survey because they do not want to seem rude when asked to participate. However, once they have the questionnaire they may remember that they are in a hurry to get dinner on the table or to meet friends to see a movie. Because they are in a hurry, participants may skip any confusing questions or just neglect to turn over the survey to finish the second page. Using a researcher-administered method a researcher will notice these omissions and prompt the participants to answer all the questions on the form. In fact choosing helpful and encouraging administrators can increase response rates (Blohm et al., 2007).

There are some groups of people who may distrust any form of marketing research. This would include those groups who may feel disenfranchised from mainstream society. As a result of this feeling of disenfranchisement and the distrust that follows, members of these groups are least likely to participate in surveys. By having someone who is of a similar background personally conducting a survey, members of these groups are much more likely to participate.

Advantages of researcher-administered surveys

- Clarify confusions and misunderstandings
- Prompt participants to complete all the questions in a survey
- Establish a rapport with difficult to reach groups of participants

13.1.2 Self-administered surveys

Some survey methods use paper questionnaires or online survey forms that are self-administered. With these methods there is no researcher physically present during the surveying process. One of the major advantages to using paper and online surveys is that self-administration is much cheaper, as there is no need to pay for a researcher's or assistant's time. Another advantage to using a self-administration surveying format is that a researcher cannot lead a participant in any way to respond with a specific answer to a question. Of course a good researcher is not going to tell a participant how to answer a question. However, when explaining a question to a participant, a researcher may still unintentionally influence their answer. A third advantage of a self-administered survey is that a participant can take their time to complete the form. If they are interrupted during the process of completing the survey, they can even leave the form and come back and complete it at another time.

An additional advantage of having a self-administered survey is that the method allows a participant privacy. When a researcher administers the survey, a participant may be concerned about that researcher's response to their answer. This would be particularly true of answers to questions about personal behavior. However, even with a routine question, participants may want to provide a more positive answer when personally responding to a researcher.

Advantages of self-administered surveys

- Less cost because there is no need to pay for a researcher's time
- A researcher cannot lead a participant to provide a specific response
- A participant can complete the form at their own pace
- There is no concern about a researcher's reaction to the answers

13.2 Researcher-Administered Survey Methods

Researcher-administered surveys can be conducted personally or by using the telephone. In addition, personal surveys can be conducted using computer technology rather than paper questionnaire forms. When in the field conducting interviews, the success of researcher-administered surveys will depend on being organized and treating everyone with respect. In fact, even the tone of voice used can affect whether people are willing to cooperate (Van Der Vaart et al., 2006). A well conducted survey can be repeated over the years to determine trends in consumer preference. An interesting example of this type of change is shown in the box below.

SURVEYS CAN TELL WHAT A BRITISH CUSTOMER BELIEVES IS IMPORTANT

A survey on customer satisfaction in the UK ranked John Lewis stores as Number One. The ranking may not have surprised those who shop at the store. After all, John Lewis has built a reputation on treating customers well. However, what is interesting is that this year's survey, in comparison to previous surveys, demonstrates that customers assess

---

customer service differently. Ten years ago survey participants listed staff friendliness and helpfulness as important criteria when assessing the level of customer service. In the most recent survey, these attributes were not considered as important.

Does this mean that customers now do not mind rude staff? No, the answer is that customers now take for granted that staff will be friendly and helpful. Instead, the survey revealed that product knowledge is now considered an important criterion of customer service. This is not surprising when one considers that customers can now come into a store with product information they have gathered online. No customer wants to be in a position of knowing more about the product than the sales staff!

Source: Murphy, 2006

13.2.1 Personally-administered surveys

Personal surveying is the predominate method of collecting data in Europe while in the USA it has not been so widely used (Brace, 2004). One of the reasons for its popularity in Europe may be that continent's more concentrated population centers. In the USA the population is more dispersed over a wide geographic area, making telephone surveying a more popular methodology.

Personal surveying has important advantages over telephone surveying as a methodology. With personal surveying researchers are able to use prompt cards or other visual stimuli that will assist participants with their answers. For example, if a question asks if participants have purchased a specific brand of shampoo, a picture of the brand can be shown. Many people can more easily remember a product visually, by remembering what the bottle looked like, than by remembering a specific brand name. If a survey is about consumer preference in the color or style of a product, researchers can have the product ready to view. For food products, participants could be given a sample to taste before they respond to the survey questions. If a research question involves consumer preferences for types of promotion, examples of print ads or video clips of broadcast ads can be shown.

13.2.2 Location of personal surveying

There are a number of different locations where personal surveys can be administered. The natural location for research that involves current customers would be at a business or organization itself. For example, if the organization commissioning the research is a sports team wanting to know more about their fans, the survey could be administered at one of their games. If the organization is a retailer wanting to know about product preferences, researchers could survey shoppers at their store. Of course these locations would only reach current and not potential customers.

For some types of research studies, particularly those dealing with consumer behavior, a participant's home may be the ideal location. This location is particularly useful when the participant is required to answer questions about a product's usability. Having the product nearby in the home, while the survey is being taken, should assist the participant in providing an informed answer. Of course having participants take a researcher-administered survey in their home requires advance permission, scheduling issues, and travel time and cost.

Another location for conducting surveys would be at a place with a number of retail businesses. This type of research is often referred to as 'mall-intercept surveys'. A large regional shopping mall is a favorite location for conducting personal surveys, as a mall will generally attract a demographically diverse group of shoppers. A large mall will also attract customers from a wide geographic area who will provide a mix of urban, small town and rural potential participants. A large mall will also have a variety of different types of retail, dining and even entertainment options that should draw a psychographically diverse population. While there researchers should chose a number of different times to administer the survey, as different age groups may shop at different times of the day. In addition, they should station themselves beside different businesses that attract a variety of types of shopper. Using personal surveying, researchers stop potential participants and survey on the spot or direct them to a separate area with comfortable seating.

A final location for conducting personal surveys is at a public place where potential participants are gathered. This might be a community park or another civic amenity such as a swimming pool or zoo. Surveys could also be administered on a street corner where a targeted sample of potential participants passes by. Another idea is to conduct a personal survey at a public or community festival. The choice of location would depend on what type of event attracts the required population. Of course it will be necessary to get permission from the city before such surveying takes place.

13.2.3 Computer-aided personal surveys

Technology has provided a means to discard the paper questionnaire form traditionally used when conducting personal surveys. Instead, a computerized tablet is used by researchers to read questions and record answers. A researcher or assistant would still be present but the answers would be recorded electronically. There are important advantages for researchers in using this form of electronic data collection. Researchers will save money as there will be no data entry costs and the recorded answers can be downloaded directly into a computer program for analysis. Besides the cost savings, direct downloading increases reliability by excluding data entry errors. Complex survey forms will often be written with directions for a participant to skip ahead to a specific question based on their response to a previous question. With an electronic form this will happen automatically, minimizing confusion. In addition, the sequencing of questions can be randomized. This is an important consideration if there is any concern that question sequencing might be influencing the resulting answers.

13.2.4 Researcher-administered telephone surveys

The most significant advantage of a telephone survey over personal surveying is that it allows participants to be geographically dispersed. A phone survey can reach potential subjects wherever they live at little extra cost. In addition, participants can be reached that researchers may not be able to survey at a business or in a public place. For example, the elderly may be easier to reach by surveying them at home over the phone rather than in public.

Another advantage of telephone surveys over personal interviewing is that the telephone allows a participant to remain anonymous. As a result, participants may provide information that they may not wish to provide to someone personally. They may also be more willing to provide negative feedback, which they may feel would be rude if delivered in person.

Problems with conducting telephone surveys

There are, however, significant challenges that researchers must overcome when conducting phone surveys. Contacting potential participants is an increasing problem due to the growing number of individuals who rely on their cell phones rather than having a land line. Researchers can purchase phone lists for land lines, but not cell phones. In addition, when calling a home phone on a land line market researchers at least know that individuals are at home and could potentially participate in a survey. Even if market researchers had access to cell phone numbers, using them for a cell phone survey would probably result in a poor response rate. People may be answering their cell phones in a store, or whilst driving, or may even be at work. Individuals thus engaged would usually not be receptive to the idea of taking time to participate in a survey.

Another difficulty is the number of people who have caller ID. Such households may not even answer the phone if a number is not recognized. Another issue that researchers must consider is privacy laws. The popularity of Do Not Call lists means that many households cannot be called for commercial marketing research.

13.3 Methods of Conducting Self-Administered Surveys

Surveys can be self-administered by providing participants with a form using the postal service, email and websites, or even pdas. The mail survey has been the traditional means of delivery for self-administered surveys. However, using technology to deliver questionnaires is becoming increasingly popular. A survey form can be sent to participants in the body of an email and then returned electronically when completed. Another means of delivering the questionnaire electronically is to send potential participants an email with a link that directs them to a website to take the survey. Even text messaging on cell phones and pdas is now being used to ask survey questions. Below is one example of how text messaging is implemented in conducting research.

TEXT MESSAGING RESEARCH

How can instant messaging be used to generate research data? Let me text message you the ways!

1　A moderator may use instant messaging to interview a research subject.
2　During online focus groups, a moderator may use instant messaging to ask for more in-depth information from a single participant.
3　Instant messaging can also be used to notify potential subjects that an online quantitative survey is available.
4　During an online survey, certain responses might result in a moderator text messaging a participant to chat.

Instant messaging has become the most popular format of telecommunication among young people. Marketing researchers are now exploiting the advantages of text messaging, as speed is important in certain industries that rely on trends. Text messaging allows a research study to be completed in 24 hours. If the research takes too long, it will be too late to introduce the concept!

Source: Vence, 2006

13.3.1 Mail surveys

One of the primary means of delivering a self-administered survey form to participants is the postal service. There are significant advantages to using mail surveys, which is why they continue to be used by researchers despite the growing popularity of electronic delivery of questionnaires. A mail survey will reach designated households as everyone has a physical address, while not everyone has an email address. There is no problem obtaining a list as there are commercial companies whose business is providing such information to researchers. Marketing researchers could also use a publicly available source such as a voting registration list. The alternative is using a commercial or publicly available list. In addition, mail surveys can be conducted internationally which allows for cross-cultural comparisons (Alam, 2006).

Problems with conducting mail surveys

Of course the success of a mail survey depends on the quality of the mailing list that is being used. A poor quality list that does not target the right households or has old addresses will not save money, as the responses will not provide the needed information or even arrive at households.

While one advantage of using a mail survey means there is no researcher to bias responses, the lack of personal communication can also be a disadvantage. When using a mail survey researchers have no means to encourage completion or to explain questions that respondents might find unclear. Another issue with mail surveys is that researchers must wait for responses to be returned in the mail. The research will take more time to complete as researchers must wait whilst not knowing if participants are going to respond – or if they have thrown the form away and more participants will need to be sought.

13.3.2 Web-based self-completion

Emails are generally not widely used for delivering questionnaire forms because of practical issues. An email attachment that is large enough to contain all the text and formatting for a questionnaire may be too large for a potential participant's computer to handle. In fact, such a large attachment may be screened out as SPAM. However, electronic delivery using email is appropriate for short questionnaires targeted at groups that are familiar with the organization and therefore likely to respond. Most electronic survey forms though will be on separate websites and email will only be used to send the relevant website link that provides access to the form.

There are commercial online survey software packages that can be purchased that will assist in the design of a survey, collect the responses and tabulate the results. The newest products are relatively inexpensive and easy to use. While the fact that the form is electronic does not change the survey questions, it can change the way the questions and answers are presented. Visuals can be incorporated and the sequence of questions can be easily varied.

The major difference in using an online survey versus a mail survey is that the survey results appear immediately. This allows researchers to track the number of responses and send email reminders to those who have not responded. It also allows researchers to change any of the questions that seem to be causing confusion or to reconsider any of the questions that are not being answered.

Difficulties with conducting online surveys

There are also disadvantages to online surveys. First, respondents must have computer access. They must also be computer literate and feel comfortable responding online. While it may be true that a majority of people have computer access, not all types of jobs require people to be in front of a computer. In addition, not everyone enjoys being online. For those individuals who are not online every day because of their job or personal interests, completing an online survey will mean that they must go online specifically for that purpose, which is not as easy as picking up a pen or answering the phone.

Another disadvantage is that the potential participants who wish to respond to online surveys will be skewed toward younger, better educated individuals. This is fine if a research question addresses a product that is of interest to younger people. However, if a research sample calls for responses from a variety of demographic and psychographic types, online may not be the best methodology to motivate a response (Deutskens et al., 2006).

13.4 Motivating Participation

The response rate is the number of people who respond to a survey compared to the number of respondents who are eligible to participate. Low response rates should be expected (see the box below). In some research studies the sample can be as low as 10 per cent. This is the reason why more sample participants are selected than are needed to meet the sample size requirement. However, there are a few ways in which this response rate can be improved.

LOWER RESPONSE RATES HAVE RESEARCHERS WORRIED

The problem of ever smaller survey response rates was discussed in a meeting between the heads of the five largest global research firms, along with the top executives from those industries that rely on research. They came together to address two major problems: groups who do not respond to surveys and the overall shrinking rate of response. Most agreed that those groups who do not respond to surveys are largely made up of young ethnic minority males. However, all groups are less likely to respond than in the past with overall response rates as low as 10 per cent not uncommon. As a result surveys tend to reach the same respondents repeatedly.

An example or a problem that results from these phenomena is P&G's research effort. The company has spent $200 million on research using 600 different research companies all trying to get accurate information on consumer preferences. However, dramatically different results were returned by a mail and online survey of a new coffee concept. The online survey rated a new coffee concept as being seventh out of twelve while a mail survey rated the new idea as being top. These dramatically different results were returned even though each survey sample was supposed to represent the same population. In addition, the company found that two online surveys conducted one week apart resulted in different product recommendations!

What are the reasons for these problems? First there is 'opinion fatigue'. Online surveys are now so quick and easy to generate that people are getting too many requests to respond and therefore will decline to participate. Second, the people who are willing to respond to any survey are a very small proportion of the population. Only 0.25 per cent of the population provides 32 per cent of online responses, according to a British research company.

(Continued)

What is the answer? One research company achieves high response rates by paying participants very well. Another researcher suggested the use of shorter surveys of only three questions. Interestingly, no researcher or company recommended conducting research to determine what would motivate more consumers to participate.

Source: Neff, 2006

Of course, the research question and process are of critical importance to marketing researchers. However, this is not true for potential participants. Busy people walking down the street will usually not be pleased when they are stopped and asked to complete a survey form. The first impulse of anyone answering the phone, only to discover there is a researcher on the line, will be to hang up. Imagine people with too little time picking up their mail or clicking on to their email – they will quickly sort through, looking for personal correspondence and work-related items. What is left is usually termed 'junk' mail or SPAM and will be quickly discarded.

However, there are reasons why individuals *will* participate, including a desire to assist others, a general interest in giving their opinions, or for personal gain. If the purpose of the research is to help in finding a solution to a problem, those directly concerned with that problem may be willing to help for altruistic reasons. For example, if a survey is to determine people's attitudes toward global warming those interested in environmental issues are likely to respond. Sometimes research for commercial products may even elicit responses because the use of a specific product is of personal interest to a participant. Subjects such as the use of technology and a choice of entertainment options may motivate participation because the topic is associated with an interesting activity. In addition, some people are always interested in giving their opinion. They may find that the attention they receive fulfills an inner need to be noticed. However, these two reasons will not always be present and therefore researchers must consider the need to motivate participants by using a financial or product incentive in order to complete both a researcher-administered and self-administered survey.

13.4.1 Providing information to potential participants

Some people may choose to participate in a survey because of personal interest in a product or because they believe the results of the survey will help others. Therefore it is of critical importance that any information about who is sponsoring the research and how the results will be used is communicated to potential participants. For personally-administered surveys, this information should be provided verbally. For both mail and online surveys, researchers should enclose or attach a letter that includes this information.

If a covering letter is sent along with a survey form to provide credibility, it should be on a letterhead from either the research firm or the business or organization sponsoring the research. An email request should provide contact information, to allow someone who wants to verify the identity of the sending or sponsoring organization to do so. Both the letter and the email should explain why that particular person or household has been chosen. People are more likely to respond positively if they can understand why they have been chosen to participate. For example, the letter or email might explain that the survey is being sent to people who work in education or the medical profession. Even if researchers are using a random sample, there will still be a reason why a specific population was chosen.

The letter or email should explain the purpose of the research in terms that someone unfamiliar with such research terminology can understand. This language issue is so important that the covering letter or email should be as carefully tested as the survey form. The explanation should also include information on the research methodology in order that participants will know how the data are being gathered. If the research is of a sensitive nature, information on confidentiality should be given. This should include a reassurance that no participant will be identified by name, that only tabulated total results will be released, and that all forms will be destroyed on conclusion of the study.

The next issue that should be addressed is how participants will benefit from completing the survey form. Some research on social or political issues, while not benefiting individuals directly, will benefit society as a whole. In this case, the letter or email should appeal to the altruistic nature of participants. If this is not the case, the letter or email should describe any financial or alternative incentive that is being offered to those completing the survey.

To encourage completion, the letter or email should discuss the length of the survey and the projected time it should take to complete. Also, to encourage completion it has been suggested that an addressed and stamped letter be included for mail surveys. For online surveys the link for the survey's website should be easily located. It is just as important that even the envelope that contains the survey or the subject line in the email communicates the purpose of the research. After all, no one specifically picks up their mail or reads their emails hoping for the opportunity to participate in a survey (De Rada, 2005). Finally, the letter or email must be brief, must use simple everyday language, should look attractive and must be visually designed to be read easily.

Covering letter or email components

- Place on an official letterhead or provide contact information in an email
- Explain who is being sent the letters (sample) and how they were selected
- Explain the purpose of the research
- Provide information on the methodology
- Assure confidentiality
- Communicate how society or participant will benefit
- Describe the length of the form and the length of time to complete it
- Include mailing instructions and an envelope or a website link
- Place information on the envelope or email subject line

13.4.2 The use of incentives

If the subject of the research is something rather mundane, such as the frequency of auto maintenance or a soft drink consumption preference, most recipients will probably not wish to participate in the survey. In this case researchers must consider the use of an incentive to motivate responses (Teisl et al., 2006). This incentive could be indirect, such as the chance to win a prize. In this case, a respondent who completes the survey may be entered in a prize draw. Because most people will understand that they will probably not win, the prize must be so exciting that the chance of winning will motivate participation. Therefore the incentive chosen should be of particular interest to the population sample being targeted by the research survey

(Saunders et al., 2006). For example, a survey targeting frequent travelers could use as an incentive the possibility of a free trip to the Caribbean, as most people would find this an attractive enough incentive to motivate their participation even if they only had a slim chance of winning.

The incentive could also be direct. A free product, such as a CD, soft drink or poster, could be given to anyone who completes the survey. As this can be expensive, a discount coupon for a product that the company supplies could be offered. For example, for a survey on auto maintenance preferences researchers might offer a coupon from the sponsoring company for a free oil change if the form is completed. This incentive has the advantage of motivating completion and also providing promotion for the company. If researchers do not wish to tie the coupon to a specific company as it may affect participants' answers, a voucher that could be used at one of several companies could be offered instead.

13.5 The Survey Process

The survey process is similar for both researcher-administered and self-administered surveys. First the research question must be written. As with all forms of research this will be a team effort between researchers and management. The research question will help to determine the profile of the sample that will be needed to participate in the research. The next step will be to decide upon the method of conducting the survey, whether the method is researcher- or self-administered. The survey will then be written and tested. The times and locations for researcher-administered surveys must be chosen to meet the needs of participants. For self-administered surveys, the dates for mailing or emailing a survey will need to be decided.

For researcher-administered surveys the next step will be to identify staffing needs and hire and train the personnel who will conduct the survey. After the personnel are hired and trained, the survey can be conducted. For self-administered surveys, the survey is now mailed or the website is opened, after which a researcher will wait for the responses to be returned. Once the data have been returned – either by the survey taker, through the mail or electronically – the results are then analyzed and the report is written (see Figure 13.1 below).

13.5.1 Training survey takers

The success of researcher-administered surveys depends on the skill of survey takers. These survey takers do not need to be professional researchers. Large corporations can use the services of a commercial call center. Small businesses or research companies that only occasionally conduct surveys can hire employees by the hour. This type of part-time job could be attractive to college students or the retired. However, because these employees will not have experience in conducting surveys, it is important to conduct training before the survey process begins.

From the start training should inform the survey takers of the purpose of the research. Survey takers will be more motivated to have participants complete a survey if they understand the importance of the research question. The second step in the training is to explain the structure of the survey and the reasons for the questions. The role of the supervisor or lead researcher should be explained, namely that they are there to assist with difficult participants and to provide general support. The survey takers should also be taught the general rules for conducting successful surveys.

Once training has been completed, the survey takers should first administer the survey on each other. In addition, the supervisor should role-play uncooperative or rude potential participants

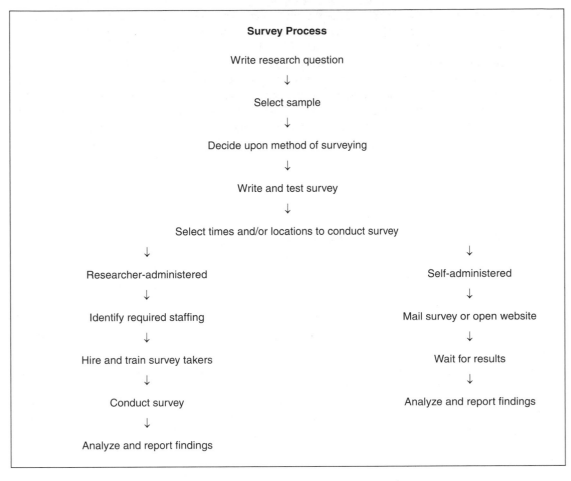

Figure 13.1   The Survey Process

so that survey takers learn how to diffuse such situations. Once survey takers are on the phone or out in the field, the first surveys should be supervized and monitored.

Training survey takers

- Describe the research topic
- Explain the survey structure and the reasons for the questions
- Define the role of the survey taker and the supervisor or lead researcher
- Practise role playing survey taking
- Supervize and monitor first surveys

13.5.2 Conducting a survey

The survey process for both phone and personal surveys should proceed through the same steps. Survey takers should first be trained to introduce themselves and their organization. They then should explain the purpose of the research and the sample selection process. This information will be from a script written by the researchers. The survey takers should next determine eligibility with one or two screening questions. These can be as simple as asking if the person speaking is head of a household, or in a specific age range, or if they have children living in their household.

After eligibility has been determined survey takers should explain the length of the survey in terms of the time requirement, not the number of questions or pages. They must then obtain consent to proceed with the survey. While the survey is being conducted, a survey taker should be prepared to explain confusing questions without leading a participant to provide any specific response. Finally, a survey taker should always sincerely thank a participant for their assistance.

The process of conducting researcher-administered surveys

1 Make the introduction
2 Explain the purpose and sample
3 Determine eligibility with a screening question
4 Explain the time requirement
5 Obtain consent
6 Conduct the survey, clarifying questions when needed
7 Thank the person for their participation

There will be occasions when a survey taker contacts a potential participant who reacts to the request to participate in the survey with rudeness or even hostility. A survey taker should never respond back in kind, as it may damage the reputation of the organization conducting the research. Instead, a survey taker must remember not to take the response personally and simply move on to the next call. At times, some of these people may wish to speak to a supervisor, realizing that the survey taker is not the one responsible for the survey call. Supervisors should always be available to handle these calls and soothe any irate callers.

Summary

1 A researcher or an assistant can administer survey forms or these can be self-administered. The methods for administered surveys include in person, computer-aided personal surveying and by telephone. The advantages of these methods include the ability to clarify misunderstandings, to prompt completion and to establish rapport. Self-administered surveying includes mail and web-based forms. The advantages to self-administered surveys include less cost, an inability for researchers to bias the response, and participants' ability to complete at their own pace and convenience.
2 Personal surveying has the advantage of allowing the use of visual prompts. A researcher can also demonstrate product use. Computer-aided personal surveys use a hand-held device to collect answers. This reduces the cost of data entry while also making complex question sequencing easy to understand. Telephone surveys suffer from low response rates but they still have the advantage of reaching certain groups and providing anonymity.

3   Mail and email surveys are inexpensive and with this methodology there is no danger of an interviewer biasing the response. The success of both mail and email surveys depends on the quality of the mailing or email list used to reach participants. Online surveys can be inexpensive to create and should provide researchers with the ability see results immediately and to track response rates. In addition, results can be analyzed immediately. The disadvantage is that a sample may be skewed towards young people.

4   To motivate completion, information that is provided to participants should explain the reason for the research and why a certain subject has been chosen. It should also assure confidentiality and provide contact information for those who wish to assure themselves regarding the legitimacy of the research. Information should also be provided on any financial or product incentive that will be given to the research subject.

5   The survey process starts with writing the research question, selecting the sample, and the method of surveying. If the survey is to be administered, the process must include the training of survey takers. Survey takers should train by practising giving the survey to each other. The trainers should monitor the first surveys conducted by the survey takers.

Key Terms

computer-aided surveys   a survey taker records an answer electronically using a small hand-held computer screen

researcher-administered survey   form of survey taking, including personal and by phone, where a researcher is present while a subject answers the questions

self-administered survey   form of survey taking, including paper and online, where a researcher is not present when a participant answers the questions

Discussion Questions

1   What would be the advantages of conducting self-administered surveys of professors about their teaching methods?

2   Why would you recommend either researcher- or self-administered surveys when conducting a research study that used recent immigrants to the country as a sample?

3   Where would be the best location to hold personal interviews on a personal care product? Why?

4   Why is it becoming more difficult to get people to respond to any survey?

5 What would be the advantages and disadvantages of using online surveys on the current employment of school leavers and university graduates?
6 Which population groups would be most willing to complete online surveys? Why do you believe this is the case?
7 What information would be important to include in a covering email or letter when conducting a survey of students' opinions of their professor?
8 Why would it be critical to train survey takers who were going to conduct a survey of students?

Recommended Reading

Buchanan, Elizabeth (2004) *Readings in Virtual Research Ethics: Issues and Controversies.* Hershey, PA: Information Science Publications. This book contains various articles on the ethical issues involved in conducting online research, including online surveys, internet ethnography and email interviews.

Graeff, Timothy (2003) *The Marketing Research Handbook: A Guide to Conducting Consumer Research.* Dubugue, IA: Kendall/Hunt Publishing. Provides learning exercises for the reader to reinforce the research concepts and also gives sample surveys to analyze.

Grover, Rajiv and Vriens, Marco (eds) (2006) *The Handbook of Marketing Research: Uses, Misuses and Future Advances.* London: SAGE. This book contains articles by 48 marketing experts with an emphasis on how surveys, among other techniques, can be used to gain useful insights into consumer behavior.

Gwartney, Patricia A. (2007) *The Telephone Interviewer's Handbook: How to Conduct Standardized Conversations.* San Francisco, CA: Jossey-Bass. Addresses the issue of how to interview over the phone in spite of the growing reluctance of people to participate. Also covers the topics of professionalism and ethics.

Oppenheim, A.N. (1999) *Questionnaire Design, Interviewing and Attitude Measurement.* New York: Continuum. A very thorough treatment of both the design and conducting of survey research with an emphasis on how questions can be written to successfully measure consumer attitudes.

Sue, Valerie M. and Ritter, Lois A. (2007) *Conducting Online Surveys.* London: SAGE. Evaluates the advantages and disadvantages of online surveys and also provides information on the available software options.

PART 4

Analyzing and Reporting Findings

14 Analyzing Verbal and Other Qualitative Data

Learning Objectives

1 Explore the difference between the analysis of quantitative and qualitative data
2 Discuss the types of information that can be revealed through analyzing data
3 Explain the process of transcribing recordings
4 Learn the methods of coding qualitative data
5 Discuss the software available to assist with qualitative coding and analysis

INNOVATIVE RESEARCH DISCOVERS THE 'YUCK' FACTOR

If you are a grocery store owner, one of the decisions you have to make is how to arrange the products in your store. The most common system is to put similar products together for convenience. However, researchers have discovered another issue, which they call the 'contagion' factor. All shoppers buy products, such as cat litter and toilet bowl cleaner, that elicit feelings of disgust but need to be purchased anyway. But who would have guessed that lard was also a product that causes people to feel uneasy?

Researchers learnt about the contagion factor by placing products, one of which is a neutral product and one a 'disgust' product, next to each other in a grocery cart. They then asked participants if they would purchase the products. This exercise was done a number of times with the different products in different arrangements. The researchers discovered that when neutral products were next to a 'disgust' product they were rated as less acceptable. The 'disgust' product was 'contaminating' the neutral product.

Questions: What recommendations for additional research would you make to a grocery store based on these findings? Can you think of any other unique research that another type of retail establishment could conduct?

Source: Morales and Fitzsimons, 2007

14.1 Analysis of Quantitative versus Qualitative Data

The data from quantitative research are in the form of numbers that can be averaged, compared and contrasted. The resulting statistics are used to represent the level of a form of consumer behavior or consumer preference within a targeted population segment. Management may not understand how the statistics were obtained, but they can easily understand the averages and percentages and, therefore, trust the resulting information.

In contrast, qualitative research results in verbal data and images including recordings, written words and sometimes photos or videos. These data cannot be statistically manipulated, compared and contrasted. In addition, the analysis does not result in easily understood percentages. For this reason, management may well misunderstand and mistrust the resulting analysis (Johnson, 2007).

Rather than proving facts using statistics, the analysis of qualitative data has as its focus the search for meanings. This is because qualitative research is used to answer the question of 'Why?' The answer will always be more complicated to explain to management than just a percentage or average. In fact sometimes the reasons for consumer behavior that are uncovered through research can be quite surprising. The box below demonstrates how important these insights are, particularly for small businesses.

HOW IMPORTANT IS RESEARCH FOR SMALL BUSINESSES?

Why do 50 per cent of Canadian small businesses fail within their first five years? An article on the 11 most common mistakes made by Canadian entrepreneurs lists lack of market research as the number one error that can cause a business to fail. Because the entrepreneurs didn't first conduct research of the existing environment, they sometimes didn't even know they had competitors when they started their businesses! They also didn't research the marketplace and as a result didn't know who to target as potential customers. As a result, these Canadian businesses often had to change their definition of their target market once they were already in business. Not knowing your competitors or customers is a very expensive, and often fatal, mistake! This mistake could have been avoided if marketing research had been conducted! Here's a list of most common mistakes that lead to business failure:

1   Failure to conduct marketing research
2   Failure to understand the impact of fast growth
3   Lack of cash flow
4   Poor communication with partners
5   Poor record keeping and administration
6   Ignorance of tax credits
7   Failure to network
8   Unfocused sales strategies
9   Poor grasp of marketing
10 Staffing difficulties
11 Hesitancy to reach out for help

Source: Glandfield, 2006

Table 14.1 Differences in analysis

Quantitative Analysis	Qualitative Analysis
Statistics that describe behavior	Recommendations based on concepts and categories
Analysis of quantitative data occurs after research has been completed	Analysis of data occurs while research is still being conducted
Statistics are manipulated for new meanings	Data are repeatedly analyzed by researchers for new insights

14.1.1 The art of qualitative research

Qualitative research, as with quantitative research, is conducted in order to answer a research question. However, a skilled qualitative researcher may find more in the data than just the answer to a research question. Quantitative research is usually conducted using a survey methodology. This limits the responses of participants to the issues on the survey form. Because the subjects involved in qualitative research are allowed to provide any additional information they feel is important, there will be a wealth of data. These data may provide new insights to help answer the research question. In fact, it may turn out that the subjects have an entirely different view of the solution to a problem or a new opportunity.

Because the research process may reveal unexpected ideas and opinions it is important that regular meetings are held between researchers and the management of a company during the research process. These meetings will be to share the unexpected insights that have resulted from the research. This will give the company's management the opportunity to discuss whether they wish to have these insights further explored by adjusting the research methodology.

The analysis of qualitative data is also unique because it starts without predetermined categories in which to place ideas or opinions. Rather, new insights will reveal themselves as the data are repeatedly analyzed by researchers. The goal of such analysis is a full description of the attitudes, values and opinions of consumers. The differences between analyzing quantitative and qualitative data are summarized in Table 14.1.

14.2 The Analysis Process

The steps involved in analyzing qualitative data include organization of the data, review of the data, coding, and analysis. The most significant difference between quantitative and qualitative analysis is that with qualitative analysis, rather then merely quantifying responses researchers are looking for patterns or themes in the data. Sometimes management may misunderstand the qualitative research process (see the box below).

WHAT DATA CAN AND CANNOT TELL US

There has been frequent criticism against focus groups as a research methodology. However Eric Johnston, a qualitative market researcher, has some counter arguments. He cites three main criticisms against focus groups and gives his response in the magazine *Marketing News*.

(Continued)

Criticism 1: Focus group research can't predict whether a company's future product will be successful.

Response: No research can predict the future. Nor should research findings be the final decision maker. Decision making is management's job. They should use focus groups data, along with other research findings and their own experience, when making product development decisions.

Criticism 2: Focus group discussions evoke rational responses from consumers whereas purchase decisions are irrational.

Response: A well run focus group is not merely a question-and-answer session. Its purpose is to get beyond the rational by using group interaction between members. In addition, focus groups often use projective techniques whose sole purpose is to elicit emotional responses.

Criticism 3: Reliance on focus group research means that innovative ideas proposed by employees will be ignored.

Response: Focus groups should never be used as a substitute for company creativity. However, focus groups can be used to learn how consumers might react to a groundbreaking idea. A negative reaction means that the idea may need more work – not that it should be abandoned.

Source: Johnston, 2006

While the analysis of qualitative data is more art than science there are still distinct steps to the process. First, researchers must organize the data. The next step is to transcribe any verbal information onto tape. Once the data are organized and transcribed researchers review the material by reading through it with no preconceived idea of what will be found. After this initial review researchers will again examine the data, all the while coding common concepts. Once this level of coding is complete, the researchers will again review the material to find any concepts that need to be broken down into more than one category. They will then analyze these concepts and categories by questioning what relationship they have to the research question. The final step is to interpret this information into recommendations for action.

14.2.1 Data organization

Data organization involves both the collection and the transformation of the collected information. Organization of data according to research question can be particularly important for qualitative research, as the findings may need to be compared with the findings from quantitative data on the same subject (Harradine and Ross, 2007). Some of the data resulting from the research might be lists that have been collected on large pieces of paper. Focus groups commonly use this method so that everyone present can view the responses being provided to questions asked by the moderator. The lists are commonly written in marker pen in large print and then hung on walls around the room. These lists must be taken down, labeled and dated. Each label should include the research question that resulted in the list of information. The date of the focus group and the name of the researcher should also be noted on each piece of paper.

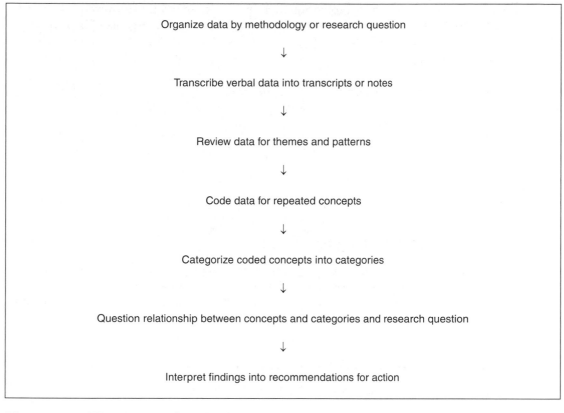

Figure 14.1   The process of analyzing qualitative data

Once these pieces of paper are back in the office, the data should be typed. If the lists include additional notations, such as item numbering when participants have been asked to prioritize, this information must also be added to the typed list. Sometimes arrows or other visual notations will be on the paper. If they cannot be typed they should be described in the typed document. This typed list cannot totally duplicate all the information contained on the original sheets and, therefore, these should be saved in case they are needed for analysis.

Written materials from any other projective techniques should also be collected. These may be ideas written on index cards, cartoons with speech bubbles or sentence completion forms. Drawings made by participants should also be organized and saved by having them scanned into a computer program. These scanned drawings will also now be available to be added to the final report. Digital photographs that have been taken by participants can also be downloaded into the computer, both for analysis and for future use in the final report or presentation.

When all the material has been written down data from focus groups it can be organized by research question. If more than one group was conducted, the information should also be organized by group. Projective data should be organized by technique. For example, all sentence completion forms and all drawings should be kept together. Interview transcripts should be organized by research question. Intercept interviews must be organized by location and expert interviews by topic. Observational research forms are usually organized by the location where the observations took place. Ethnographic research materials should be organized by site visit, while the material produced by grounded theory research needs to be organized by topic.

Organization of data

- Focus groups organized by research question and group
- Projective techniques organized by technique
- Interviews organized by topic
- Intercept interviews organized by location
- Expert interviews organized by topic
- Observational research organized by location
- Ethnographic research organized by site visit
- Grounded theory research organized by topic

14.2.2 The art of transcribing recordings

Qualitative interviews and focus groups will both result in tape recordings that will need to be transcribed. If possible, a word for word transcription should be produced. However, if there is a great deal of taped material this may not be economically feasible. A good transcript will allow a company to experience the research process as if they were there (see the box below).

WOULDN'T YOU LIKE TO KNOW WHAT THEY SAY ABOUT YOU?

Sports Marketing provides information to companies that manufacture sports equipment on how their product is selling in comparison to the competition's. Besides the usual quantitative data, Sports Marketing also gathers qualitative data through expert interviews with a panel of 300 retailers. The retailer group is interviewed twice yearly on sales and marketplace trends. They are also asked to rate their suppliers of sporting goods. These reports allow the manufacturers to see how their products compare to their competitors' in the minds of retailers.

However, in addition the reports contains qualitative information such as direct quotes and comments about the brand. For the retailers, it is almost like eavesdropping on what store owners are saying about you. What is the cost of such a service? A complete product report, such as on the bike industry, costs $4,000.

Source: Delaney, 2005

It is best if the researcher who moderated the focus groups or conducted the interviews listens to the tape before transcription. While a researcher is actually conducting an interview or moderating a focus group, part of their awareness will have to be focused on that process. Listening to the proceedings afterward they can simply focus on what is being said. While they are busy conducting the research, it is always difficult for a researcher to retain all that is happening.

Listening to the tape will refresh a researcher's memory of what was said. In addition, the tone of voice used and even the silences between speech can provide insights.

After listening to the tape, transcribing the material is the next step in the analysis process. While a researcher is listening to a tape, they can be typing up notes on the main points being made. Once the transcription process starts, the researcher can pause the tape while they make notes on new insights or memories. For example, there may have been a focus group member who spoke rarely but followed the proceedings closely with evident interest. This gives more weight to his or her opinions than if the researcher remembered that the focus group participant seemed bored and distracted. It is difficult for researchers to take notes on behavior during a focus group or interview, as it can disrupt the proceedings and make participants feel uncomfortable. Therefore these notes should be added to the transcript. The same or different participants will frequently repeat information, and a researcher can quickly pick up patterns and develop a shorthand notation process.

Transcribing tapes is much more than just a technical task, which is why it is best if a researcher prepares a transcript personally. The goal of transcription isn't a word for word perfect transcript. Instead, while the transcription is taking place, a researcher should concentrate on recording information that addresses the research question. While the conversation may stray and other topics be discussed, these topic areas are important only in how they relate to the main research question. For example, if the research concerns the cost of a product, such as cell phones, participants may start discussing where they like to shop. A researcher will then analyze this conversation for its relevance to the research question on cost, by noting whether the stores mentioned are discount outlets or high priced specialty stores. Information on a great sale on shoes that was added by one participant can be ignored.

When transcribing a tape, it is not important to note the names of speakers as they do not need to be identified personally. However, it is still important to attribute comments to individuals to determine if there is consistency in the comments they provide throughout the focus group. Instead of names, a researcher can add a code or a number to represent each speaker. In addition, comments on tone of voice or emotion can be added using the same system.

One means of adding such detail is to type the transcript in a column format. The first column will have the words spoken during the session, whether interview or focus group. The second column will contain the researcher's notes on who is speaking, their tone of voice and any other observations noticed by the researcher when the research was conducted. The third column will be used for coding purposes. Because this column transcript will be referred to frequently during the analysis process, it is important to leave additional space where handwritten comments can be added.

14.3 Coding Qualitative Data

Once the transcriptions are complete, researchers should review all of the data. This review should be conducted with an open and relaxed frame of mind. At this stage of the analysis, researchers must let the data reveal insights rather than impose ideas that were formed while conducting the research. While the impressions formed during the research are important and should be retained, it is also important for researchers to look at the data with fresh eyes. It might be that comments and ideas which were initially overlooked can now be seen as being important. An example of a research study that required repeated review of the transcripts is shown below.

Once data have been transcribed and reviewed, researchers will begin to code. Coding is used to note the repetition of ideas, opinions or facts. The first coding will be conducted to examine the data for answers to the research question. For example, the research question might have asked how a visit to the dentist could be made more pleasant. A focus group of clients would be asked for their ideas for improvements that could be made to a dental clinic. A transcript would be coded for the times when any mention of the ideas for improvements was mentioned. These instances are coded so that researchers can then return to the information to analyze if many of the responses gave similar ideas or if any unique suggestions were provided.

The transcribed notes will then be analyzed again to code other topics that arose during the research. For example, besides discussing ideas for improvements, researchers might find that on multiple occasions trouble reaching the dental office due to a lack of convenient parking or public transportation options was mentioned. Another issue discussed might have been the services now offered at a new, competing, dental office. By coding these data, researchers may find that it is this new competition that received the most mentions. Below is an example of how data are being collected from online sources.

An example of this process in action is the research of shopping habits conducted by Virtual Surveys in the UK. Bloggers were asked to keep a week-long diary of their shopping habits. Content from the blogs was then shared amongst the group anonymously. The blog members then commented on each others shopping habits. Of course, even online an experienced moderator is still needed to keep the discussion lively and on track.

Source: *Marketing*, 2007

The first step in the analysis of all of the written material is coding for the main concepts that appear in the transcripts. Researchers read through the documents to see if there are any concepts that are raised repeatedly. If a study involved the reasons why students leave university before completing their studies, the main concepts that might appear could be 'money', 'studies too difficult' and 'unfriendly staff'. However, a more surprising concept that might be discovered would be 'got good job offer'. This analysis takes skill, as the wording used in each individual comment may not directly describe the concept and it will certainly take more than one reading of the material by a researcher before all of the concepts become clear. It is a researcher's responsibility to notice the similarities in comments and that they may all belong to a single concept.

Categories

Once researchers have finished coding for concepts, they may find that some need to be further broken down into categories. These concepts and categories are important as they are the building blocks from which researchers will make their recommendations for action. For example, many comments in a transcript may involve the concept of the price of a product. Several participants may state that they don't buy a product unless it is on sale. Other participants may state that they buy a competing product because it is cheaper, while some may state directly that the price of a product is too high. While all of these involve the price of a product, a researcher may decide they are too dissimilar and break them down into three categories: 'don't buy because can't afford, 'competing product purchasers', and 'non-purchasers'. The researcher may then make different recommendations for attracting each of the first two groups and recommend no action on the third.

Researchers can code transcripts using highlighting markers with a different color for each concept and category, or alternatively the concept and category name can be noted in the margins of a document. As researchers code the material for the answer to a research question, each time a researcher comes across a statement that deals with the issue of the price being more than a consumer is willing to pay this will be coded. However, with qualitative research there may be other concepts that arise that are worth noting (which is one of the benefits of qualitative research). For example, in the discussion on price, a researcher might note that several consumers expressed how much they enjoyed the design of the product. While the research question had not addressed the seasonality of price sensitivity, this would still be useful information for management.

Table 14.2 Building categories

Transcribed notes →	Concepts →	Categories
Like the color Great appearance I love lots of chrome!	Style →	Style
Over my budget Wish I could afford it More expensive than my current car	Price →	Product cost
Takes too much gas Insurance probably expensive Requires specialized shop	Price →	Operating expense

14.3.1 Using coding to develop recommendations

Once coding is completed, all material will be reviewed again to develop recommendations based on the coded concepts and categories. For example, a research question might have asked 'Why do consumers not purchase automobiles produced by our company?' The coded material may have revealed infrequent comments made on color, appearance, and amount of chrome. All of these comments the researcher will code under one concept – 'style'. Other comments made about the cost of the automobile a researcher will code under the concept of 'price'. Further analysis might now reveal that the concept of 'price' is actually two categories. One involves comments on the cost of the automobile, while the researcher might find that a separate category is now needed for those comments that involve the cost of maintaining such an automobile, including comments about gas mileage, insurance and repair costs. Based on this coding researchers might recommend that promotional material should address the reasonable cost of maintaining the vehicle and not just the low purchase price. Table 14.2 shows one example of how concepts and categories are built.

14.3.2 Software tools for coding

Software tools that assist in the analysis of qualitative data are now available. However, marketing researchers must decide if it is worth the money to purchase such software. If a research process has only involved one or two focus groups or interviews, the time saved in using software may not justify its cost and the time it will take for researchers to learn to use it. In this case, researchers may decide to rely on hand coding and analysis.

If researchers conduct qualitative research on an ongoing basis or have a large qualitative research study planned, then it may be worth their while to purchase and use coding software. While these software packages can save researchers the tedium of coding, they do not replace the analytical process of determining the concepts and analysis of the concepts and categories that result in recommendations.

A software package designed for qualitative research will help with the development of a system of coding and then applying the system to the transcribed text. It will also allow researchers to add brief comments to the data. These comments might explain nonverbal behavior that a researcher had noticed while the comment was being made. Researchers will also be able to link different codes between transcripts, memos and notes on different focus groups, interviews and projective techniques. The software can also help in the preparation of final reports by displaying coded categories in a graph format. If there is a sufficient amount of data, once it is coded the number of responses that include a particular type of content can be quantified for management (Srnka and Koeszegi, 2007).

This process is started by a researcher selecting text in a transcript that belongs to a specific concept, which the researcher then names. Once this task is done the software will then search all the data files for identical text and code these occasions as the same concept. For example, the comment that a product is 'too expensive' will be coded as belonging to the concept of 'price'. The software will search all the transcripts and other written material for similar comments. In addition, the software can search for additional phrases that have the same meaning. Terms such 'costs too much' and 'not worth the price' can be added to the same concept.

14.4 Analysis of Qualitative Data Content

After the data have been organized, transcribed and coded, the next step in the process of analysis is to determine if there are any relationships between the concepts and categories. The purpose of developing relationships is to generate new ideas to answer a research question. These new ideas will be the basis for making recommendations for action. For example, one qualitative research study was used to examine the cultural effects of the country of origin of a product on British consumption behavior. As a result, it was noted that country of origin was important for some groups of products (Balestrini et al., 2003).

After all, management will want actionable recommendations from a study, not just analysis. A report that simply describes researchers' impressions will not be considered useful enough to justify the cost of the research. Possible recommendations might involve how to target new types of consumer segments, descriptions of the process of consumer behaviors, a comparison and contrast of consumer motivation, or an hypothesis of a relation between variables that will need to be verified by future quantitative research. Below is one example of ethnographic research that was used to provide such recommendations.

ETHNOGRAPHY GOES VIRTUAL

Every producer of retail goods knows that the placement of an item on a store shelf or a display rack will affect consumers' purchase behavior. One way to test this consumer behavior is to change store placement and displays to see how this affects sales. Of course, this is an expensive testing technique if the new placement negatively affects sales!

Frito-Lay decided they needed to conduct shelf placement research but they opted to conduct ethnographic research in a virtual, rather than a physical, store. A virtual convenience store was created online that would be used to test not only product shelf placement but also pricing and new product ideas. 'Shoppers' were recruited to visit the

(Continued)

---

store through outsourced panels. When online, the research subjects were shown shelves that displayed not only Frito-Lay but also competing products and brands. The shoppers were not informed that the research was being conducted by Frito-Lay, only that they were free to purchase any product. Shoppers made their snack food purchases by clicking on the display. Different store displays were shown to see how placement affected product choice. In addition, after shopping was completed, some shoppers were surveyed online about their product choices.

Frito-Lay believes this online ethnographic research is more effective than interviewing, as shoppers would have a difficult time remembering their snack food purchase behavior. Did it work? Not only did Frito-Lay learn about shelf placement, they also made both pricing and packaging changes based on this research.

Source: Enright, 2006

14.4.1 Consumer segments

Coded qualitative research data can be analyzed for information on possible new market segments to target. A company may be aware of how to market their product to their current demographic and geographic segments, but qualitative data might reveal entirely new psychographic segments of which that company was unaware. These new segments will have been identified based on common values and attitudes that have been verbalized or displayed during the qualitative research process.

For example, a research focus group on a product for older consumers might have found that people aged 65–75 years old do not consider themselves as being older. Because they are still leading active lives, this segmentation category based on age may have no meaning for them. Instead, they may identify themselves as 'active adults' who just happen to be retired or on their second career. They may also think that they have no attitudes in common with people in the traditional category called 'senior citizens'.

Likewise, qualitative research data may uncover segments of individuals who identify with various types of hobbies. What they will all have in common is a specific interest, say in crafts, and will therefore identify themselves by this, for example as 'crafters'. As a result, researchers might recommend that a company commissioning research on this topic considers producing products aimed at this new segment.

Qualitative research might also uncover new usage categories. In discussions of food consumption, it might be found that food ordinarily consumed at breakfast is also enjoyed at other times of the day. Based on a finding that cereal is also eaten at the office, researchers might recommend a new promotional campaign based on this usage.

14.4.2 Consumer behavior processes

Besides new market segments, qualitative research can provide insights into consumer behavior processes. A company that makes readymade dinner entrées may be interested in the meal preparation processes of today's busy dual career families. Analysis of ethnographic data might reveal that parents would like to have everyone sit down for meals together, but that children have their own diet preferences. Using this knowledge, researchers could recommend that a company produces prepackaged dinners with a choice of side dishes so that everyone can eat together and yet still have the food they each want. If it is found that parents still want to have their families maintain a little formality when dining, researchers might then recommend that the packaging includes decorative paper napkins.

An observational study on how people drive their cars might find that drivers need cup holders that can keep their beverages hot or cold when they spend long periods of time in the car. In addition, observing children traveling in their car seats may have revealed a need for a small storage area for their food. These are ideas that might not otherwise have been discovered in quantitative survey research. However, analyzing the data from qualitative research can reveal useful ideas such as these that can be recommended to companies.

14.4.3 Comparing and contrasting consumer traits

While researchers are analyzing data, they may note some differences in the consumer behavior process based on demographic or psychographic traits. For example, a qualitative research study might have been specifically designed to examine and compare the differences in cell phone usage for different age groups. These types of differences will appear in qualitative data from focus groups, interviews or ethnographic studies. In this case researchers might perhaps find that women were using the photo feature to take pictures while shopping of possible purchases for their home that they can then view later. Meanwhile, it may also be found that males were using their cell phone cameras to take candid photos of their friends. These are ideas that can be developed into recommendations.

14.4.4 Development of hypotheses

Another recommendation that may result from an analysis of qualitative data is an hypothesis about the relationship between two variables. This hypothesis cannot be said to be proven, based on the qualitative research. However, it might be so intriguing that the researchers recommend quantitative research be conducted to determine the validity of this hypothesis. For example, qualitative research might find that the consumers who are nonusers of a product believe that the product is too expensive to operate. This fact could then be tested further with survey research.

14.4.5 Analysis of ethnographic and observational research data

The information provided by ethnographic and observational research will not be in a verbal format. Instead, the data will be in the form of notes on behavior, photos or video. Observation forms and notes must also be analyzed, but not by coding for words. Instead researchers will be looking for unique or repeated behavior that has been noted on the forms or in the photos or videos. Researchers can look for these data concerning the process of using a product, new ways of using a product, where consumers use a product and the mistakes they make when using a product – all of which may have been noted on the forms (Gummesson, 2007).

For example, observational research of consumers shopping at a clothing store can show how they travel through the store, which products they tend to buy first, and how long they spend in the store. If researchers notice that people seem to have a problem finding the fitting rooms, better signage may be recommended. In addition, if it becomes obvious that certain clothing racks are not being visited, it might be recommended that the store layout be changed. All of this information can then be used by management to make the store more user friendly.

Often ethnographic research may reveal that people use a product in a way that was not originally intended by the company that designed that product. These insights can be used to make recommendations on the redesign of a product or the development of a totally new product. For example, an ethnographic study may have been conducted on students living together in university-owned housing. An analysis of videos taken during the study may have found that students like to study while lying on their beds. From this study, it might be recommended that better lighting be provided above beds. After all, good research should result in increased revenue as shown in the box below.

EFFECTIVE RESEARCH PAYS FOR ITSELF IN NEW ZEALAND

There were four winners in the Market Research Effectiveness awards in New Zealand. These winners were chosen on the basis of the financial return provided to companies commissioning research.

In first place was the research conducted by Focus Research for Frucor. The campaign to introduce Just Juice Bubbles resulted in a product introduction that had sales of 170 per cent of the target. The campaign was successful because Focus Research and the marketing department of Frucor worked together both on the research and the resulting marketing strategy. Frucor didn't just want statistical analysis, they wanted to partner with a research firm that would help them translate the findings into business success. Thus Focus Research worked in partnership with Frucor to design a product that included the customer preferences discovered during the research.

Strategic partnerships are important if the kind of impressive result discussed above is to be achieved. Research Solutions held a seminar for their clients, the media and other contacts about why some research projects lead to strong financial gains for a company. The four factors that were identified were trust, risk taking, researchers having access to all departments of a company throughout the marketing research process, and listening to the researchers.

A company must trust researchers enough to not only ask their opinions but also to listen when those researchers make recommendations about the research methodology. Playing it safe when designing a research plan leads to safe findings that result in safe actions. Instead a company should listen and explore researchers' ideas on the best way to obtain the necessary data. To make the best possible use of market researchers' expertise, a company should ensure that researchers have access to decision makers in other departments of that company, including finance. Lastly, a company is paying for researchers' expertise. Therefore, they need to listen to the research findings even when these are not what they expected to hear.

Source: *NZ Marketing Magazine*, 2006

Summary

1 The differences between analyzing qualitative and quantitative data include the fact that the analysis of quantitative data results in statistics that describe behavior. However, qualitative data are analyzed for insights into the motivation for behavior. Quantitative data are analyzed at the conclusion of research while qualitative data are analyzed while research is conducted. The analysis of qualitative data is an art that relies on the knowledge and skill of researchers. The analysis must only be conducted by researchers as they alone will have experienced the incidents that occurred during the research. In order that these incidents are not lost, researchers should hold debriefing meetings as soon as the research study has been concluded and even during the research process.

2 While qualitative analysis is an art, there is still a process to be followed. First the data must be organized and any verbal information transcribed. The data are then reviewed and coded for concepts and categories. Finally, the relationship between concepts and categories is questioned and the findings interpreted into recommendations for action. Data are organized based on the methodology and notes are then transcribed. This transcription can be verbatim or in note form. The transcription should be in a format that allows researchers to easily add insights and coding. The transcription is then reviewed for insights.

3 The most important step in the qualitative analysis process is the coding of the data. Both repeated and isolated incidents and comments are coded by theme and named as concepts. This can be done through physically marking the words and then distinguishing the type of comment by words or colors. From these coding will be built categories with common elements. There is now software that helps to make this task more manageable, but the ideas for the coding of concepts and categories must first come from researchers.

4 Analysis of coded data will include questioning the relationship between categories, and looking for insights that can be interpreted to answer the research question. The interpretation might reveal information on new potential consumer segments. It also might reveal information on consumers' behavior processes. Consumers could thus be analyzed for an interpretation of traits. In addition, hypotheses between variables may be established. Finally, analysis of nonverbal ethnographic and observational data can be used.

Key Terms

categories   distinct groupings of data within a single broad concept

coding   reviewing the transcribed material and then using colors or words to indicate comments that address similar themes

concepts   comments that are noted on transcripts that all address a similar broad theme

transcription   typing either the exact words or a summarization of what is being said while listening to a tape of research participants

---

Discussion Questions

1   Why is the analysis of qualitative data an entirely different process from the analysis of quantitative data?
2   Why is it important to organize the data from qualitative research as soon as possible after completion of the study?
3   Why is it recommended that a researcher transcribe the tapes of a research study consisting of focus groups of potential students on any problems they have had with administration?
4   Why is coding of verbal transcripts as much an art as a science?
5   For a qualitative study of student athletes' attitudes toward their coaches, can you think of some concepts of data that might arise from the coded data?
6   Would you recommend using software to help with coding? Why or why not?
7   If you were reviewing the data from a qualitative research study on the relationship between students and music, what kinds of interpretation of the data might result?
8   Why is it essential that the person who conducts the ethnographic research analyzes the findings?

Recommended Reading

Auberbach, Carl F. and Silverstein, Louise B. (2002) *Qualitative Data: An Introduction to Coding and Analysis.* New York: New York University Press. While writing from the perspective of psychology, this book is still a good source of information on coding and analysis.

Burber, Renate, Gadner, Johannes and Richards, Lynn (eds) (2004) *Applying Qualitative Methods to Marketing Management Research.* Basingstoke: Palgrave Macmillan. A book that focuses on qualitative methods, with interesting information on analyzing the resulting data so as to be able to make recommendations for solving problems.

Daymon, Christine and Holloway, Immy (2002) *Qualitative Research Methods in Public Relations and Marketing Communications.* London: Routledge. While covering all expects of the research process, this explains the analysis process for researchers beginning their careers.

Denzin, Norman K. and Lincoln, Yyvonna S. (2003) *Collecting and Interpreting Qualitative Materials.* London: SAGE. Describes how to analyze visual material as part of the qualitative research process and also discusses computer-assisted analysis for qualitative research data.

Huberman, Michael and Miles, Matthew B. (eds) (2002) *The Qualitative Researcher's Companion.* London: SAGE. A collection of articles by experts in the field of qualitative research, this book has chapters on data analysis and interpretation.

Patton, Michael Quinn (2002) *Qualitative Research and Evaluation Methods.* London: SAGE. A thorough treatment of all aspects of qualitative research, the final chapters of this book have excellent information on the interpretation and analysis of findings.

Strauss, Anselm and Corbin, Juliet (1998) *Basics of Qualitative Research: Techniques and Procedures for Developing Grounded Theory.* London: SAGE. A sound reference book on all aspects of grounded theory, it also focuses on how to evaluate the results of research studies.

15 Analyzing Numerical Data

Learning Objectives

1 Explore the difference between measurement scales
2 Describe the data analysis process including the pre-analysis review, coding and the entry of data
3 Explain descriptive statistical analysis including frequency, central tendency and dispersion
4 Explain how statistical tests can be used to prove an hypothesis false

---

WHAT ARE YOUR VIEWS OF THE BRITISH NATIONAL PARTY? WOULD YOU REALLY SAY?

Research by YouGov, an internet-only research group, has found that responses to sensitive questions will vary based on the media through which they are asked. In the UK they found that people are more likely to give socially 'wrong' answers on an online survey than with other survey formats. They also found the same response pattern in the USA. People in both countries are much more likely to respond to questions with illiberal answers online. Does this mean that researchers are finally getting the 'real' answers? Not necessarily, the fact that online surveys pay and can be completed quickly and easily has resulted in a group of people that participate in many online survey forums and may be skewing results. Online surveys now comprise 20 per cent of UK fieldwork in market research, even though only 63 per cent of households have internet access.

Question: Is the fact that companies are relying heavily on online surveys a matter for concern?

Source: Grande, 2007

15.1 Measuring Differences

Qualitative marketing research methods analyze consumers' psychographic characteristics including attitudes, opinions, values and ideas. These characteristics are difficult to express using numbers. On the other hand, quantitative marketing research methods analyze consumers' current or future behavior which can be expressed using numbers or percentages. When analyzing the data from quantitative research, consumers' physical characteristics such as gender, age, religion, ethnicity, income, education level, or even their height, hair color or weight, can be quantified. In addition, consumers' behavior can be quantified by frequency of purchase, consistency of purchase, place of purchase or size of purchase. Using statistical analysis researchers will explain behavior using numbers rather than words. Furthermore, if the sample for a population is sufficiently large and properly selected, researchers will be able to say with some certainty that the research findings are probably true for the total population (Hellebusch, 2006).

15.1.1 Scales of measurement

A computer will be used to tabulate the results of a survey, but the findings will still need to be analyzed. Before the methods of analysis can be discussed it is important to understand measurement scales, as the type of scale used in designing the answer will affect the type of statistical analysis used.

People use measurement scales on a daily basis. When consumers decide to purchase a rug for their bathroom floor, they may decide to use their own feet and pace out the floor space to be covered. When they go to the store they can again measure off the space using their feet and find a rug that fits. Of course it is simpler to use a measuring tape already marked off with standard units of measurement. In research it is also easier to use standard measurement scales. The four standard measurement scales researchers have available are nominal, ordinal, interval and ratio. There is a very good reason why it is important to understand the differences in measurement scales, as the choice of statistical procedure to analyze the data will depend on the scale being used.

The nominal scale
The nominal scale is used for characteristics that can be defined as different states of being. Male and female, for example, are two characteristics that are measured by the nominal scale. There are only the two states and a research participant must be one or the other. University graduate and non-university graduate are another example. A research participant can be one or the other, but not both. Nominal data are usually analyzed by simply counting the responses. A research study might find that of a study of 100 people on their favorite hobbies, 62 were male and 38 were female. The report might also state that of the 100 participants, 78 did not graduate from university while 22 did graduate. When analyzing central tendency, the mode will be used.

Ordinal measurement scale
The ordinal scale is used when there is not just an absolute difference, such as male or female, but rather a degree of difference, such as preference. A question using the nominal scale would be 'What type of pizza do you prefer?' This question, using an ordinal scale, would ask consumers to rank order their favorite types of pizza. Analyzing these data would provide a ranking such as participants' favorite type of pizza topping is pepperoni, followed by cheese, and then

sausage. While this measure provides information on ranking, what this type of measurement does not show is how much more popular pepperoni pizza is than cheese or sausage. When analyzing central tendency, the median will be used.

The interval scale

Using an interval scale will provide more information than just ranking. An interval scale adds a unit of measure with a start and finish, and the difference between each unit of measurement being the same. Researchers construct the scale by creating the starting and ending point of the scale and the units of measurement. In this type of ranking participants are given a choice of degrees. The question might ask if the pizza was very delicious, delicious, good, all right, or inedible. While the construction of the scale is arbitrary, it is assumed that the amount of difference between 'delicious' and 'very delicious' is the same as the amount of difference between 'good' and 'all right'. With this type of data researchers will be able to provide an average opinion of the pizza by all survey participants.

When constructing questions that will provide interval data, researchers can use a category rating scale, Likert scale or differential scale. A category rating scale gives a rating such as excellent, very good, good, poor, very poor, awful. In a Likert scale, five to seven choices are given that measure a participant's opinion or agreement with a statement. This could be strongly agree, agree, undecided, disagree, strongly disagree. A number is attached to each category that allows researchers to provide an average. A semantic difference scale is also commonly used in interval measurement question construction. In this type of measure two opposing statements are made with seven points in between. A participant chooses where they stand on the subject by circling a number. An example of a semantic difference scale is an answer to the question 'How would you rank our pizza?' The possible responses would be given as: delicious 1-2-3-4-5-6-7 inedible. When analyzing central tendency, the mean will be used.

The ratio scale

A ratio scale has given start and end points that already exist and are not created by researchers. A consumer's weight is an example of a ratio scale, as no person's weight can be zero pounds. There is also an upper limit on what a human can weigh and still survive. On a ratio scale there is also the ability to measure exactly the difference between units. A person who weighs 200 pounds is exactly twice as heavy as a person who weighs 100 pounds. A person who spends $900 on food per month spends exactly twice as much as a person who spends $450 on food. The use of the ratio scale in marketing is not as common as the use of the interval scale because marketing often asks questions about peoples' preferences and opinions using an interval scale. When analyzing central tendency, the geometric mean will be used.

15.2 The Process of Quantitative Data Analysis

After a survey has been conducted, researchers will be faced with either a pile of survey forms or, if the survey was entered directly into a computer, an electronic file. Researchers must now begin the task of analyzing the data. This process of data analysis will begin with a pre-analysis stage where researchers will review the data, including its validity, completeness and accuracy. They will then code any open-ended questions and enter all the data into a computer software program.

Using an electronic form can save time at this stage because the data will already have been entered onto a computer. Another advantage to online surveys is that researchers can monitor the data as they arrive (see the box below). However, the electronic file still needs to be reviewed for completeness and any responses to open-ended questions must be coded. This is also true of online forms that ask for complaints or suggestions (Thomas, 2006).

ONLINE SURVEYS: SOME ISSUES ARE THE SAME – HOWEVER SOME ARE UNIQUE

Conducting a survey online can save a company time and money. However, when conducting a survey online the suggestions that make a survey successful are the same. The need for careful planning, an understanding of the sample population and well written survey questions hold true whatever the delivery mechanism. Yet some extra advice needs to be provided to researchers conducting online surveys.

First of all participants must be notified that the survey form is available online. For existing customers, web links on a company website work well. For potential customers emails can be sent.

Second, participants can be encouraged to finish the survey form by showing them their progress. Since they do not have the ability to page ahead as on a paper survey form, a visual, such as a percentage bar, will let survey takers know how far along they are in the survey.

Third, because survey takers can type in responses, researchers may be tempted to add many open-ended questions. However, such questions take more time and effort for participants to answer. Too many open-ended questions may result in participants abandoning the survey.

Finally, online surveys allow researchers to monitor progress. They can check to see how many participants have completed the survey and how long each survey took to complete. They can also see how many participants did not complete. If the completion rate is too low, the survey may need to be adjusted. In addition, if not enough participants are finding the survey the manner of notification may need to be changed.

Source: Kottler, 2005

After pre-analysis the next step in statistical analysis is determining the frequency of responses. The analysis may be of a single variable or the frequency of more than one variable could be cross-tabulated. Once this has been completed, the data are analyzed for central tendency by calculating the mode, median or mean. Researchers will also want to know how widely the participants' responses varied from each other, so dispersion will be examined by calculating standard deviation, range and variance.

Finally, statistical tests will be performed to determine if differences in the data are due to chance or random error, or if such a difference has a statistical significance (see Table 15.1). Statistical testing can include Chi square, F-test and t-test. This statistical testing will be used to determine if the hypothesis is supported. For example, the researchers may have hypothesized that more men than

Table 15.1 Data analysis process

Pre-analysis	Review data for validity, completeness and accuracy
	Code open-ended questions
	Enter the data into a computer software program
Analysis of responses using descriptive statistics	Calculate:
	Frequency
	Central tendency
	Dispersion
Analysis using inferential statistics	Hypothesis testing for statistical significance
	Chi-square testing for goodness-of-fit

women attend the cinema. If the data show that men buy fewer theater tickets than women, statistical testing will confirm if this difference is significant enough for the alternative hypothesis to be supported. A study may contain more than one hypothesis as long as questions are written to address each (O'Neil, 2007).

15.2.1 Pre-analysis of survey data

Once survey research has been conducted, the first task confronting a marketing researcher is to review the questionnaire forms. After this review is completed the researcher is ready to code any open-ended questions. The final step in the pre-analysis process is to enter the data into a computer software program.

Review

Researchers may have taken great care in deciding upon the research question. In addition, the questionnaire form may have been painstakingly written and tested. However, unless the survey sample was very small with only a few participants, the actually conducting of the survey will have been out of the control of researchers. For an administered survey form, assistants will have been hired to conduct the survey. Self-administered forms will have been completed without any help from researchers or assistants. Because of these facts, the survey forms must be checked for validity, completeness and accuracy before the data are entered.

The issues that arise when validity is considered are whether the survey was actually conducted by an assistant and whether a participant was eligible for the survey. It is unfortunate but true that sometimes those people hired to conduct surveys may actually have completed the forms themselves. This may be due to frustration, because of an inability to obtain the cooperation of potential participants, or it may be due to dishonesty. Whichever might be the case, all forms should be checked to see if it looks as if an assistant has completed them. Clues would include answers that are extremely random or answers that are constantly duplicated. In addition, the demographic portion of a form should be checked to ensure that any eligibility requirements, such as age and education level, have been respected.

Not all survey forms will have every question answered and so should be checked for completeness. A form may be incomplete because a participant chose not to answer some of the questions or it may not have been completed because of time constraints. In addition, the form may have consisted of more than one page and a participant may not have noticed additional questions on a second page. Researchers must then decide what percentage of completion is required for a form to be included in the study or for it to be discarded.

Lastly, forms must be checked for accuracy. Researchers must review the forms to determine if the answers can be read and understood. They should be able to easily distinguish which answers have been marked. In addition, the answers to open-ended questions should be able to be deciphered.

Coding survey data

After the forms have been checked for validity, completeness and accuracy, they are ready for data entry. Since surveys are a form of quantitative research, the data need to be entered as numbers that can then be statistically analyzed. Close-ended questions should have been precoded on the survey form with the numbers that will be entered into the computer.

However, open-ended questions will require manual processing before they are ready to be entered onto the computer. To accomplish this task, researchers should begin by listing all the answers that were given to an open-ended question, and then consolidate the responses. For example, if a question asked for reasons for shopping at Crossroads Mall, the responses might be consolidated into the groupings of 'convenient location', 'variety of stores', 'parking' and 'special events'. Each grouping is then assigned a numerical code and it is this code that is entered into the computer.

Data entry

If a survey is web-based, the data entry step is not required as the answers are entered automatically. Some paper forms are now designed so that the results can be electronically scanned. Data entry for traditional paper survey forms can be performed by anyone with the skill to use a computer. A software package such as SPSS can be used for statistical analysis. SPSS is commonly used in business and the social sciences. The program is user friendly with built in tutoring features.

15.3 Data Analysis using Descriptive Statistics

Once the data have been entered into the computer software program, marketing researchers are now ready to start the process of analyzing the data. They should never forget that the purpose of the analysis is to provide information that can be used for making strategic decisions (see the box below). There are two types of statistical analysis that can be used and these are descriptive and inferential. Descriptive analysis collects, summarizes and presents a set of data. This type of analysis is simple for researchers to conduct and for management to understand.

IS GREEN PURCHASING HERE TO STAY? GLOBAL STATISTICS HELP MARKETERS WITH STRATEGY

How do companies know if a trend is real? They watch the statistics that are compiled by research firms and stories in the media. Concern for the environment is not new. Green themed advertising campaigns started in the 90s but there wasn't much interest on the part of consumers. Therefore 'green' products didn't sell. But they do now, with companies from Airbus to Proctor & Gamble bringing products to market that are aimed at the environmentally aware consumer.

(Continued)

How did they know that the time was right to sell these products? The polls show that people are increasingly aware of the issue. In fact, a poll of UK and US consumers found that the change in attitude on environmental issues showed the largest shift of any research that the company has conducted. Who is greenest? A survey taken in 2006 by the Pew Research Center found that consumers in Japan, India, France and Spain were most concerned about environmental issues.

Source: Neff and Thompson, 2007 and Grande, 2007

Descriptive statistics help researchers to see patterns in research data. A basic concept used to analyze consumer characteristics and behavior is frequency, including one-way frequency and cross tabulation. Using frequency researchers can identify how many participants' responses were similar. A second concept is central tendency, which includes the mode, median and mean. In addition, dispersion of central tendency must be examined including range, variance and standard deviation.

Data analysis

- Frequency: one way, cross tabulation
- Central Tendency: mode, median, mean
- Dispersion: range, variance, standard deviation

15.3.1 Frequency

Frequency can be understood using the example of a survey question that asked why consumers shopped at Abdul's Sporting Goods store. The survey question may have provided the answers to choose from – good prices, the best selection and helpful service. If 1,000 people were surveyed Abdul would want to know what percentage of consumers selected each response. However, some people will not respond to a survey at all. In fact the response rate will differ based on cultural values (Lyness and Kropf, 2007).

The first issue faced by the researchers helping Abdul is that not all of the 1,000 survey forms may be useable as some of the participants may not have answered the question, while others may have attempted an answer but the mark they made is difficult to interpret. In addition, some respondents may not have completed the questionnaire. As a result, of the 1,000 survey forms completed perhaps only 950 will be useable. When the data are analyzed for one-way distribution (how many people responded to each potential answer to the question) it may be found that helpful service is the most frequent response. A distribution table of the data would look like Table 15.2 below.

This information will quickly inform Abdul of the ranking of the responses, with helpful service being top, followed by best selection and then good prices. However, it is difficult when just reading the numbers to understand how much more important to the participants was service over selection. Adding a percentage to the table makes the relationship between the responses easier to grasp as most people can see the relationships between percentages more quickly than

Table 15.2   Frequency table with percentages

	Number	Percentage
Helpful service	521	55%
Best selection	287	30%
Good prices	142	15%
Total	950	100%

Table 15.3   Frequency table for question allowing multiple responses

	Number	Percentage
Helpful service	588	62%
Best selection	345	36%
Good prices	162	17%
Total	1095	115%

those between raw numbers. The percentage is calculated off of the total number of responses used (950) rather than the total number of respondents (1,000). The percentages show that helpful service is almost twice as important as best selection.

The survey question asking consumers for their motivation for shopping at Abdul's could have been designed to allow for multiple responses. The question would have read 'Which of these reasons are why you shop here?' In this case the numbers would look different as some people might tick more than one response. The responses look like Table 16.3.

Because the question allowed respondents to tick more than one answer, the total response is now 1,095. However, the percentage is still calculated on 950 respondents which is why when added together, the responses total more than 100 per cent.

These different frequency results demonstrate the importance of carefully planning the survey questions and answers. In the tables above, the ranking did not change. However it is possible that allowing multiple responses will change the frequency ranking. If more than one response is allowed, researchers may wish to ask respondents to rank them in preference. In this way respondents who tick both service and price can demonstrate which of the two is most important.

Cross tabulation

The first step in calculating frequency is to determine which responses were chosen most often. What one-way frequency analysis does not describe is how data collected in the survey are related. For example, Abdul may want to know the ages of the shoppers choosing each response. Cross-tabulation is a simple and yet powerful tool that can be used by researchers to understand how variables are related to each other. The term 'cross-tabulation' results from the fact that one variable is crossed with another to see the relationship between the two.

In the example of Abdul's Sporting Goods store, the researcher knows that the reasons people shop at the store are service, selection and price. The researcher will have also asked various

Table 15.4 Cross tabulation table

Age:	18–29		30–49		50+		Total	
Service	122	34	187	65	104	34	445	46%
Selection	51	14	50	17	24	41	205	21%
Price	185	52	51	18	76	25	312	32%
Totals	358		288		204		962	
	38%		25%		32%			

demographic questions, including the age of each shopper. If Abdul wants to target young shoppers aged 18–29 to shop at his store, he will be most interested in the opinions of young people. By using cross-tabulation he can determine what the main motivating variable is for this age group. (see Table 15.4 above).

With a small sample, tabulation can be handled with simple math and the table could be constructed manually. More often a software program such as SPSS will be used. The advantage of using this kind of software is that the data can be cross-tabulated using multiple variables simultaneously. The cross-tabulation in Table 15.4 shows that, for all shoppers, service is most important at 46 per cent. However, the group aged 18–29 considers price as being most important at 52 per cent, while for shoppers aged 30–49 service is most important. For shoppers aged 50 plus, selection was most important at 41 per cent.

15.3.2 Central tendency

People often use the term 'average' when they are referring to a middle ranking. However there are a number of ways to measure average or central tendency that include mode, median, and mean.

Mode

Mode refers to the response that is the most common for all participants. Mode is used when describing nominal data, which can have one of either two states of being, but not both. In the research for Abdul's store discussed above, the respondents may have also been asked their gender. The question might have found that of the 950 survey participants who responded to the question on gender, 505 were male and 445 female. Obviously gender cannot be averaged, as the answer would always be exactly half or 500. Instead the concept of mode (most frequent response) is used, with the mode being male instead of female.

Median

Median is the response that measures the halfway point of the responses. Median is used in ordinal data, where there is a degree of difference. In the question on motivation for shopping at Abdul's, best selection is the median response as one answer received more responses and one answer received less responses. Median cannot be used when analyzing nominal data as there are only two possible responses so there cannot be a midpoint.

Mean

Mean is the average of all of the responses. The mean is calculated by adding all the responses and then dividing by the number of participants. If the survey participants were asked their age, it would be simple to determine mean age. The ages of all the participants would be added together and then divided by the number of responses, or 950.

Central tendency measures

- Mode: the most frequent response
- Median: the response that divides a series of responses in half
- Mean: the average of the responses

15.3.3 Dispersion measures

One of the issues that researchers must analyze is how varied the responses are from the calculated mean. To do so researchers use the concepts of range, variance and standard deviation. These statistical concepts allow researchers to compare the dispersions of two sets of data. While two sets of data may at first seem similar because they have the same mean, researchers know that the individual responses that comprised the mean may be dispersed very differently. The ways to examine this issue of dispersion of responses include range, variance and standard deviation. The amount of dispersion may depend on the way the rating or ranking question was structured (Coelho and Esteves, 2007).

Range

Range is the easiest dispersion measure to understand and tells researchers how widely answers are dispersed. To calculate range, the smallest value expressed in the survey is subtracted from the highest value. This gives the range of responses. The data below in Table 15.5 give the amount of money spent on lunch by male and female students. Both have the same mean of 11 whether the currency is in dollars or pounds or Euros, and yet just by looking at the figures there is obviously a difference between the spending patterns of male and female students. To calculate range, the lowest figure is subtracted from the highest figure. The range for the females is 6, while the range for the males is 16.

Table 15.5 Calculation for range

	Females	Males
	7	3
	9	5
	9	8
	10	9
	11	10
	12	11
	12	13
	13	14
	16	15
	13	22
Mean	11	11
Range	9	19

Variance

The variance of the set of numbers around the mean helps researchers to understand how dispersed each individual response is from the mean. One way to calculate this number would be to subtract each individual data number from the mean and then add the differences. However, this will not work because the negative numbers and the positive numbers will always cancel each other out and the answer will be zero. To solve this dilemma, the difference between each individual data number and the mean is first squared and the answers are then summed. The final step is to divide the sum by the number that is one less than the number of responses. This step allows researchers to compare the variance between data sets that have different numbers of responses. The final number calculated is the variance.

Table 15.6 Calculating variance

	Females		Males	
	7	16	3	64
	9	4	5	36
	9	4	8	9
	10	1	9	4
	11	0	10	1
	11	0	11	0
	12	1	13	4
	12	1	14	9
	13	4	15	16
	16	2.5	22	21
	11.0	56	11.0	264
Variance		6.22		29.33
Standard deviation		2.49		5.42

Most females and males spend between the mean plus or minus the standard deviation. Females: 8.51–13.49, Males: 5.58–16.42.

Standard deviation

The higher the variance, the more dispersed are the responses in the set of data. As can be seen by looking at the data, the males' spending pattern is more dispersed. The problem with the variance number is that being squared, the number no longer has any meaning. If the square root of the variance is calculated the answer will be the standard deviation, which is in the same units, currency, as the original numbers.

If the standard deviation is added and then subtracted from the variance, this tells researchers that this range is where most responses will fall. The standard deviation for the females is 3.72 and for the males is 4.05. If the standard deviation is greater in one data set than the other, then the responses provided by the participants in that sample will have varied more widely. While this is easy to see in the small sample of ten numbers, it would not be easy to see in a set of 950 numbers.

If these standard deviation numbers are then added and subtracted from the mean, they will show where most of the responses lie. For females, this is between the price of 8.51 and 13.49.

For males, it is 5.58 and 16.42. Two sets of data can have the same mean but still have very different standard deviations.

15.4 Data Analysis using Inferential Statistics

The other type of statistical analysis that researchers can conduct uses inferential statistics. These statistical methods go beyond just describing the data discovered during the research. Of course, no marketing research study that uses a sample can 'prove' anything with absolute certainty. What the analysis of quantitative research data can do however is indicate whether an hypothesis is most likely to be false. Using inferential statistics, researchers can perform statistical tests to determine if responses from a sample can be used to draw conclusions about an entire population. In fact more than one statistical test can be conducted on the same set of data (Park et al., 2007).

15.4.1 Statistical testing process

The first step in using statistical analysis to indicate the truth of a hypothesis is to state the hypothesis, or guess, about some characteristics of consumers or their behavior. The research methodology will then be designed to ensure that these characteristics, whether about people or their behavior, are measured. Once the research study has been completed and the data entered onto a computer, the measured variable for the sample of participants will be compared with the expected outcome stated in the hypothesis.

The type of test that will be used to determine if the difference is significant depends on both the type of measurement that was used and the type of resulting data. These tests can be used on their own or in combination (van Wezel and Potharst, 2007). The z-test is used to determine if the differences in proportions or mean of characteristics are statistically significant or not, while the t-test also looks for statistical significance but between the means of two unrelated groups. The z-test is used in marketing when one segment of consumers is being studied.

15.4.2 Hypothesis

An hypothesis is a guess that is made by the company or individuals commissioning the research. Perhaps an academic publisher has come up with a new textbook product that can be read electronically. The question is whether they should spend the money to develop and introduce the product? Qualitative research has indicated that many students would be interested in this product. However, the finance department of the company has stated that at least 20 per cent of students will need to purchase the product to make it financially viable.

This first hypothesis is the null hypothesis and will be stated as what the company does not wish to be true. (The symbol H_0 is used to designate the null hypothesis.) The null hypothesis is considered true until proven false. For the publisher in this example the null hypothesis is that less than 20 per cent of students will be interested in purchasing the product. The alternative hypothesis would be that 20 per cent or more of students will be interested in purchasing the product. (The alternative hypothesis is designated H_1.) One hypothesis is the opposite of the other and so both cannot be true.

Formulas for stating the hypotheses

H_0: π = < 0.20
H_1: π = $\geq$ 0.20

The statistical tests cannot be used to prove the hypothesis true. This is impossible as the only way to know with 100 per cent accuracy if an hypothesis is true is to survey the entire population. If the null hypothesis is proved false, then the alternative hypothesis (that 20 per cent or more of students will be interested) can be accepted as being true. The null hypothesis needs to be expressed in such as way that its rejection leads to the acceptance of the preferred conclusion – developing the new product. These stated hypotheses are an example of a one-tailed test, the kind most commonly conducted in marketing research.

The publishing company surveyed a sample of 1,100 students (more than the sample size of 1,024 that would have been needed to make the study valid at 95 per cent confidence) and found that 22 per cent stated they were interested. While this is over the required 20 per cent, researchers know that taking a sample will never be as accurate as asking everyone. However, the question remains – if 22 per cent is so close then is it simply error that made it over 20 per cent?

Therefore, the next step is to calculate whether the difference between the hypothesized outcome and the survey outcome is statistically significant. While the word 'significant' usually means important, in statistics it means 'true'. The test to find if it is significant would be automatically calculated by a statistical computer software program such as SPSS. However, the formula is actually easy to understand. To calculate the significance all that is needed is three numbers: the hypothesized percentage, the sample percentage, and the standard error of the percentage. Researchers already have two of these, the hypothesized and sample percentages. To calculate the standard error of the percentage, the researcher would use the following formula.

Formula for calculating standard error

σ_p = $\sqrt{\pi\,(1 - \pi)/n}$
σ_p = $\sqrt{.20\,(1 - .20)/1100}$ = .010

Using this number as the standard error, the z-score can be calculated.

Formula for calculating z-score

Z = $(p - \pi_h)/\sigma_p$
2.0 = $(.20 - .22)/.010$

This z-score (sometimes referred to as the p-value) can be compared with the numbers found on a table of z-scores to determine if it indicates that the null hypothesis is not true. It is standard procedure to have the computer software do the comparison. However, a rough calculation can be done by remembering the standard numbers for confidence levels. For a 95 per cent confidence level the number was 1.96 and for 97 per cent confidence 2.58. The z-score of 2.0 tells the researchers that they can not say with 95 per cent confidence that the null hypothesis is not proved false. Therefore the company will not go ahead with production. Interestingly, if the company wanted to be 97 per cent confident – the company would not start production. The same type of calculations can be done for comparing a hypothesized mean and the mean that was found by surveying the sample.

Steps in the analysis process

- State the hypothesis
- Conduct the research
- Compare the measured value with the hypothesized value
- Decide the necessary level of confidence
- Choose a statistical test for significance
- Calculate the test value
- State a conclusion and any recommendations

15.4.3 Level of confidence

The possibility that the null hypothesis will be rejected as false when it is indeed true is called a Type I Error, which is signified by using the lower case Greek alpha (α). The amount of possibility that a Type I error has been committed is called the level of significance of the statistical test. Researchers must decide on the amount of risk they are willing to tolerate of committing a Type I error. There are standard levels of risk that are considered acceptable when conducting statistical analysis. These standard levels, or value of α, are 0.01, 0.05 or 0.010. Another way to express these values is that there is a 1 per cent, 5 per cent or 10 per cent chance of the hypothesis being rejected when it is indeed true. The traditional value used by researchers is 0.05, or there is a 5 per cent risk that the null hypothesis is false, but it isn't rejected.

Another type of error, Type II, happens when the null hypothesis is not rejected when it should be. The Greek letter beta (β) is used for this type of error. A statistical test to check for Type I errors is called a one-tailed test, while a statistical test to check for Type II errors is called a two-tailed test. Most researchers will only use a one-tailed test.

15.4.4 Chi-square tests

The Chi-square test is used for what is called 'goodness-of-fit' when analyzing frequencies of responses in a frequency table using cross-tabulation. Marketers often want to know if a there is a relationship between a specific group of consumers and some preference for a product benefit. Marketers also may want to know if men or women prefer the product in a smaller size bottle, or they may want to know if young consumers would prefer the product in a new color. While these statements could be presented as hypotheses this is not necessary. In fact, when using Chi-square all researchers need to do is think – the computer will handle the rest.

Using the example of the publishing company and the textbook, the company believes that men will be much more interested in the product than women. The researchers will use SPSS to calculate a cross-tabulation of preference (yes or no) with gender (male or female). The computer, based on the proportion of men to women in the sample, will calculate what the expected percentages would be if there was no difference in preference versus if gender makes a difference.

It would be simple to compare these numbers using percentages if the groups were all the same size. However, this is unlikely to be true. For this reason the Chi-square test can be used to determine if there is a statistically valid difference in the relationship between age and reason.

Summary

1   Quantitative research produces statistical findings that, if the sample is sufficiently large and has been carefully chosen, can be used to support a null hypothesis. The measurement scales that can be used are nominal, with two states of being, and ordinal, which also shows preference. In addition, interval scales provide a standard unit of measurement, and ratio, which has a given start and end point.

2   The process of qualitative data analysis starts with the pre-analysis of data including review, coding and data entry. Descriptive statistical analysis includes frequency, central tendency and dispersion. Inferential analysis includes analysis of statistical significance used to test an hypothesis.

3   Frequency analysis provides a count of the frequency of responses. Cross tabulation shows the number of responses along with at least one other variable. Central tendency analysis of the data includes the mode (or most frequent response) the median response, and the mean (or average). Dispersion measurements include range, variance and standard deviation.

4   Data analysis can also be used to test the hypothesis, or guess, made before the research begins. The purpose of the analysis is to try to prove the hypothesis false (and the alternative hypothesis true) with a certain level of confidence. A z-test is used to determine if there is significance in the difference in the expected hypothesized result and the result and from the surveyed sample. A Chi-square test finds the goodness-of-fit in a frequency table between two variables.

Key Terms

continuous variables   variables whose units of measurement can always be cut into ever smaller units

discrete variables   variables that can be measured in distinct units

interval scale   measurement scale with standard units of distance between preference choices

nominal scale   measurement scale with only two states of being

ordinal scale   measurement scale that provides information on preference

ratio scale   measurement scale with a natural start and end point

Discussion Questions

1 What survey questions would you ask about students' attitudes toward downloading music using all four measurement scales?
2 What type of errors can be found when survey forms are reviewed before data entry?
3 What kind of problems can result from researchers skipping the pre-analysis stage?
4 Which variables would you cross-tabulate with students' opinions on the ethics of downloading music: age, gender, postal code, income, or education level? Why should you test for goodness-of-fit?
5 How would you describe the mode, median and mean of the answers to a question on income level?
6 If a study finds men and women spend the same mean amount of money on clothes, what additional information would standard deviation supply?
7 Why do researchers try to prove the null hypothesis false rather than true?
8 Why does a student need to know about statistical testing even if he or she doesn't understand how the math is calculated?

Recommended Reading

Foster, Jeremy, Barkus, Emma and Yavorsky, Christian (2006) *Understanding Advanced Statistics*. London: SAGE. This book provides an explanation of advanced statistical models used for analysis that can be conducted using computer programs.

Good, Phillip I. and Hardin, James W. (2006) *Common Errors in Statistics (And How to Avoid Them)*. Chichester: Wiley. A more advanced treatment of statistics, with an emphasis on the mathematics behind statistical theories.

Kault, David (2003) *Statistics with Common Sense*. Westport, CT: Greenwood. Introduces statistical concepts through their application in real life without overly emphasizing the theory behind the statistics.

Lee, Eun Sul and Forthofer, Ron N. (2006) *Analyzing Complex Survey Data*. London: SAGE. A thorough approach to the many issues involved in analyzing qualitative data, including variance estimation, data requirements and preliminary analysis.

Levine, David M. and Stephan, David F. (2005) *Even You Can Learn Statistics: A Guide For Everyone Who Has Ever Been Afraid of Statistics*. Upper Saddle River, NJ: Pearson Prentice Hall. Starts with an explanation of key statistical terms and then describes the types of statistics, analysis, testing and presentation of statistical findings.

Stevens, Robert E. (2006) *Concise Encyclopedia of Church and Religious Organization Marketing*. Binghamton, NY: Best Business Books. This book is a good reminder that marketing is now used by religious organizations. Chapters on survey research and analysis are included.

16 Report Writing and Presentation

Learning Objectives

1 Explore the importance of the written research report
2 Describe the organization of the four sections of the written report
3 Explain how to write a professional research report
4 Discuss how best to communicate information during an oral presentation

INTERNATIONAL AUTOMAKERS ARE LISTENING IN

Ford, Chrysler, and Toyota all have a new way of researching consumers' attitudes and preferences: they are researching blogs. Ford is using BrandIntel, a research company located in Toronto, to track what consumers are saying about Ford's styling and performance plus their overall impressions of the company. To obtain this information BrandIntel monitors daily conversation in blogs and discussion groups, looking for comments on over 200 product attributes. Chrysler also uses the services of online marketing research firms. However, Chrysler focuses on monitoring the views of influential auto enthusiasts. They use this information or early 'buzz' about their autos to design their ad campaigns. Meanwhile Toyota uses a company called Buzz Metrics to monitor what is being said about their models. Toyota believes that what is said on blogs and in discussion groups is so influential in motivating consumers to purchase that their new FJ Cruiser SUV was introduced without using any traditional media.

Question: With the growth in new ways to gather consumer opinions online, should the information and recommendations from a research company be presented in some other format than the traditional written and oral report?

Source: Halliday, 2007

16.1 The Importance of a Written Report

Marketing researchers do not conduct research just for the sake of 'knowing'. Research is conducted to find a solution to a problem. Even though the data have been collected and analyzed, marketing researchers' work is still not done. After all, the analysis that the marketing researchers have completed does not solve management's problem. Instead, it is the raw material that provides the insights that researchers will use to make the recommendations that will solve the problem (Schlaikjer, 2007). Once researchers have completed the analysis and developed the recommendations, the next step is to communicate this information in a written and oral format that is both understandable and actionable.

Researcher responsibilities after completion of a research study

- Analyze data for relevance to research question
- Make recommendations for action based on the data
- Prepare a written and oral report to communicate the data, analysis and recommendations

16.1.1 Reasons for preparing a report

Unfortunately, too often researchers do not allocate enough time or importance to this last step of report preparation. Perhaps this is because researchers enjoy the research process more than report preparation and writing. As a result, researchers might simply prefer to move on to the next research project.

However, there are important reasons why a written report is necessary. First the report gives legitimacy to any recommendations by describing the research methodology. There is also a need to preserve information for the future. A report also communicates recommendations while providing documentation that can be used to clarify any misunderstandings. After all, the company that commissioned the research will be paying for recommendations that can be implemented to improve their performance, rather than just facts based on findings (Schultz, 2005).

Of course today there are other methods used to present research findings than a traditional written report. For example, reports can be prepared in the form of videos. This type of report is more common when conducting research with trendy products and young research participants. A video can capture 'attitudes' that are difficult to communicate in writing.

Reasons for a written report

- Explanation of research terminology and methodology
- Preservation of knowledge for future employees
- Documentation of actionable ideas based on research
- Clarification in case of misunderstanding

Explanation

Researchers must prepare a thorough report as management may not be able to understand the research methodology or the analysis process without a clear explanation. Terms such as 'stratified sample', 'projective techniques' or 'confidence level' may have no meaning to those whose responsibility it is to make decisions based on the research. Without an explanation of these terms the data will either be meaningless or misunderstood. Marketing research is also used in fields other than just consumer marketing. For example, a study done on political issues may well have a reader who is familiar with political strategy but unfamiliar with research methodology (Wring, 2006).

Preservation

A second reason for a written report is so that the knowledge that is obtained from the research continues to be available in the future. The research data and recommendations need to be maintained for both the marketing department and management. All companies have personnel changes and it is particularly common for marketing professionals to change positions frequently. Even the manager who commissioned the research may be promoted or leave the company. If there is no written report, the new manager will have no access to the knowledge that resulted from the research effort. In this case duplicate research may be conducted.

Documentation

An important purpose of the report is not only to report data or information. The written report is where the recommendations that result from the data and analysis are explained. These recommendations are the result of marketing researchers' analysis and interpretation of the data. These recommendations should be reported as actionable ideas that management should consider implementing.

Clarification

A final reason for writing the report is to ensure that the marketing researchers who have conducted the research have a document that details findings and conclusions in case of future misunderstanding. If management makes a decision that causes a future loss of revenue, it might be easy to state that the decision was based on research conducted by the marketing department. If there is a written document this misrepresentation can be clarified.

16.1.2 Types of research report

One size does not fit all when preparing research reports. More than one type of report may be needed. First, preliminary reports may be prepared to reassure those who commissioned the research that any efforts are on track. In addition, different groups of individuals will have a desire and need for varying levels of detail in the report. These groups include the marketing staff, management, company employees and participants. When preparing the various reports required researchers should consider carefully both the length of the report and how it is to be disseminated.

Preliminary report

If the research process spans a considerable length of time, a marketing researcher may prepare a brief preliminary report. A preliminary report can assure management that the research is preceding as planned. Having read the report, those who originally commissioned the reseach may decide to make changes in the methodology based on the preliminary results that have been presented. It is better to find that management wants changes before the process is complete. Of course a more detailed report will be prepared after the research and analysis have been finished.

Marketing staff report

A report being prepared for the marketing staff of an organization should contain all details of planning and methodology. Marketing researchers will be interested in all of the results and analysis, whereas management will only be interested in the main findings. This document will also be used for reference when planning future research.

Management report

A report prepared for the management of an organization will provide an overview of the research process. Management will generally not have the time or inclination to involve themselves in all the details of the process. However, they will usually want more information on any findings and recommendations. A shorter report that leaves out most of the technical details has the advantage of being less expensive both to write and reproduce. In addition, researchers should remember that a shorter report is more likely to be read and understood. Because managers are busy with many responsibilities, a long report may be put aside to be read 'later' when there is more time. Unfortunately, this 'later' (with ample free time for reading the report) may never arrive. Researchers working together with management from the beginning of the research process will prove advantageous for both (see the box below).

RESEARCH + MANAGEMENT GOALS = SUCCESS

Marketing research practice now emphasizes partnerships between researchers and management. Today researchers understand that their research must deliver more than numbers. Research findings must translate into concrete benefits for companies by helping them achieve business goals. If not, management will not commission research again. Ten tips to ensure that the research findings are seen as useful by management are:

1. Align market research with the marketing plan.
2. Link market research with business results.
3. Link business activities with future business results.
4. Integrate the voices of customers and employees into the strategy process.
5. Link customer attitudes with customer behavior.
6. Engage stakeholders in the research process.
7. Define success measures.
8. Track those measures.
9. Create a process for driving insight.
10. Create a process for driving improvements that produce action.

Source: Rosenberg and Wikstrom, 2006

Employee report

If the research report recommendations involve a change in the product line or targeting a new consumer segment, a company may wish to share the research that resulted in these recommendations with their employees. If the company wants the support of its employees in making changes, the employees need to understand the research that resulted in the recommendation.

However, company staff may not be interested in all the details of how the research was conducted, so the report needs to kept short. This type of report can also be posted on internal websites so it is shared with everyone in an organization.

Participant reports

When conducting the research, participants may have expressed a wish to learn about the outcome of the research. This is especially true if the research was undertaken for a nonprofit organization. If they are interested, participants should be provided with a short summary of the findings. After all, it is the participants who made the research possible. However, participants should not be provided with a copy of the recommendations as this is information that belongs to the company or organization commissioning the research.

16.2 Components of a Written Report

Reports may vary in writing style, but all reports should contain an introduction, a section on methodology, any findings and recommendations, and appendices (see Table 16.1 below). The introduction will identify those involved in the research and provide a brief overview of the contents. The next section of the report will explain the research question, objectives and methodology. The third section would discuss the research findings and recommendations. The appendices will provide background information that will more fully explain the report's contents.

16.2.1 Introduction

The introductory material contained in a report will include a title page, a letter of transmittal, a table of contents and an executive summary. The report will start with a title page that provides the name of the research study, the date of the report submittal, the names of the researchers, the names of the people or organization that commissioned the research and contact information for both groups. A letter or memo of transmittal will be included for marketing research studies that were conducted by an outside firm. The letter of transmittal formally concludes the research study and transmits ownership of the information contained in the report to the management of the company. The letter will also describe the legal ownership of any supporting material, such as tapes or completed survey forms. Because of the sensitive nature of some research, the commissioning organization may wish to have this information destroyed and in this case the letter will also state that this has been done.

The report should next contain a table of contents and should be indexed in some way so that each section can be easily found. This table of contents and the indexing are useful when the report is discussed in meetings, as each section can be easily and quickly located. A table of contents should not only list the main sections, such as the introduction and findings, it should also list the pages for any subtopics under the main topics. A table of contents should also provide a separate listing for any graphs and tables. The more detail that is provided in a table of contents, the more easily material can be found.

An executive summary quickly states the research question, the methodology, findings and conclusions. As most people in positions of management are under time pressure, the

Table 16.1   Components of research report

Introduction	Title page
	Letter or memo of transmittal
	Table of contents
	Executive summary
Research methodology	Introduction
	Research question
	Research objectives
	Sample selection
	Methodology
Findings and recommendations	Findings
	Recommendations
Appendices	Further details on sampling procedure
	Examples of methodology
	Full presentation of data

executive summary is essential to communicate quickly what a report contains. In addition, if the executive summary does not communicate effectively that the research methodology, findings and recommendations are important, the report may never be read. While included early on in the report, the executive summary is actually the last part that is written. An example is provided below.

SAMPLE EXECUTIVE SUMMARY

The report addresses the research question of 'What benefits do older travelers aged 62–75 want from a summer cruise experience?' The research objective was to design a vacation package that could be promoted to older travelers to increase market share and overall revenue by 10 per cent. The research found that activity preference depended on age, with older travelers preferring local cultural experiences. The recommendation is therefore that the company design holiday packages that have interactions with local people, such as the opportunity to learn local crafts.

16.2.2 Research methodology

The body of a report will include information on the research question, the research objectives and the research methodology. First, the problem that resulted in the research being conducted should be explained and the main and any secondary research questions should be stated. Since the findings and recommendations should directly address the research question, it should be highlighted from the body of the report by using bolding or italics so it can be easily referred to later.

The research objectives should also be explained. If they are not included, anyone reading the report may wonder why certain aspects of the research findings are not discussed further in the recommendations. For example, a research objective might have been to discover what percentage of current customers would be interested in buying a product but produced in new colors. The findings might contain information discovered during focus groups that customers are not aware of the company's promotional material. While this interesting fact might be included it will not be expounded upon, as it was not the purpose for conducting the research.

This section of the report should also describe the sample selection process. It should clearly explain how it was determined who should participate in the study and how these specific individuals were chosen from the total population. The legitimacy of the findings of a quantitative study depends upon whether the appropriate people were asked to participate. Even for qualitative research, if the wrong people are asked to participate in the research, the information will not be relevant. Therefore, to give legitimacy to the research findings and recommendations, it is important to describe the profile of participants and how they were selected.

Finally, the body of a report will explain the research methodology. For a survey this will include how the questionnaire was developed and tested. The report will also inform the reader of how many surveys were conducted, the method of contact and the dates of the research. For a focus group, similar information will be included but the name of the moderator will also be given. Readers may be less familiar with research techniques such as observation, projective techniques, and ethnography. If less well known research techniques have been used, the report will need to explain the methodology in more detail.

16.2.3 Findings and recommendations

The next section should discuss the research findings and recommendations. This section should include a summarization of the research findings. It should not provide all the data that were compiled during the research process, instead it should summarize the data that were used to develop the recommendations.

Research always provides a wealth of information. However, providing all the detail at this point in the report will only confuse the reader. For example, a survey might have been conducted to discover what activities consumers want to experience on a cruise ship. The research will have also asked survey respondents demographic information. During the analysis stage, researchers discovered that the geographic location of consumers' homes made no difference to preference. This fact will be stated. However, there is now no need to present a detailed breakdown of the home location of each participant in the body of the report. This data can be added in the appendix. On the other hand, if age was a very important variable that affected what activities people wanted to experience detailed information on age and activity preference should be included in the body of the report.

Recommendations are the most important component of a research report. After all, researchers are not paid just to collect data. They are also paid to analyze and interpret the data. The recommendations should directly address the research question and the research objectives. The concern that research proves useful and it doesn't just sit on someone's desk is not new (Christian, 1962). There has been increasing attention paid to this issue, as some business owners do not know how to use research for obtaining recommendations, as is shown in the example below.

16.2.4 Appendices

The final section of the research report will provide the full data that were obtained during the research process. These could be in the form of printed tables of data or the data can be provided on a CD. It will also include information that provides further details on the research sample and methodology. For example, details on the research sampling method can be explained. If referrals were used, the organization and individuals contacted can be listed. Examples of the research methodology such as survey forms, projective techniques or focus group scripts can also be included.

16.3 Writing a Professional Report

If the research report is going to be read, instead of just sitting on someone's desk, it is important that it be readable, interesting, and concise. A report that contains too much jargon, is poorly organized and is visually unattractive will not be read. This is especially the case because most people have multiple tasks to accomplish each day and will complete the easiest task first.

Readable

Issues that researchers should consider before writing a report must include the writing style. It is as important that a report be written in the right style as that it provides the right information. Before beginning to write a report, researchers should determine for whom the report is being prepared. If a report is being written for someone in the marketing department, a more professional style will be used. Here it can be assumed that the reader will be familiar with research terminology. However, if the report is being written for someone who runs a small business researchers must write in a more colloquial style while being careful to explain every term.

Interesting

Any report should also be interesting to read. Researchers should not just state facts but also give examples of interesting incidents that occurred during the research process. This type of detail will help to bring the information to life in the mind of the reader. Another way to add interest to a report is to use photos of the participants as they were involved in the research process. If this is not possible actual quotes can be used to give readers the feeling that they were at the research sessions.

Concise

A report should be kept as short as possible whilst still including all necessary information. It should also be arranged so that readers can process the amount of information they wish without necessarily reading the entire report. This can be accomplished by providing a well written executive summary and clearly labeling each section. In addition, headings and subheadings should be used throughout the report so that a specific issue can be found quickly.

16.3.1 Using visual material

The research findings section will contain a wealth of detailed numerical data. A report writer should use visuals to help communicate this information whenever possible. These visuals will assist readers in understanding the relationship between different sets of data. For example, readers can quickly visualize the relationship if 46 per cent of the respondents were female while 54 per cent were male. Readers would not have a problem understanding that slightly more participants were female than male.

However, if part of the research question addressed the age of the survey respondents this demographic data can be quite detailed. For example, if 12 per cent of the respondents who used the product were aged 18–22, 16 per cent were aged 23–29, 26 per cent were aged 30–39, 23 per cent were aged 40–49, 14 per cent were aged 50–59 and 9 per cent were 60 or older, it is extremely difficult for readers to visualize quickly and see the relationship among these numbers. To assist readers, such detailed data can be presented in the form of tables, charts and graphs.

Tables

A table simply lists numbers in rows by categories. Individual numbers will still be discussed in the body of the text. However, if the report writer uses a table they will not need to mention all the numbers. In the example given above, the writer might include in the body of the report that the largest age group of product users was 30–39, at 26 per cent, with 23 per cent of the users aged 40–49. The writer might then add that the smallest group was aged 60 or older, at 9 per cent. This comparison thus makes the point that most users are middle-aged. The remaining numbers, while still relevant in showing the distribution, should not be discussed in the body of the report as it makes it too difficult to read.

Pie charts

A pie chart is a visual method to present raw numbers and their relationship as percentages of a whole. A pie chart is simply a circle that is divided into areas that are represented by size. Pie charts are useful when representing numbers that make up a whole, such as the percentage of customers in different age groups. The different sections of a pie chart should be shown in various colors or in shades of gray for each group. Using color to differentiate the sections makes a pie chart easier to read and use.

Pie charts are static, in that they do not show changes over time. However, constructing more than one pie chart can be used to show how data have changed. For example, a pie chart can be constructed using current data on the age of product users and another can be constructed using data from a previous time period. These two pie charts are then easy for a reader to compare visually. Using the two pie charts would visually show the loss and gain between market segments. For example, younger purchasers' share could be seen to decrease which could forecast problems in the future.

Bar charts

Bar charts represent the values of different items so that these can be easily compared. The difference from pie charts is that bar charts do not necessarily show items that are part of a known whole. However, a bar chart will be used to show the relative size of the raw numbers of people in each age group who are product users. A bar chart can be shown with the bars vertical or horizontal. Bar charts can also be used to show changes over time by combining two sets of numbers collected at different dates. Each set of data can be shown next to each other on the chart.

Line charts

A line chart is designed to show changes in data over periods of time. Time is shown on the horizontal axis, while the numerical measurement is shown on the vertical axis. A line chart can show the percentage change in a product's sales by any measurement of time, such as by the day, month, season or year. The advantage of a line chart is that it can easily display movement in a value over time for more than one variable. For example, a company may collect sales data for five different products all of which could be shown on the same line chart. This could then reveal if there is any relation between changes in sales figures. For instance, when one product falls in sales, does another increase?

16.4 An Oral Presentation

An oral presentation is an opportunity for researchers both to explain and to 'sell' to management any research findings and recommendations. An oral presentation also allows researchers to provide a more effective description of the research methodology. This is because during an oral presentation a presenter, by observing their audience, can become aware of when they are encountering difficulties and can explain any confusing details more fully. In addition, a presenter can more clearly explain how report recommendations are related to any research findings. Finally, an oral presentation provides a means to clarify any misunderstandings about the research process.

Table 16.2   Sample outline for 30-minute presentation

Introduction 10%	Identify research participants
(3 minutes)	State time allotted for presentation
	Inform audience when questions can be asked
	Describe contents of presentation
Methodology 20%	Statement of research question and objectives
(12 minutes)	Brief explanation of sample selection procedure
	Description of methodology
Recommendations 60%	Description of findings
(18 minutes)	Recommendations for action
Conclusion 10%	Restatement of research question and main recommendation
(3 minutes)	Thanks and questions

Reasons for oral presentation

- A clearer explanation of methodology
- An oppportunity to explain the tie between research findings and recommendations
- An opportunity to clarify misunderstandings

16.4.1 Presentation structure

Presentations, just like written reports, must have a structure for two reasons. A structure helps the audience anticipate, and concentrate on, information that is of particular interest. A structure also helps a presenter stay on topic. No one would throw together a written report at the last minute as its poor organization would leave readers confused. It would be quite obvious to them that researchers had not taken time to present the material in a logical manner.

However, people do throw presentations together at the last moment and believe that their audience will not notice. Unfortunately a poorly prepared oral presentation will leave listeners just as confused as a poorly prepared written report. A well prepared presentation will have four major components: an introduction, methodology, findings and recommendations, and a conclusion. It is important when planning a presentation that most time is devoted to the recommendations section. Table 16.2 shows a sample outline for a presentation. Please note how the time has been divided to ensure that all topics will be covered before the conclusion of the presentation. Not all sections are given equal time as not all have equal importance.

Introduction

The presentation's introduction should identify the researchers and the commissioning company. It also should explain how long the presentation will take. During the introduction the presenter should inform the audience whether questions may be asked during the presentation or if the audience should keep their questions until the end. The introduction should then very quickly state the research question and describe what information the presentation will contain. For example, in a 30-minute presentation, the introduction should only last about three minutes.

Methodology

The section of the presentation on methodology is where the presenter will first state the research question and objectives. The presenter will then briefly inform the audience of how the research participants were selected. The presentation should not be used to describe the technical details of the sampling procedure. If the audience is interested, the report will contain all the necessary information. The purpose of describing the sampling procedure during the presentation is simply to give credibility to the findings and recommendations. The same holds true for the methodology, although more time should be spent on this topic so the audience will better understand how the findings were obtained. At this point in the presentation, a sample survey form can be distributed, projective techniques can be displayed, or a short video clip from a focus group can be shown.

Findings and recommendations

The presenter should spend more time presenting the findings and recommendations. They can use visuals such as graphs to quickly show to the audience what has been learned from the research. The presentation should never try to explain all the findings, as there simply isn't the time and the audience will get lost in the details. In addition, it is the presenter's responsibility to sift through all the findings to determine what is relevant for answering the research question. However, any findings that have an impact on the recommendations should be presented. The box below discusses how researchers and management can work together.

WHEN CAN RESEARCH BE CONSIDERED EFFECTIVE?

The answer to this question is clear to those market researchers who attended a seminar sponsored by Research Solutions, based in New Zealand. In their opinion, marketing researchers must 'come out from behind their pie charts' and become partners with the organization commissioning the research. What does such partnership mean? A true partnership was defined as exhibiting four factors.

First, the partnership must be based on trust. This means that management must trust more than the numbers. Of course a good market researcher will produce accurate findings but management must also trust the recommendations made by researchers.

Second, management must be willing to risk making changes based on research findings. This risk-taking approach must start at the research proposal stage. If the research proposal is written to allow only a conservative research approach, no breakthrough findings can possibly result.

Third, researchers must be in contact not just with management and marketing but also with other departments throughout a company. This must be the case because the recommendations that result from the research will impact on more than just the marketing department. The decisions will impact on finance, production and even human resources. If these departments do not trust the marketing researchers, they are more likely to argue against taking action based on their recommendations.

Fourth, management must accept that research findings are based on consumers' viewpoints, which can be surprising and sometimes uncomfortable for management to hear. It is not the responsibility of researchers to only bring good news.

Source: Focus Research, 2006

Conclusion

The conclusion to a presentation should be brief. The presenter should restate the research questions and the main recommendations. They should also thank the audience for their attention. The presenter should allow adequate time to answer any questions. The audience should also be informed of who it is they can contact if they have any questions in the future.

16.4.2 Presentation rules

A presentation has a different purpose than that of a written report. Giving a good presentation is a skill. However, presenting is a skill that can be learned. Everyone understands that being able to produce a clear, concise and interesting written report takes time and effort.

However, too often presentations are afterthoughts that people expect will happen automatically once they are in front of an audience. After all, while not everyone is skilled in writing, everyone can speak. Yet nothing could be further from the truth.

The general rules for an effective presentation are to be interesting, organized, and brief. A presentation should never be thought of as simply an oral presentation of all the information in a written report. The purpose of a presentation is not just to communicate information. After all, the audience at a presentation can read the written report for themselves. The purpose of a presentation is to 'sell' the ideas contained in the report by persuading an audience to act upon its recommendations. If an oral presentation is successful, the audience should be eager to read the written report for more details.

16.4.3 Unforgivable sins made during presentations

A successful presentation depends on preparation (see the box below). In addition a good presentation must be interesting. If it is not interesting, the research recommendations may be ignored because the audience simply lost their attention and they have not been heard. Everyone has probably had the experience of having to sit through a poorly prepared presentation. There are a few unforgivable sins that are guaranteed to result in a poor quality presentation.

BEFORE IT EVEN BEGINS

Everyone knows that a good presentation requires preparation. However, not everyone knows that there are other issues that must be considered if a presentation is to proceed flawlessly. These include:

Know the audience – including who they are, what they already know about the subject, what they want to learn from the presentation, and what management wants them to learn from the presentation.

Know the surroundings – including the comfort of the room, where the audience will sit, where the presenter will stand, whether the layout will allow the presenter to circulate around the room and the availability of flip charts, white boards and computer equipment.

Know the presentation – including the length of time required by practicing the presentation while using the required equipment, either alone or in front of others.

(Continued)

In fact, if possible a presentation should be practiced in front of a similar audience in the same room that will be used later. A practice presentation will mean that when the actual presentation is given, the presenter will be relaxed and able to concentrate on the audience instead of the presentation.

Source: Polonsky and Walker, 2004

A presenter should never insult an audience by reading anything longer than a short quotation. After all, the audience came to hear an oral presentation and they could have stayed in their offices to read the report on their own. In addition, audiences should never be frustrated by being shown any PowerPoint slides that can't be easily read. They should also never be bored – life is difficult enough without struggling to stay awake during a presentation. A presenter should never be so rude as to ignore the audience, nor should they overwhelm an audience with too much detail. Bear in mind that humans can only assimilate so much information at a time. Finally, a presenter should care about the information that is being presented. After all, if the presenter does not care, why should the audience?

Unforgivable sins committed during oral presentations

- Reading out the report
- Presenting PowerPoint slides that are unreadable
- Boring the audience
- Not interacting with the audience
- Using too much supporting material
- Not being emotionally involved with the presentation's contents

16.4.4 Using visuals during a presentation

Because of today's multimedia environment, people have become accustomed to receiving information in more than one form at the same time. It is now common for the evening news, and even other programs, to include a scroller at the bottom of the TV screen which people can read while they are watching the show. In addition to the broadcast and scrolling information on the main screen, a small inset screen will provide even more information. People seem to have no problem understanding these multiple sources of information. After all, in everyday life people routinely listen to music on their iPODs while performing other tasks (Sadler-Trainor, 2005).

So it is not surprising that people have a difficult time simply listening to a verbal presentation with no other visual interaction. Even the most interesting oral presentation may leave an audience with their minds wondering as to what they need to pick up at the grocery store on their way home from work. Therefore, using visual material not only helps to communicate the research information it also helps an audience stay focused on a presentation. Visuals used during a presentation may be computer generated. However low-tech methods, such as using a whiteboard, flipcharts, handouts and photographs, can be just as effective.

Low-tech methods

PowerPoint is probably the best known method of presenting visual information during oral presentations. However low-tech methods can also be used, including writing on a whiteboard, using flipcharts, and distributing handouts with relevant information and photographs of products or research participants. Whiteboards and flipcharts can be used to draw attention to important facts. If a surprising 78 per cent of consumers surveyed were unaware of a company's new promotional campaign, this number can be written out in red on the board or paper. The number becomes a clearly drawn exclamation point for this fact.

Even if a presenter chooses to use PowerPoint during a presentation, it is still useful to use a low-tech method such as handouts of the slides. If PowerPoint is not used handouts are even more important. Audience handouts, which should only list the main findings and recommendations, serve two purposes. They can be used to reinforce what a presenter is explaining and they can also provide a place for an audience to write notes as they are listening. Handouts can also be used that contain other material, such as maps of the study area or copies of the survey form or projective techniques. Photographs of the product under discussion can also assist an audience in better understanding the relevance of data. These photographs can be used as displays around the room where a presentation is taking place.

High-tech methods

High-tech presentation aids include the projection of an online source, videos and PowerPoint. Using a PC and a projector, presenters can bring up on screen material that is online. For example, if the research involved perception of a company's image the home page of that company's website can be shown. Video clips of participants, perhaps in focus groups or involved in ethnographic research, can also be used during a presentation. The use of videos is becoming increasingly common when making research presentations. Videos will bring the material to life in ways that other material cannot. Sometimes research studies have relied on videos to record events or behavior that are then analyzed. Of course these studies should include some of the video clips in the presentation (vom Lehn, 2006).

Benefits

PowerPoint slides can be used to help an audience comprehend information. However when these are badly used, which they often are, they will only confuse and distract an audience. There are some general rules on the use of PowerPoint that everyone should follow. First, presenters should remember that PowerPoint is best used for showing the summarization of data in charts and graphs. PowerPoint's worst use is for displaying large amounts of text. As PowerPoint is a visual media, the fewer words that are used the better. For example, a PowerPoint slide could be used to show an insightful quote made by a focus group participant. In addition, a few keywords that came up frequently as answers to an open-ended question on a survey can also be shown. These could then be discussed by the presenter. If PowerPoint is used, it should combine using slides with projecting other types of images.

Problems

PowerPoint is used inappropriately if too much information is put on a slide. Not only will the slide be difficult to read, it will also distract the audience from what is being said by the presenter. If a presenter gives an audience time to read a slide before a presentation resumes, it wastes time in that presentation. It will also mean the presenter will have to reestablish the connection with the audience when the presentation resumes. In fact inexperienced presenters sometimes use PowerPoint slides as a shield to hide behind. While providing an audience with factual information is important, it is the persuasive ability of a speaker that 'sells' an idea.

Summary

1   Marketing research is conducted to find answers to questions which will lead to recommendations for future action. This information is usually communicated through a written report and oral presentation. Reasons for the written report include the need to explain the research methodology, to preserve the knowledge for future employees, to document the actionable ideas that resulted from the research and to provide clarification in case of future misunderstandings. A researcher may wish to prepare reports of different lengths for other researchers, management, staff and participants.

2   A research report will consist of an introduction that will identify those involved in the research and provide a brief overview of the contents. The methodology section of a report will explain the research question, the objectives and the methodology. The third section, which is the most important part of the report, will discuss the research findings and recommendations. The appendices will provide background information that will more fully explain the report's contents.

3   A professional report is readable, interesting and concise. If this is not the case, the report will not be read and, therefore, the recommendations will not be implemented. Numerical data should be communicated using tables and charts. These will help readers visualize the relationship between groups of data.

4   An oral presentation is needed to explain the methodology, the relationship between the findings and the recommendation, and to provide an opportunity to clarify misunderstandings. The presentation will include an introduction, methodology and findings, recommendations and a conclusion. A presentation should be interesting, organized and brief. Both low-tech and high-tech visuals should be used to better communicate information.

Key Terms

executive summary   quickly states the research question, the methodology, findings and conclusions

management report   shorter report that leaves out most of the methodological details but provides more information on the findings and recommendations

participant report   a short summary of the findings sent to participants or posted on the organization's website

preliminary report written to assure management that the research is proceeding as planned

visuals graphic representation of numerical data that helps the reader understand the relationship between numbers

---

Discussion Questions

1 What types of reports would need to be prepared as the result of a survey study of students' sports preferences?
2 Why is the recommendations section considered the most important component of a written report?
3 If you had conducted a quantitative survey study on students' plans for their summer holiday, what type of information would you include in the appendices?
4 Why should the writer of a report be concerned that the report is readable, interesting and concise?
5 Why should quantitative information be presented using tables and charts?
6 Why should a researcher take the time to prepare an oral presentation when the audience can read the written report at a time and place of their choosing?
7 What type of confusion or misunderstandings could an oral presentation address in a research report with a controversial recommendation that students should have more holiday time?
8 Why should either low-tech or high-tech information be used when making an oral presentation?

Recommended Reading

Brown, Michael (2003) *Making Presentations Happen: A Simple and Effective Guide to Speaking with Confidence and Power.* London: Allan and Unwin. A book that provides advice on how to remove stress from the presentation process. It includes information on building audience rapport, persuading an audience and using technology.

Harvard Business School (2004) *The Results Driven Manager: Presentations that Persuade and Motivate.* Harvard: Harvard Business School Press. An excellent resource on all aspects of making presentations with helpful hints and problems to avoid.

Harvard Business School (2006) *Written Communications That Inform and Influence.* Harvard: Harvard Business School Press. Another excellent resource that covers all types of writing, including proposals and reports.

O'Hair, Dan, Rubenstein, Hannah and Stewart, Rob (2007) *A Pocket Guide to Public Speaking*. Bedford: St Martin's Publishing. A short, basic book that covers the steps involved in preparing and delivering a presentation.

Patten, Mildred (2001) *Questionnaire Research: A Practical Guide*. Los Angeles, CA: Pyrczak. Provides information not only on preparing questionnaires but also on the presentation of statistical findings and writing final reports.

Rea, Louis M. and Parker, Richard A. (2005) *Designing and Conducting Survey Research: A Comprehensive Guide*. San Francisco, CA: Jossey-Bass. A book on survey research written for the nonprofit and public sector. Includes information on writing reports that increase accountability.

Wolcott, Harry (2001) *Writing Up Qualitative Research*. London: SAGE. Exactly what the title states, this book focuses exclusively on writing up research findings and recommendations.

Bibliography

Agafonoff, Nick (2006) 'Adapting ethnographic research methods to ad hoc commercial research', *Qualitative Market Research: An International Journal*, 9 (2).

Alam, Ian (2006) 'Service innovation strategy and process: a cross-national comparative analysis', *International Marketing Review*, 23 (3).

American Marketing Association (2006) 'Marketing definitions'. Retrieved 13 February 2006 from www. marketingpower.com/content4620.php

Anderson, Jon (2007) 'Single servings: one-on-one interviews have their advantages', *Marketing News*, 15 May.

Andreasen, Alan R. (2002) *Marketing Research that won't Break the Bank: A Practical Guide to Getting the Information You Need*. San Francisco, CA: Jossey-Bass.

Andriani, Lynn (2007) 'Love for sale', *Publishers Weekly*, 28 May.

Arora, Neeraj (2006) 'Estimating joint preference: a sub-sampling approach', *International Journal of Research in Marketing*, 23.

Arthur, Damien (2006) 'Authenticity and consumption in the Australian Hip Hop culture', *Qualitative Market Research: An International Journal*, 8 (2).

AskCensus (2006) Retrieved 12 March 2006 from www.census.gov

Atalik, A. (2007) 'Customer complaints about airline service: a preliminary study of Turkish frequent flyers', *Management Research News*, 30 (6).

Auchmutey, Jim (2004) 'Mini-watermelons? "Sweet!" say consumers', *The Atlanta Journal-Constitution*, 8 July.

Balestrini, P., Gilbert, D. and Gamble, P. (2003) 'Is Europe a brand? An exploratory study of consumer perceptions', *Journal of International Marketing and Marketing Research*, 28 (3).

Barnett, Tim and Valentine, Sean (2004) 'Issue contingencies and marketers' recognition of ethical issues, ethical judgments and behavioural intentions', *Journal of Business Research*, 57.

Beckett, Whitney (2007) 'New technology weeds out pieces early', *Women's Wear Daily*, 17 January.

Berger, Arthur Asa (2004) *Ads, Fads and Consumer Culture*. Lanham, MD: Rowan and Littlefield.

Blohm, Michael, Hox, Joop and Koch, Achim (2007) 'The influence of interviews' contact behaviour on the contact and cooperation rate in face to face household surveys', *International Journal of Public Opinion Research*, 19 (1).

Boone, Jon (2007) 'Students faulted in job-hunt research', *Financial Times*, 8 May.

Brace, Ian (2004) *Questionnaire Design: How to Plan, Structure and Write Survey Material for Effective Market Research*. London: Kogan Page.

Bray, Hiawatha (2004) 'Firms guage attitudes online: service track perceptions of people, products'. Retrieved 29 May 2006 from www.boston.com/business/technology/articles

Burgess, Steven Michael and Steenhamp, Jan-Benedict (2006) 'Marketing renaissance: how research in emerging markets advances marketing science and practice', *International Journal of Research in Marketing*, December.

Carson, David, Gilmore, Audrey, Perry, Chad and Gronhaug, Kjell (2001) *Qualitative Marketing Research*. London: SAGE.

CASRO (2007) 'Survey research databases'. Retrieved 19 February 2007 from www.casro.org/surveyres data.cfm

Canniford, Robin (2006) 'Moving shadows: suggestion for ethnography in globalised cultures', *Qualitative Market Research: An International Journal*, 8 (2).

Chen, Qimei, Rodgers, Shelley and Wells, William D. (2006) 'Telenography proves itself legitimate', *Marketing News*, 1 February.

Chen-Courtin, Dorothy (1998) 'Look before you leap: some marketing research basics', *ArtsReach*, June/July.

Chon, Gina (2007) 'Bling-bling Buick', *Wall Street Journal – Eastern Edition*, 11 January.

Christian, Richard C. (1962) 'Industrial marketing: where is the payout on research dollars?', *Journal of Marketing*, 26 (1).

CILT (The National Centre for Languages) (2007) 'Frequently asked questions'. Retrieved 13 January 2007 from www.cilt.org.uk/faqs/langspoken.htm

Claritas (2006) '66 Primz marketing segments'. Retrieved 24 November 2006 from www.claritas.com

Clegg, Sue, McManus, Mike, Smith, Karen and Todd, Malcolm (2006) 'Self-development in support of innovative pedagogies: peer support using email', *International Journal for Academic Development*, 11 (2).

CNN Online (2007) 'London named world's top business center by MasterCard', CNN Com. Retrieved 30 April 2007 from http://edition.cnn.com/2007/BUSINESS/06/13/global.economy/index.html

Coehlo, Pedro S. and Esteves, Susana P. (2007) 'The choice between a five-point and a ten-point scale in the framework of customer satisfaction measurement', *International Journal of Market Research*, 49 (3).

Collier, Andrea King (2004) 'African-American readers and black writers find opportunities in large untapped market', *Writer*, 1 July.

Cornwell, Lisa (2004) 'The quest for a better, more profitable banana experience', *The Ottawa Citizen*, 2 July.

Cowlett, Mary (2007) 'Breaking down the data', *Marketing*, 14 March.

CPANDA 'Quick Facts About the Arts' (2006) Retrieved 22 December 2006 from www.cpand.org/arts-culture- facts/index

CR Quick Take (2004) 'CR investigates: best cars for kids', *Consumer Reports*, April.

Daengbuppha, Jaruwan, Hemmington, Nigel and Wilkes, Keith (2006) 'Using grounded theory to model visitor experiences at heritage sites: methodological and practical issues', *Qualitative Market Research: An International Journal*, 9 (4).

De Rada, Vidal Diaz (2005) 'Measure and control of non-response in a mail survey', *European Journal of Marketing*, 29 (1/2).

Delaney, Ben (2005) 'Sports Marketing Surveys sells suppliers qualitative sales data', *Bicycle Retailer & Industry News*, 1 March.

DeNicola, Nino (2007) 'Find best participants through use of pre-groups', *Marketing News*, 15 May.

Deutskens, Elisabeth, de Ruyter, Ko and Wetzels, Martin (2006) 'An assessment of equivalence between online and mail surveys in service research', *Journal of Service Research*, 8 (4).

Dibb, Sally and Michaelidou, Nina (2006) 'Using email questionnaires for research: good practice in tackling non-response', *Journal of Targeting, Measurement and Analysis for Marketing*, 14 (4).

Donath, Bob (2004) 'Undercover audits tell more than customer satisfaction', *Marketing News*, 1 February.

Douglas, Susan P. and Craig, C. Samuel (2007) 'Collaborative and iterative translation: an alternative approach to back translation', *Journal of International Marketing*, 15 (1).

Durante, Richard and Feehan, Michael (2006) 'Watch and learn: ethnography yields useful, strategic insights', *Marketing News*, 1 February.

Economist (2007) 'A magic portion?', *The Economist*, 6 January.

Ember, Carol R. and Ember, Melvin (2001) *Cross-Cultural Research Methods*. Alta Mira Press.

Enright, Allison (2006) 'Best practices: Frito-Lay gets real results from a virtual world', *Marketing News*, 15 December.

ESOMAR (2006) *Esomar Highlights*. Retrieved 15 January 2006 from www.esomar.org

EUCLID (2006) 'ACRONIM: Arts and cultural Research On-Line International Matrix'. Retrieved 22 December 2006 from www.euclid.info/acronim

Farrar, Steve (2004) 'Brenda's loyalty lays her private life secrets open', *The Times Higher Education Supplement*, 2 April.

Faulkenberry Summers, Myra (1992) 'Thinking small: researchers must tailor their expectations along with their exercises to conduct effective focus groups with kids', *Marketing Research*, 6 (2).

Fielding, Michael (2006a) 'Change with the times: ARF exec discusses future of ad research', *Marketing News*, 15 March.

Fielding, Michael (2006b) 'Ethnography proves fruitful in emerging economies', *Marketing News*, 1 September.

Focus Research (2006) 'Effective research', *NZ Marketing Magazine*, 25 (10).

Foddy, William (1995) *Constructing Questions for Interviews and Questionnaires: Theory and Practice in Social Research*. Cambridge: Cambridge University Press.

Folgers (2006) 'Folgers redefines coffee category with the introduction of Folgers Simply Smooth, the first nationally available stomach-friendly coffee'. News release, retrieved 18 December 2006 from www.pginvestor.com

Fost, Dan (2003) 'Louis Borders: Older and Wiser Webvan Founder Eases Back into the Fray with Web Content Venture', *San Francisco Chronicle*, 30 July.

Francis, June N.P., Lam, Janet P.Y and Walls, Jan (2002) 'The impact of linguistic differences on international brand name standardization: a comparison of English and Chinese brand names of Fortune-500 companies', *Journal of International Marketing*, 10 (1).

Freeborn, Theresa (2004) 'Research fills in the blanks', *Credit Union Magazine*, July, pp. 46–7.

Frukhtbeyen, Irina (2005) 'More than 80% of dads involved in "everyday" household purchases', PR Web news release news wire, 3 October.

Gelb, Gabriel M. (2006) 'Online options change biz a little – and a lot', *Marketing News*, 1 November.

General Mills (2004) 'Our careers: marketing research'. Retrieved 2 December 2006 from www.generalmills.com/CareerOpportunities/ourcareers-marketing

Glandfield, Bob (2006) 'The 11 most common blunders', *The Globe and Mail*, 17 April.

Grande, Carlos (2007a) 'Advertisers see women as green shoppers', *Financial Times*, 18 April.

Grande, Carlos (2007b) 'National news: net polls more likely to find taboo views', *Financial Times*, 16 May.

Grande, Carlos (2007c) 'Big Brother family pioneer research', *Financial Times*, 29 May.

Grande, Carlos (2007d) 'Consumption with a conscience', *Financial Times*, 19 June.

Grant, Ian and O'Donohoe, Stephanie (2007) 'Why young consumers are not open to mobile marketing communication', *International Journal of Marketing*, 26 (2).

Grapentine, Terry and Klupp, Mary (2004) 'Refining the research microscope', *Marketing Research: A Magazine of Management and Applications*, 16 (2).

Gummesson, Evert (2007) 'Commentary: access to reality: observations on observational methods', *Qualitative Marketing Research: An International Journal*, 10 (2).

Hackley, Chris (2003) *Doing Research Projects in Marketing Management and Consumer Research*. London: Routledge.

Halliday, Jean (2007) 'Car talk: Ford listens in on consumers' online chatter', *Advertising Age*, 5 February.

Hansen, Kasper M. (2007) 'The effects of incentives, interview length, and interviewer characteristics on response rates in a CATI-study', *International Journal of Public Opinion Research*, 19 (1).

Hanson, Dallas and Grimmer, Martin (2007) 'The mix of qualitative and quantitative research in major marketing journals, 1993-2002', *European Journal of Marketing*, 41 (1/2).

Harradine, Rod and Ross, Jill (2007) 'Branding: a generation gap', *Journal of Fashion Marketing and Management*, 11 (2).

Harris, Ken and Margraff, Megan (2007) 'A new dimension in retail analysis', *Brandweek*, 14 May.

Harrison, Tina, Waite, Kathryn and Hunter, Gary (2006) 'The internet, information and empowerment', *European Journal of Marketing*, 40 (9/10).

Hellebusch, Stephen (2006) 'Know sample quantity for clearer results', *Marketing News*, 15 September.

Henderson, Naomi R. (1992) 'Trained moderators boost the value of qualitative research', *Marketing Research*, June.

Henderson, Naomi R. (2006) 'What if? Researchers should begin to ask questions about the future of focus groups', *Marketing Research*, Spring.

Herzog, Hanna (2005) 'On home turf: interview location and its social meaning', *Qualitative Sociology*, 28 (1).

Hofstede, Geert (2001) *Culture's Consequences: Comparing Values, Behaviors, Institutions and Organizations across Cultures*. London: SAGE.

Hofstede, Geert and Hofstede, Gert Jan (2005) *Cultures and Organizations: Software of the Mind, Intercultural Cooperation and its Importance for Survival*. New York: McGraw-Hill.

Honomichl, Jack (2006) 'Honomichl Global Top 25', *Marketing News*, 16 August.

Hooker, John (2003) *Working Across Cultures*. Stanford, CA: Stanford Business Books.

IMS Health Inc (2004) 'IMS to acquire United Research Shanghai'. Press release, retrieved 30 September from www.imshealth.com

Ipos MORI (2006) *The International Student Experience Report 2006*. Retrieved January 2007 from www.ipsos-mori.com/polls/2005/unite-international.shtml

Johnson, Bradley (2006) 'Forget phone and mail: online's the best place to administer surveys', *Advertising Age*, 17 July.

Johnson, Laura (2007) 'Technology: indirect observation yields insights', *Marketing News*, 15 May.

Johnston, Eric L. (2006) 'Don't blink: focus groups criticized for wrong reasons', *Marketing News*, 1 September.

Keegan, Sheila (2007) 'Viewpoint: the commercial-academic divide: never the twain shall meet', *The International Journal of Market Research*, 49 (1).

Kim, Myoung, Hye Kim, Kyeong Cha and Lim, Jeeyoung (2007) 'What makes Koreans happy? Exploration on the structure of a happy life among Korean adults', *Social Indicators Research*, 82 (2).

Kottler, Richard (2005) 'Eight tips offer best practices for online MR', *Marketing News*, 30 (6).

Kraft Foods (2004) 'Nabisco introduces 100 calorie packs as a way of counting calories when reaching for a snack'. Press release, retrieved 11 January 2004 from www.kraft.com/newsroom/07122004.html

Kraft Foods (2006) 'Nutrition and taste add up for Kraft South Beach Diet Foods in 100 calories portions'. Retrieved 13 March 2006 from www.kraft.com/newsroom/08172006.html

Lee, Nick and Broderick, Amanda J. (2007) 'The past, present and future of observational research in marketing', *Qualitative Market Research: An International Journal*, 10 (2).

Lemmens, Auelle, Courx, Christophe and Keimpe, Marik G. (2007) 'Consumer confidence in Europe: united in diversity?', *International Journal of Research in Marketing*, 24 (2).

Lowes, Lesley and Gill, Paul (2006) 'Participants' experiences of being interviewed about an emotive topic', *Journal of Advanced Nursing*, 55 (5).

Lyness, Karen S. and Brumit Kropf, Marcia (2007) 'Cultural values and potential nonresponse bias: a multilevel examination of cross-national differences in mail survey response rates', *Organizational Research Methods*, 10 (2).

Market Research Society (2006) 'Code of conduct and guidelines'. Retrieved 21 January 2006 from www.marketresearch.org.uk/standards

Marketing (2007) 'Age of the 2.0 focus group', *Marketing*, 17 January.

Marr, Merissa and Fowler, Geoffrey A. (2007) 'Disney rewrites script to win fans in India', *Wall Street Journal – Eastern Edition*, 11 June.

Martin, Roger (2007) 'How successful leaders think', *Harvard Business Review*, June.

McGorry, Sue Y. (2006) 'Data in the palm of your hand', *Marketing Education Review*, 16 (3).

McManus, John (2004) 'Stumbling into intelligence', *American Demographics*, 1 April.

Miles, Louella (2006) 'Is your data false?', *Market Research*, 10 May.

Miller, Claire Cain and Olson, Parmy (2007) 'Tesco's landing', *Forbes*, 4 June.

Morales, Andrea C. and Fitzsimons, Gavan J. (2007) 'Product contagion: Changing consumer evaluations through physical contact with "disgusting" products', *Journal of Marketing Research*, Volume XLIV, May.

Moser, Alan (2005) 'Take steps to avoid misused research pitfall', *Special Report: Marketing Research*, 15 September.

Murphy, Claire (2006) 'Serve them right', *Marketing*, 2 February.

Nancarrow, Clive, Tinson, Julie and Webber, Richard (2007) 'Roots marketing: the marketing research opportunity', *International Journal of Market Research*, 49 (1).

National Retail Foundation News Release (2006) Retrieved from www.nrf.com (accessed 23 July).

NZ Marketing Magazine (2006) 'Effective research', *NZ Marketing Magazine*, 25 (10).

Neff, Jack (2006) 'They hear you knocking, but you can't come in', *Advertising Age*, 77 (40).

Neff, Jeff and Thompson, Stephanie (2007) 'Eco-marketing has staying power this time around', *Advertising Age*, 78 (18).

O'Neil, Julie O. (2007) 'The link between strong public relationships and donor support', *Public Relations Review*, 33 (1).

O'Sullivan, Terry (2005) 'Advertising and children: what do the kids think?', *Qualitative Marketing Research: An International Journal*, 8 (4).

Owen, David (2007) 'Touching down in London', *Financial Times*, 3 February.

Papadatos, Caroline (2006) 'The art of storytelling: how loyalty can build emotional connections to their brands', *Journal of Consumer Marketing*, 23 (7).

Park, Hye-June, Davis Burns, Leslie and Rabot, Nancy J. (2007) 'Fashion innovativeness', *Journal of Fashion Market and Management*, 11 (2).

Pires, Guilherme, Stanton, John and Cheek, Bruce (2003) 'Identifying and reaching an ethnic market: methodological issues', *Qualitative Market Research: An International Journal*, 6 (4).

Piron, Francis (2006) 'China's changing culture: rural and urban consumers' favorite things', *Journal of Consumer Marketing*, 23 (6).

Pollack, Andrew and Martin, Andrew (2006) 'FDA tentatively declares food from cloned animals to be safe', *The New York Times*, 29 December.

Polonsky, Michael Jay and Walker, David S. (2004) 'Making oral presentations: some practical guidelines and suggestions', *The Marketing Review*, 4.

Proctor & Gamble (2006) 'Letters for Santa provide first-ever glimpse at what kids really want this holiday season'. News release, 11 December.

Purdy, Christopher H. (2006) 'Fruity, fun and safe: creating a youth condom brand in Indonesia', *Reproductive Health Matters*, 14 (28).

Ramsey, Elaine, Ibbotson, Patrick and McCole, Patrick (2006) 'Application of projective techniques in an e-business research context', *International Journal of Market Research*, 48 (5).

Retail Week (2004) 'Trend spotting – follow the leader', *Retail Week*, 9 July.

Ries, Al and Ries, Laura (2004) *The Origin of Brands: Discover the Natural Laws of Product Innovation and Business Survival*. New York: HarperBusiness.

Robben Island (2006) 'Market segmentation study for Robben Island Museum, quantitative/qualitative and desk research, May 2005'. Retrieved 16 December 2006 from www.robben-island.org.za/tenders/downloads/2005-05-03-research-brief.doc

Rosenberg, Erice and Wikstrom, Yvette (2006) '10 tips align research business objectives', *Marketing News*, 5 September.

Rossiter, James (2007) 'Shopping mall developer moves into Cambodia', *TimesOnline*. Retrieved 12 June 2007 from http:/business.timesonline.co.uk/tol/business/industry-sectors/construction-and-property/article 1923089.ece

Rowley, Ian and Tashiro, Hiroko (2007) 'Testing what's hot in the cradle of cool', *Business Week*, 7 May.

Sadler-Trainor, Genevieve (2005) 'A visual overdose? Communications in public relations', *Public Relations Quarterly*, 50 (4).

Sands, Roberta G. and Krumer-Nevo, Mical (2006) 'Interview shocks and shockwaves', *Qualitative Inquiry*, 12 (5).

Saros (2007) 'Welcome to Saros'. Retrieved 4 February from www.sarosresearch.com/main-index.html

Sarye, Shay (2001) *Qualitative Methods for Marketplace Research*. London: SAGE.

Saunders, J., Jobbber, D. and Mitchell, V. (2006) 'The optimum prepaid monetary incentives for mail surveys', *Journal of the Operational Research Society*, 57 (10).

Schlaijker, Erica (2007) 'Research buyers give the lowdown on what they really want', *Honomichl Top 50*, 15 June.

Schonlau, Matthias, Fricker Jr, Ronald D. and Elliott, Marc N. (2002) *Conducting Research Surveys Via E-Mail and the Web*. Santa Monica, CA: RAND.

Schultz, Don E. (2005a) 'Academic research process still offers value', *Marketing News*, 39 (13).

Schultz, Don E. (2005b) 'Viewpoint: we can do better', *International Journal of Market Research*, 47 (6).

Schwarz, Norbert, Grayson, Carla, and Knauper, Barbel (1998) 'Formal features of rating scales and the interpretation of question meaning', *International Journal of Public Opinion Research*, 10 (2).

Science in the Box (2006) Proctor & Gamble 'Consumer research'. Retrieved 27 November 2006 from www.scienceinthebox.com/en_UK/research/consumerresearch_en.html

Seidler, Sharon (2003) 'Qualitatively speaking: conducting qualitative research on a global scale', *Quirk's Marketing Research Review*, December.

Shakar, Avi and Goulding, Christina (2001) 'Interpretive consumer research: two more contributions to theory and practice', *Qualitative Market Research: An International Journal*, 4 (1).

Shapiro, Arthur (2004) 'Let's redefine marketing research', *Brandweek*, 45 (25).

Siesfield, Anthony G. (2005) 'Take on a new role', *Marketing News*, 15 September.

Singer Company History (2007) retrieved 21 January 2007 from www.singerco.com/company/history.html

Singer, Matthew E. (2006) 'Writer's loci: learn how to craft a winning proposal', *Marketing Research*, Fall.

Singer, Natasha (2007) 'Hey, Sleepy, want to buy a good nap?', *The New York Times*, 1 February.

Smith, Craig (2006) 'Reaching out', *Marketing*, 7 June.

Spangenberg, Erice B., Grohmann, Bianca and Sprott, David E. (2005) 'It's beginning to smell (and sound) a lot like Christmas: the interactive effects of ambient scent and music in a retail setting', *Journal of Business Research*, 58.

SRBI (2005) 'Inside America's largest minority', *Time*, 22 August.

SRI (2006) 'Welcome to VALS'. Retrieved 14 November 2006 from www.sric-bi.com

Srnka, Katherina J. and Koeszegi, Sabine T. (2007) 'From words to numbers; how to transform qualitative data into meaningful quantitative results', *Schmalebach Business Review*, 59 (1).

Starbucks Timeline and History (2007) Retrieved 21 May 2007 from www.starbucks.com/aboutus/timeline.asp

Stroud, Dick (2005) *The 50-Plus Market*. London: Kogan Page.

Stroud, Dick and Kelly, Nathalie (2005) 'And age shall not not weary them', *Marketing Week*, 11 March.

Sutherland, Lucy (2004) 'South Shore entrepreneur Marta Loeb: Mum's the word: researcher tracks young mothers' buying habits', *Packaged Facts*, 3 October.

Swartz, Jon (2001) 'Popular Online Grocery Pioneer Webvan Shuts Down'. *USA Today*, July 10.

Sweeney, Arthur and Perry, Chad (2004) 'Using focus groups to investigate new ideas: principles and an example of internet-facilitated relationships in a regional financial services institution', in *Applying Qualitative Methods to Marketing Management Research*. Basingstoke: Palgrave Macmillan.

Teisel, Mario, Roe, Brian and Voida, Mike (2006) 'Incentive effects on the response rates, data quality and survey administration cost', *International Journal of Public Opinion Research*, 18 (3).

Tetrad (2006) 'United States Demographics'. Retrieved 25 October 2006 from www.tetrad.com/demographics/usa

TGI Surveys (2007) 'What is TGI?'. Retrieved 11 January 2007 from www.tgisurveys.com/about.htm

Thomas, Brenner (2006) 'Talking back: new guest technology changes feedback process operations', *Hotel and Motel Management*, 1 May.

Tuckel, Peter and Wood, Michael (2001) 'Respondent cooperation in focus groups: a field study using moderator ratings', *International Journal of Market Research*, 43, Quarter 4.

Tuckman, Bruce (1965) 'Developmental sequence in small groups', *Psychological Bulletin*, 63 (6).

Vallaster, Christine and Hasenöhrl, Susanna (2006) 'Assessing new product potential in an international context: lessons learned in Thailand', *Journal of Consumer Marketing*, 23 (2).

Van Der Vaart, Wander, Ongena, Vi Lee, Hoogendoorn, Adriaan and Dzjkstra, Wil (2006) 'Do interviewers' voice characteristics influence cooperation rates in telephone surveys?', *International Journal of Public Opinion Research*, 18 (4).

Van Wezel, Michiel and Potharst, Rob (2007) 'Improved customer choice predictions using ensemble methods', *European Journal of Operational Management*, 181 (1).

Vence, Deborah (2006) 'In an instant: more researchers use IM for fast, reliable results', *Marketing News*, 1 March.

Vom Lehn, Dirk (2006) 'Embodying experience: a video-based examination of visitors' conduct and interaction in museums', *European Journal of Marketing*, 10 (11/12).

Vyas, Shuchi (2006) 'P&G unveils $6 bn diaper brand in India', *The Economic Times Online*. Retrieved 3 January 2007 from http://economictimes.indiatimes.com/articleshow/792655.cms

Wasserman, Todd (2003) 'Sharpening the focus', *Brandweek*, 44 (40).

Weinberg, Bruce D. and Davis, Lenita (2004) 'Exploring the WOW in online-auction feedback', *Journal of Business Research*, 58.

Welch, David (2004) 'Not your father's … whatever', *Business Week*, 14 March.

World Association of Research Professionals (2006) 'Guidelines on interviewing children and young people'. Retrieved 1 February 2006 at www.esomar.com

Wring, Dominic (2006) 'Focus group follies? Qualitative research and British Labour party strategy', *Journal of Political Marketing*, 5 (4).

Wynter, Gordon A. (2006) 'Truth or consequences: go beyond tradition in assessing research's validity and reliability', *Marketing Research*, Fall.

Young, Robert and Javalgi, Fajshekhar G. (2007) 'International marketing research: a global project management perspective', *Business Horizons*, 50.

Zhou, Kevin Zhang, Chenting, Su and Yeqing, Bao (2002) 'A paradox of price-quality and market efficiency: a comparative study of the US and China markets', *International Journal of Research in Marketing*, 19 (4).

ZIBA Design (2006) 'ZIBA Design's search for the soul of the Chinese consumer', *Business Week*, 25 September.

Index

academic institutions 92
academic researchers 93
Academic Search Elite 100
accuracy 89
advertising agencies 64, 67
Advertising Research Foundation 66
American Association for Public Opinion
    Research 66
American Marketing Association 4, 7
American Statistical Association 66
analysis and findings 59
appendices 59, 269
applied research 7, 16
assumptions 37, 38–9, 40, 50

back translation 75, 83
bar charts 271
basic research 7
blogs 99, 101
budget 60
business library 89, 97
Business Source Premier 100

cartoon completion 31, 162
categories 231, 237, 243
causal questions 148, 156
causal research approach
    25, 27, 33
census 178, 191
central tendency 252, 254
checklist choice questions 203
children 13
chi-square tests 249, 259
close-ended questions 199
cluster sampling 186, 191
code of conduct 13, 16

coding 198, 207, 209, 235–6, 243, 251
competitor analysis 11
complete observer 165
complete participant 166
completeness of forms 250
component sorts 162, 173
computer-aided personal surveys
    216, 225
concepts 237, 244
confidence 188
consequence questions 149, 156
consumer behavior processes 26, 28,
    48, 71, 240
consumer segments 240
consumers 21–2, 80
contextualism 81, 83
continuous variables 260
convenience sample 110, 122
corporate marketing departments 10
Council for American Survey Research
    Organizations 66
Council for Marketing and Opinion
    Research 66
covering letter 220
credibility 89, 101
critical thinking 37–8, 50
cross-tabulation 253
cross-cultural research 70
cultural
    dimensions 73, 83
    environment 77
    groups 70
    values 72, 80
custom research firms 64–5, 67
customer complaint forms 43
customer database 43

data entry testing 199
data entry 180, 205–1
data organization 232
deception 14
decision-making process 45, 50
declarative research question 46
demographics 116
descriptive questions 148, 156
descriptive research 24–6, 33, 57
descriptive statistics 251
design errors 179
design preferences 71
determining sample 188
dichotomous choice 202, 209
discrete variables 260
dispersion 252, 255
distribution 22, 48
documentation 60

educational institutions 87
electronic survey forms 206,
    218, 249
electronically scanned 251
email 59, 217–8
emotional makeup 77
employee research report 264
environmental analysis 11
ethics 13, 16, 80, 168
ethnic groups 90, 131, 153, 162, 168
ethnographic research 32–3, 168–9, 173,
    234, 241
European Automobile Manufacturers
    Association 87
executive summary 267, 277
expert interview 30, 146, 151, 156
exploratory research 24–26, 33, 57
external environment 21, 33l, 89, 98
external research provider
    61, 63, 65

false assumption 39
fill-in-the-blanks questions 202
finance department 43
financial records 43
findings and recommendations 25, 268

focus group 27, 30, 78–9, 116, 124, 139, 232–3
    advantages 125
    analysis 132
    conducting 131
    disadvantages 126
    methodology 128
    online 137
    participant 108
    preparation 128
    script 130, 139
follow-up questions 14, 30 126, 143
forced choice questions 202, 209
formal presentation 59
frequency 249, 252
F-test 249

geographic characteristics 120
global research industry 65–6
government agencies 87, 92, 94
grounded theory 23–3, 171, 173
group dynamics 134–5

hand-held devices 30
highlighting 237
Hofstede's dimensions of culture 75
human resources department 43
hypothesis 26, 33, 125, 143, 145, 241, 257

images 230
incentives 114, 122, 221
in-depth interview 30, 145, 150, 156
indexing 265
individualism versus collectivism 79, 81
inferential statistics 257
information 12, 33
intercept interview 30, 147, 150, 156
internal data 27, 38, 42, 50, 53
internal interviews 42, 44
internal research 45
internet 26
interrogative research question 46
interval scale 248, 260
interview 30, 78, 141–44
    participant selection 109
    stages 142

interviewer 144
invitation to participate 115

JSTOR (Scholarly Journal Archive) 100

key words 99
knowledge 12, 33

language 72–3, 221
letter of transmittal 265
level of confidence 259
level of cultural difference 72
LexisNexis Academic 100
life insurance 6
lifestyle publications 95
Likert scale 248
line charts 271
local research firms 73
location 131, 137, 154, 215

mail surveys 218
management report 264, 277
management 231
Market Research Society 66
market segment 22, 24
marketing concept 6, 16
marketing department 21
marketing information database 42, 92
marketing plan 11, 16
marketing research association 65–7
marketing research 16
    definition 7
    departments 21, 62
    firms 92, 94
    international 69
marketing research job responsibilities 10
marketing staff report 264
marketing, definition 4
masculinity versus feminity 80–1
mean of population 186
mean 254
median 254
methodology 54, 57, 71, 199
mode 254
moderator 30, 126, 129, 139
    characteristics and skills 133–4

motivating participation 219–20
multiple choice 203

networking 96
nominal grouping technique 135–7, 139
nominal scale 247, 260
non-directional questions 149, 156
nonprobability sampling 24, 192
nonprofit organizations 20, 30, 53
nonrandom sampling 108
nonsampling errors 179, 192
normal distribution 189

observational research 14, 16, 33, 163, 173
    data 241
    form 167, 233
    participant selection 109
    process 166, 168–9
observations 31
observer training 167
online research 26, 89, 98, 276
online search engines 99
online sites 138
online sources of data 71, 97
online survey software packages 218
open-ended questions 29, 200, 248, 251
oral presentation 271
ordinal measurement scale 247, 260
organization chart 63
outline 272

participant
    identifying organizations or groups 113
    interaction 126
    involvement 169
    report 265, 277
    testing 199
participant profile 108, 116, 122, 139, 150
participating observer 166
personalized webpage sites 99, 101
personally-administered surveys 215
Pharmaceutical Marketing Research Group 66
phone calls 59
pie charts 271
planning 36
population 180, 190, 192

postal codes 187
power distance 77, 81, 83
PowerPoint 275–6
pre-analysis 250
precision 188
prejudice 82–3
preliminary report 263, 278
presentation rules 274
presentation structure 272
pretesting 198
pricing 49
primary data 23–4
primary research needs 53
privacy 26
PRIZM 118
probability sampling 24, 182, 192
product development 8, 125
production concept 5, 17
production department 43
professional recruiters 109, 122
projective research process 163–4
projective techniques 31, 79, 33, 115, 159,
    173, 233
promotion 24, 4
proportionate sampling 186
proposal timeline 60
psychographic 117
purposive sampling 110, 112, 113, 122

qualitative data analysis 233
Qualitative Research Consultants
    Association 66
qualitative research 17, 26, 28–9
quantitative data analysis 248
question sequence 206
question writing guidelines 200
questionnaire design process 196
questionnaire layout 205

random number generator or table 184
range 255
ranking choice question 204, 210
rapport 132
rating question 204
ratio scale 248, 260
recommendations 25

recommendations, developing 238
relevance 89
reporting research findings 75
research
    approach 24–5, 46
    deliverables 59
    problem 54
    proposal 17, 53, 67
research data, secondary and primary 86
research industry 61, 90
Research Industry Coalition 66
research method 24, 28–9, 268
research methodology, adapting 81
research objective 54, 56, 268
research plan 24
research process 23
research question 23–4, 26, 33, 37, 40, 45–6,
    50, 53–54, 56, 71
researcher-administered survey 213, 225
response rate 219
revenue 53
routing 206–7, 210

sales concept 5, 17
sample selection process 268
sample size 187
sample 24, 27–8, 33, 178
sampling errors 179, 192
sampling frame 181
scales of measurement 247
scientific methods 9
screening participants 149
screening questions 114, 224
search terms 101
secondary data 23–4, 33, 71, 92, 96
secondary research process 101
segmentation characteristics 115, 129
selection errors 180
self-administered surveys 214, 225
self-reference criterion 76, 84
semantic difference scale 248
sentence completion 31, 161
simple random sampling 184, 192
skip interval 184, 192
small businesses, 20, 27, 30, 43,
    53, 63

snowball sampling 110–11
social sciences 9, 14
software tools for coding 238
specialized marketing research firms 9
specification errors 179
SPSS 251
standard deviation 256
standard error 258
statement of confidentiality 60
statistical testing process 249, 257
stereotyping 81, 84
story completion 161
stratified sampling 185, 192
survey process 222
survey questions 79
surveys 25–6, 28–9, 127, 195
syndicated research firm 64, 67
systematic sampling 184, 192

tables 270
target market 49
target population 180
technology 30, 170, 208, 216
telephone surveys 216
testing questions 153
thematic appreciation tests 162, 173
themes 27
trade associations 92–3, 100–1
trade publications 95
training survey takers 222

transcribing tapes 234–5, 244
translation 73–4
Tuckman's stages of group
    development 135

uncertainty avoidance 78, 81, 84
unstructured questions 156
usage characteristics 120
validity 250
VALS (Values, Attitudes and Lifestyles) 118
variance 188–9, 256
verbal data 230
videoconferencing focus groups 137
videos 25, 263, 278
visual material 270, 273, 275, 278
voter registration list 218

websites 43, 95, 100
word association 31, 160
World Association of Opinion and Marketing
    Research Professionals 66
WorldCat 100
writing questions 148
writing questions, general rules 152
writing the answers 202
written report 263
written report, components 265

Z-score 189, 258
Z-test 257